TRADITIONAL FOODS

Processing for profit

Edited by PETER FELLOWS

INTERMEDIATE TECHNOLOGY PUBLICATIONS 1997

Intermediate Technology Publications Ltd,
103–105 Southampton Row, London WC1B 4HH, UK

© Intermediate Technology Publications 1997

A CIP record for this book is available from the British Library

ISBN 1 85339 228 6

Cover photographs by Adrian Evans/Panos, Stephen Russ, and Liba Taylor/Panos

Typeset by Dorwyn Ltd, Rowlands Castle, Hants
Printed in UK by SRP, Exeter

Contents

How to use this book

The supply of processed foods forms the basis of a livelihood for individuals all over the globe, and this book documents techniques for making foods which are traditionally sold in different regions around the world. The processes for manufacturing dozens of different food products are presented in chapters according to commodity groups, with notes on quality control. These can be used:

○ To upgrade production methods in order to improve the quality or appeal of a foodstuff already being produced.

○ To find inspiration for new products, to help build up a product range in an existing small business.

○ To help new businesses to compete effectively. Diversity can be an important way of coping with changes in raw material supply and/or demand for a product and so the value of new products should not be underestimated.

To learn more about the basic concepts of food processing, look in Part One of the book. For a specific product, simply refer to the index or the appropriate chapter of Part Two. To find inspiration for a new product from this book, there are several options:

○ Browse through the whole book for ideas which might be appropriate to your situation.

○ Identify a commodity which is in plentiful supply in your area and look in the relevant chapter, or in the index, for ideas.

○ Look at the first page of each chapter of Part Two to identify foods from your continent – although you may be familiar with a product even if the researcher who supplied the details was from a different continent, and if the ingredients are available there may be products from another continent which are well suited to your own region.

○ Some of the products include notes suggesting variations to the ingredients or finishing touches, but experienced cooks will be able to experiment with any formulation to find a product they like and feel confident about selling.

It is safest to make products for which you already know there is a demand locally, but market research may reveal scope for diversification. Any product which is new to your area should be market-tested before full-scale production is undertaken. Try the product on your family and friends and, if they like it, make a small amount to offer as free samples in an appropriate place.

Make sure all the ingredients are readily available and cost the production as you would for any enterprise. Notes are provided on packaging needs and any special equipment requirements.

Preface

In many developing countries there exists considerable interest in the establishment of small-scale food processing facilities. The commonly stated aims include import substitution, better use of local raw materials and creation of employment and incomes, often in rural areas.

Many traditional foods are made from memory by small-scale producers – techniques that are handed down from generation to generation by word of mouth. One purpose of this publication is therefore to document such information in an accessible but scientific way.

It should be noted that only foods that are commonly sold by small producers in developing countries are described in the book. It does not include meals that are prepared in the home, although it does include components of meals that are pre-processed for sale (such as oils and spices).

Many of these producers are now facing competition from imported foods, or from Western foods that can be made locally. In many cases traditional foods may have a 'poorer' appearance or a lower perceived quality than the newer foods and as a result they are losing sales. The incomes and employment of traditional processors are also falling as a result. The information in this book is therefore intended to enable producers to upgrade traditional processes and to improve the product quality (in terms of both safety and acceptability) so that they may compete effectively.

The book also aims to provide good quality information for new producers when they are starting a food processing business. In some countries the markets for a basic range of processed foods have become saturated by too many producers and the opportunity therefore exists to expand the variety of foods produced. Another purpose of the book is to inform potential producers of the requirements for making a food that is new to their area.

The first part of the book describes the technologies involved in the different food processes. This is followed by a brief outline of the need for proper quality assurance and packaging. Readers who require further information on the specific topics in this section are advised to consult the list of Further reading at the end of the book.

The second section describes in detail the production stages for foods that are presented in seven commodity groups. In each entry a description of the food is followed by the principles of preservation and processing, including a production 'flow diagram' to describe the processing stages and conditions. Finally, notes are included on quality control factors, suitable packaging and a list of the equipment required.

While every effort has been made to authenticate and check the processes described in Part Two, not all have been carried out by the editor. Intermediate Technology Publications cannot therefore accept responsibility for any errors or omissions and would welcome correspondence on the correct or alternative processes.

Acknowledgements

Part Two of this book has been written by a number of consultant authors as described below and I am indebted to them for their support and cooperation in preparing this material. I would also like to thank Matthew Whitton and Ethan Danielson for the illustrations, Panos Pictures and IT staff for photographs, and Ann Maddison and Mike Battcock for editing Chapters 1 and 7 in Part Two. Finally, my gratitude to CTA (Centre Technique de Cooperation Agricole et Rurale, Postbus 380, 6700 AJ Wageningen, Netherlands) and the Overseas Development Administration of the British Government for their financial support.

Peter Fellows

Contributing authors

Africa
Dr E. Tettey, Food Research Institute, Accra, Ghana.
Dr T. Bekele, Food Research and Development Centre, Addis Ababa, Ethiopia.
Dr O.A. Oyeleke, University of Ilorin, Ilorin, Nigeria.
Mr Eyabi George Divine, Fisheries Research Station, Limbe-Fako, Cameroon.
Ms E. Mbale, Ministry Community Development, Lilongwe, Malawi.
Mrs H.N.Y. Mtinda, Ministry of Community Development, Women's Affairs and Children, Dar-es-Salaam, Tanzania.
Mr A. Lwaitama, Min Agriculture and Livestock Development, Kilosa, Tanzania.
Mrs N. Musonda, Village Industry Services, Lusaka, Zambia.
Ms L. Chitunda, National Council for Scientific Research, Lusaka, Zambia.
Mr F. Mlotha, Small Industries Development Organization, Kitwe, Zambia.
Mr N. Engelbert, Tanzanian Food and Nutrition Centre, Dar-es-Salaam, Tanzania.
Miss Stella Kankwamba, Lilongwe Agriculture Development Division, Lilongwe, Malawi.

South Asia
Dr A. Bamunuarachchi, University of Sri Jayewardenepura, Colombo, Sri Lanka.
Dr T.B. Karki, Central Food Research Laboratory, Kathmandu, Nepal.
Mr S.G. Prapulla, Central Food Research Institute, Mysore, Karnataka, India.
Mr V.S. Padekar, Academy of Development Sciences, Kashele, Maharashtra, India.

Latin America
Dr M. Molina, INCAP, Guatemala City, Guatemala.

UK
Dr C.J. Henry, Dept Biological and Molecular Sciences, Oxford Brookes University, Oxford, UK.
Mike Battcock, ITDG, Myson House, Railway Terrace, Rugby CV21 3HT, UK.

With additional contributions from:
Ms A. McCarthy and Ms M. Fisher, University of North London, UK.

PART ONE

PROCESSING STAGES

1. Introduction

Food processing can be defined as the application of scientific principles to the preservation or modification of foods to make safe, appealing products with a uniformly high quality. It also requires the creative imagination of the processor to provide customers with an interesting variety of foods in their diets.

All food processes are made up of a series of steps (sometimes called 'unit operations') which have to be followed in a particular sequence in order to make the food. If the steps are changed, or even if their sequence is changed, the process will produce a different product. Therefore, for each product described in this book there is information on the formulation (or recipe), processing methods, quality control procedures and any packaging and equipment required.

In Part One of the book, the steps that are used in processing are grouped together as follows:

○ Raw material preparation

○ Formulation of ingredients

○ Processing stages

○ Packaging and storage

○ Quality control.

In Part Two, the sequence of processing stages is shown as a 'flow diagram' for each product, and there are more detailed notes giving guidance on each stage and particularly on quality control aspects of the process.

Processing for sale

Every family processes food each day when preparing a meal. However, there are important differences to appreciate when an individual or family processes food for sale. In home processing, any variation in quality is usually acceptable to the consumers (the family); packaging is not required; the quantities involved are smaller and there is a lower level of investment in equipment. In processing for sale, the following differences exist compared with home processing:

○ The producer does not know who will eat the food, where, when or how it will be prepared or what the consumers think of it.

○ People who buy processed foods expect the quality and quantity to be the same each time. Similarly, the weight of food in a pack should be the same as that declared on the label and should be the same in every pack.

○ The food will usually need to have a longer shelflife and to achieve this, packaging may be required. A package can also be used to attract potential customers to buy the food, and to instruct them on how to prepare it.

○ Greater skills are needed in quality control techniques and marketing.

○ There may be a need for specialized equipment for particular products.

○ Each of these increases the production costs for the food.

Therefore a food that is produced successfully in the home is not necessarily easy to produce for sale.

Process	Notes
Fresh fish/ shellfish	Large fish should be gutted and cut into chunks; medium, gutted; small, used whole.
Wash	Wash to remove dirt, blood and reduce numbers of micro-organisms.
Mix salt	Various options: treatment by rubbing with dry salt, kenching or brining in 5 per cent salt solution.
Dry	Lay fish on raised platforms under the sun for 2–10 days.
Pack	Pack in paper, jute or hessian bags or in polythene bags, inside boxes for transport.
Store	In a cool, dry place.

Example of a flow diagram, showing the stages in production of dried fish

2. Basic concepts

Food processing has two main aims: to supply wholesome foods throughout the year which maintain health and provide an enjoyable diet; and to generate income for the producers. Processing starts with harvest or slaughter and finishes when the processed foods are eaten. The purpose is to extend the storage time (i.e. to preserve the food) and/or to change the colour, flavour or texture to make the food more attractive or easier to eat. Other important benefits include less food wastage and therefore an increase in the total food supply, and less danger of food poisoning.

This section examines some of the basic concepts in food technology that are important in order to achieve these aims. As preservation is an important purpose in processing, the section begins with food spoilage and food poisoning.

Spoilage of food is caused by three factors:

○ Micro-organisms.

○ Chemical reactions (e.g. rancidity of fats).

○ Enzymes (these are naturally occurring proteins that act on the food to cause changes in flavour, colour or texture).

Because micro-organisms cause the most rapid spoilage, they are considered in more detail. However, in foods that are stored for long periods, enzymes and chemical changes may be more important and a note is therefore included on some important chemical and enzymic changes.

All fresh foods have micro-organisms on their surfaces, often in enormous numbers. Micro-organisms may be divided into general groups such as bacteria, yeasts and moulds, each of which may be further divided into sub-groups. Of the many thousands of micro-organisms, three main types are of interest:

○ Those that cause food poisoning.

○ Those that cause food spoilage.

○ Those that are beneficial for processing.

Food poisoning

If some foods are not properly processed, there is a real danger that eating them will cause illness. Food poisoning may be caused by either infection or intoxication. Illness due to infection happens when live micro-organisms are eaten and they rapidly multiply in the stomach or gut. There they produce the poisons which make people ill. An important type of these micro-organisms is the *Salmonella* group of bacteria, which produce severe symptoms even in healthy people and may kill the old, the sick or the very young.

Illness caused by intoxication occurs when the toxin (a chemical poison) is produced in the food by the micro-organisms. Often there are few signs of either the micro-organism or the toxin when the food is simply looked at. If the food is then cooked or processed, the toxin can remain unaffected even if the micro-organisms are destroyed. If contaminated food is then eaten it can cause severe illness or even death. An example of this type of food poisoning occurs from eating the toxin produced by *Staphylococcus aureus*, a bacterium naturally present on all human skin, and particularly abundant in boils and skin infections.

To prevent infection or intoxication it is essential to apply strict hygiene rules when handling foods. Workers' hands should be clean and free from infections or cuts. It is strongly recommended that all workers are also provided with clean uniforms and hats. Toilets and handwashing facilities should be available. These items cost little and have a dramatic effect on the morale of the workers and the quality of products. Further details regarding handling and hygiene are given in the booklet *Making Safe Food* (see Further reading).

Food spoilage

Yeasts, moulds and bacteria can each cause different foods to spoil (Table 1). Enzymes also

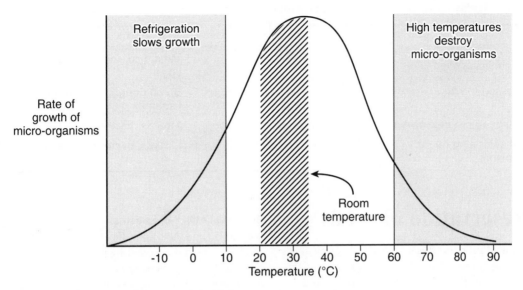

Figure 1. Micro-organism growth is high at room temperature

change the colour, flavour or texture of foods and cause spoilage. The most important factors that affect the rate at which micro-organisms and enzymes cause foods to spoil are:

○ Temperature

○ Water content of the food

○ Acidity of the food

○ Use of chemical preservatives.

A fifth factor is the presence of air, which influences the types of spoilage and food poisoning micro-organisms that can grow on foods. Air can also be important in long-term storage of some foods (e.g. cooking oils and fatty foods), where it promotes rancidity.

Temperature Higher temperatures increase the rate of spoilage by micro-organisms and enzymes, up to a maximum above which they are destroyed (Figure 1). Foods should therefore be stored in a cool place, away from sunlight or heat from fires.

When foods are heated above 60°C, most enzymes and micro-organisms are destroyed—the higher the temperature, the faster they are destroyed. However, after cooking, when micro-organisms have been destroyed, food can be easily recontaminated by food spoilage or poisoning micro-organisms and it should therefore be eaten immediately or properly packaged and stored.

Water content of food Micro-organisms and enzymes can only spoil foods if water is present. If the water is not available they cannot act, and so dry foods such as biscuits can keep for a long time. Some foods (e.g. grains) are relatively dry when harvested and can be easily preserved by removing the remaining water by drying. Other fresh foods such as fruits, vegetables and meat have a much higher water content and this can be made unavailable by drying, freezing or concentration.

Acidity of foods Foods can be grouped into two types: high acid and low acid, according to the amount and type of natural acids that are present. The level of acidity is important as it determines the types of micro-organisms which will spoil the food (Table 1). pH is the usual scale for measuring acidity. It operates from 1 (very strong acid) through 7 (pure water) to 14 (very strong alkali). Of particular interest is the figure of pH 4.5. On either side of this boundary lie two different 'environments' in which different types of micro-organisms can grow. Generally, products with a pH value of less than 4.5 (acid foods such as fruit products) are considered safe from food poisoning. Spoilage will normally be caused by moulds or yeasts and will result in visible growth on the surface. Foods with a pH value above 4.5 (low acid foods such as milk or meats) require special care in processing to avoid the risk of food poisoning.

5

Table 1 Acidity levels and the growth of harmful micro-organisms

	High acid foods	Low acid foods
Fresh foods	Fruits	Meat, fish, milk, vegetables, eggs
Processed foods	Pickles, jams, fruit juices, yoghurt, wine	Bread dough, canned meats, fish, milk
Spoilage micro-organisms	Yeasts, moulds	Moulds, bacteria
Food poisoning micro-organisms	None	Moulds, bacteria, viruses

Preservation of foods

Chemical preservatives prevent the growth of micro-organisms and therefore preserve foods. Two chemical preservatives commonly used in food processing are sulphur dioxide and sodium (or potassium) benzoate. The quantity that may be used in a food varies from country to country and advice on recommended levels should be obtained from a local Bureau of Standards. Sulphur dioxide is more effective against moulds and bacteria than yeasts and has the additional advantage of slowing down the browning or darkening of some products. It also has the advantage of being mostly driven off when food is heated. Benzoates are more effective against yeasts. As a general rule, if a product is to be opened and used up at once, a preservative should not be necessary. If a product is opened, part used and resealed, the use of a preservative can be considered. Expert advice on types and levels of preservatives should be sought. High levels of sugar (as in jam or honey) or salt (as in pickles or salted fish) also destroy micro-organisms and act as preservatives.

Beneficial micro-organisms are those that are used to change the colour, flavour or texture of a food or to help preserve it by producing acids or alcohol. All beneficial micro-organisms are safe to eat. Processes which use micro-organisms in this way are known as 'fermentations' and produce fermented foods such as bread, wine, beer (using yeasts), tempeh (using moulds), pickles, yoghurt (using bacteria) and gari, cocoa, miso and soy sauce (using mixtures of yeasts, bacteria and moulds). Some of these are included in Part Two.

Preservative action of processing methods Some types of process preserve foods by destroying micro-organisms and enzymes (for example, heating) or by inhibiting their growth (for example, freezing or drying). Others such as milling or pulping are used to change the characteristics of foods and have no preservative action. The later sections of Part One of this book describe common processing stages for small-scale production of foods in more detail.

3. Buildings and equipment

While it is better to have a new building to house any food production unit, this is not always possible. The following notes are a guide for converting an existing building or designing a new structure.

Walls and general internal finish: all internal walls should be smooth plastered in production areas to allow thorough cleaning. Ledges and rough finishes must be avoided as dust will accumulate and they are very difficult to clean. If money permits, glazed tiling on the walls, at least to a level of 4 feet from the floor, is highly recommended. If this proves impossible, selected areas (for example behind sinks or where machinery causes product splashing) should be tiled.

Birds, rodents and flying insects should be prevented from entering the building through gaps in the roof structure and/or where the roof joins the walls.

Most food processing operations involve using water, and it is very important to make sure that the **floor** is made of good quality concrete which slopes to a drainage channel. The floor area can then be washed down and drained. The drainage channel should be fitted with an iron grating that can be easily removed in order to clean the drain. The point where the drain exits from the building provides access for rats to enter it, and so wire mesh should be fixed over the end of the drain opening. The floor should also be curved to meet the wall surface and thus prevent dirt accumulating.

Good lighting is provided by fluorescent tubes but it should be remembered that under certain circumstances, machinery such as a mill with fast-moving exposed parts can appear stationary in a fluorescent light, which could cause an accident. In such cases a normal filament bulb should be used.

All **electric points** should be placed at a high level to avoid contact with water, and ideally waterproof power points should be used.

An adequate supply of **clean, potable water** from taps around the production area is essential. Unless the mains supply is reliable and clean, a high level water storage tank is required. If the mains water is cloudy at times, either two water tanks can be used or a large tank divided internally so that water in one half is allowed to settle while water from the other is being used.

As many food processing operations involve heating, **good ventilation** is needed. Large window openings covered with nylon mosquito mesh allow air into a building, especially if the direction of prevailing winds can be utilized. This also provides good natural lighting. As hot air rises, high level ventilation (with mesh covers) between the top of the walls and the roof increases air flows. If affordable, electric fans fitted on ceilings are recommended.

Layout: the various stages in a process need to be kept separate. Bottle washing, for example, is best done outside to avoid any glass splinters becoming mixed with the production process. Perishable raw materials and packaging should be stored separately and there should be some form of divided office area. Toilets must be housed in a separate building or separated by two doors from the production area. For good hygiene, workers must have access to at least handwashing facilities with soap and clean towels. A shower is highly recommended as this allows the workers to wash thoroughly at the beginning of the day.

A typical layout of a food processing room, in which raw materials move through the process (and through the room) without crossing paths, is shown in Figure 2. This helps prevent contamination of finished products by incoming, often dirty, raw materials and clearly identifies areas of the room where special attention to hygiene is necessary.

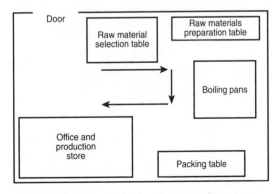

Figure 2. Layout of a food processing room

4. Sanitation and hygiene

Food and water are two of the relatively few items that people take into their bodies each day and it is therefore essential that food processors take the utmost care to prevent their products causing illness or even the death of their customers. Most countries have laws governing the hygienic requirements of food factories and these should be checked during the planning stage of a food processing project.

Three potential sources of contamination that can make properly processed foods unsafe are water supplies, unclean equipment and the operators in the production unit.

Water is used for cleaning equipment, cooling containers and as a component of some foods. In each case only potable water should be used, and therefore it may be necessary to treat water before it is used. There are two types of treatment: removal of suspended solids and removal/destruction of microorganisms. Suspended materials can be removed by allowing them to settle out in settling tanks and/or by filtering the water through specially designed water filters. Both processes are relatively slow and large storage tanks may be necessary.

Although some types of water filter also remove micro-organisms, the easiest way of destroying them in processing water is to add chlorine solution (5–8 parts per million (ppm) concentration obtained by diluting bleach to 0.02–0.04 per cent). Lower chlorine levels (e.g. 0.5ppm) are needed to prevent off flavours if the water is to be used in a product. Chlorination of water supplies can be simply arranged by allowing bleach to drip at a fixed rate into storage tanks or pipelines. The appropriate rate of bleach addition can be found by experiment, using simple chlorine paper or more sophisticated probes to check the chlorine concentration.

A less suitable alternative is to boil water for at least 10 minutes to sterilize it. This has a high fuel requirement and will therefore increase processing costs.

Processing equipment

The frequency and type of cleaning depends very much on the type of food being processed. Equipment for dry foods requires only a simple brushing down each day, whereas equipment for meat, milk and some vegetable products may need careful cleaning with both detergents and sterilants every few hours. The type of cleaning depends on the nature of the deposits on the equipment. In general, any equipment in which foods are heated will be more difficult to clean.

Different types of detergent are available for different food deposits. They do not, however, destroy bacteria or sterilize the equipment, while sterilants destroy bacteria but do not remove dirt. It is therefore important for proper cleaning that food is first removed with a detergent and the surface of the equipment is then sterilized with a sterilant. In practice the choice of detergent may be limited and it is best to try out a small quantity of what is available to make sure that:

○ It removes the food deposit.

○ It does not corrode the equipment.

○ It does not foam excessively.

○ It does not leave a taint in foods used afterwards.

Sterilants are also called sanitizers and disinfectants. In practice the most widely available sterilant is chlorine solution (also named bleach or hypochlorite). This kills a wide range of microorganisms and is relatively cheap and easy to use. The disadvantages are that it is corrosive, especially to aluminium, it may leave a flavour/odour on the equipment if not properly rinsed, and it is less effective if soils are present on the surface. It is very dangerous if it comes into contact with eyes or is swallowed. It must therefore be handled with extreme care. The strength of chlorine in cleaning solution should be 100–200ppm. If household bleach is used, it should be diluted by

¹⁄₂₅₀th to ¹⁄₁₂₅th. If bleach is not available, it may be possible to obtain sodium hypochlorite powder and dilute it to similar concentrations.

An alternative, for small pieces of equipment, is to sterilize them by immersing them in boiling water for 10–15 minutes.

Operator hygiene

The risk of operators transmitting diseases and infections through foods to customers depends on both the type of food and the hygiene practices in the food processing unit. There is a lower risk of infection in foods that are packaged and then heated (e.g. bottled juices, canned foods). The foods that carry the greatest risk of infection from operators are those that are handled after they are cooked (e.g. fried snackfoods, cooked meats) and those that are not heated before sale (e.g. sausages and other meat products, ice cream and other dairy products).

However, risk of infection can be minimized by adopting simple rules in all food processing premises.

○ Educate workers to be aware of the dangers of poor hygiene.

○ Do not allow people to work if they have a serious cold or influenza, boils or other skin infections or stomach complaints (e.g. sickness or diarrhoea). It is not sufficient to cover skin infections with a bandage.

○ All food handlers should scrub their hands thoroughly (for more than 30 seconds) using non-perfumed soap and clean water before starting work. Particular attention should be paid to ensuring clean nails. Towels should be provided and washed regularly. For processes where food poisoning bacteria are likely to be present in high numbers, workers should wash their hands regularly throughout the day. Hands should always be washed after using a toilet.

○ All tools and work surfaces should be thoroughly and regularly washed with chlorinated water throughout the day.

○ Smoking should not be allowed because bacteria from the mouth can be transferred via the cigarette to hands and hence to the food. Spitting should be prohibited for similar reasons.

○ All clothing should be clean. If necessary, aprons or coats should be provided and regularly washed.

Food handlers should scrub their hands thoroughly before starting work and regularly throughout the day

5. Raw material supply and preparation

There is a commonly held view that food processing can be done to use up rejected surpluses from fresh food markets. In most instances this is not true. Certain under- or over-sized fruits and vegetables, or those rejected because of surface blemishes, can be used if the variety is suitable, but no processing operation should be based on anything but the highest quality raw materials. It is true to say that it is not possible to improve the quality of a raw material by processing it. *Poor quality raw materials produce poor quality preserved foods.*

Handling

All raw materials should be handled with care to avoid bruising and damage. They should be transported in boxes or sacks and not thrown into piles in the backs of trucks. Foods should be kept off the ground and protected from insects, which not only eat the food but also transfer spoilage and food poisoning micro-organisms. Raw materials should be kept cool by storing them away from sunlight and they should be processed as quickly as possible before spoilage begins. Even a small amount of raw material that is spoiled by micro-organisms can quickly infect a whole batch.

Preparation

This section describes the stages in a process that are used to select and prepare raw materials for subsequent processing. When fresh foods are harvested, some are suitable for processing but others are too small, over-ripe, damaged or otherwise unsuitable. It is therefore necessary to sort foods, to separate the good from the bad and to remove contaminants such as soil, leaves, insects and inedible parts. This is known as cleaning and sorting and these stages are very cost-effective methods for improving the overall quality of food.

Cleaning removes contaminants from food and makes it ready for further processing. Peeling fruits and vegetables, skinning meat or descaling fish are all types of cleaning procedures. In vegetable processing, blanching also helps to clean the food. Cleaning should take place as early as possible in the process to prevent time and effort being spent on processing contaminants which are then thrown away. Removing rotten food at an early stage also prevents loss of the whole batch by the growth of moulds or bacteria during storage or during delays in processing.

Foods can be cleaned by wet methods (e.g. soaking, spraying) or by dry methods (e.g. winnowing, sieving). Wet cleaning is more effective than dry methods for removing soil from root crops or dust and pesticide residues from soft fruits or vegetables. However, wet procedures produce large amounts of dirty water which may cause pollution unless carefully disposed of. Clean water must be used to reduce the risk of contaminating the raw materials. Winnowing and sieving are used to clean dry foods such as grains, pulses and nuts which are hard enough to withstand the rougher treatment they receive by this method. Care is needed to avoid excessive dust, which recontaminates products and is a health hazard in itself.

Sorting Foods are sorted by size, shape, weight or colour. Like cleaning, sorting should be done as early as possible to ensure a uniform product for later processing. Sorting by size (sieving) is particularly important when the food is to be heated or dried as the rate of heating or drying depends in part on the size of the individual pieces. If there is too much variation, some pieces will be undercooked or still moist when others are properly processed. Weight sorting is more accurate than other methods, but the additional cost of the equipment can only be justified for more valuable foods (for example eggs or cut meats). Colour sorting is done by eye on a small scale as equipment is very expensive. Operators pick out discoloured foods from a sorting table or separate foods into different coloured batches for different products. Shape sorting is less common in small-scale processing but may find application in, for example, the export of fresh products such as cucumbers and bananas.

Peeling removes the skin and improves the appearance of some foods. The main considerations are to minimize costs by removing as little of the underlying food as possible, and to leave the peeled surface clean and undamaged. The three main methods of peeling on a small scale are knife peeling; abrasion peeling and caustic peeling. Knife peeling is usually done by hand using a sharp stainless steel blade, although small machines are available.

In abrasion peeling, food is placed into a rotating bowl lined with carborundum. The abrasive surface removes the skin and it is washed away by running water.

Caustic peeling uses a dilute solution of sodium hydroxide (named 'lye') heated to 80–100°C/176–212°F. Food is passed through a bath of lye which softens the skin. This is then removed by hand, by abrasion or by high-pressure water sprays. Although once popular for root crops, this method causes changes to the colour of some foods and incurs higher costs than other methods and is not now widely used. Lye is also corrosive to some metal equipment and is a danger to operators.

Recipe formulation

The correct weighing out of raw materials and ingredients is critical to the success of a small business. This step, together with adequate mixing of ingredients, has the most important effect on both the quality of a product and the uniformity of different batches of product. It is therefore worth investing in a suitable scale for weighing ingredients, ensuring that the operators responsible for formulating the batches are properly trained, and ensuring that only high quality ingredients are used. If scales are too expensive, simple scoops or measuring jugs should be used to ensure that the same amounts of ingredients are used for every batch.

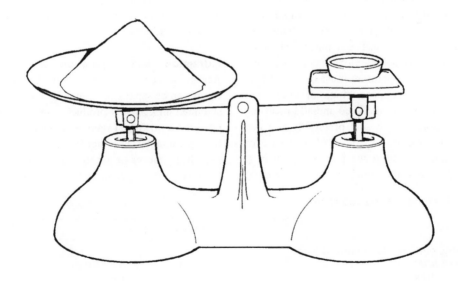

Scales or measuring jugs and scoops should be used to ensure that the same amounts of ingredients are used for every batch of the product

6. Processing methods

Size reduction

Methods of size reduction are grouped according to the size of the particles that are produced (see Table 2).

Size reduction speeds up the rate of drying, heating or cooling. When combined with sieving, it produces a narrow range of particle sizes which is important in some foods (e.g. baking flour, cocoa powder, spices and cornstarch).

Most chopping, cutting, slicing and dicing is done by hand although there are a large number of small machines available to increase the production rates and improve the uniformity of the size of pieces. Small-scale pulping, cutting and grinding equipment is also used for juice extraction from fruits, for oil extraction and for minced meats.

The process of grinding meat into small pieces or pastes (e.g. burger or sausage meat) enables more rapid cooking and allows spices and other flavours to be included. However, it does not preserve the meat and in fact causes more rapid spoilage. This is because there is more chance for bacteria from hands or dirty equipment to become mixed with the meat. Therefore, when processing meat in this way, operators must be thoroughly trained in hygienic processing, all equipment should be thoroughly sterilized and all processing should be done quickly and preferably at a low temperature (e.g. below 10°C/50°F using ice or refrigeration) to slow down bacterial growth. It can be seen from the above factors that ground meat products have the potential to cause food poisoning and it is strongly recommended that these products are not attempted unless the production staff are fully aware of the potential risks involved and trained to avoid them.

In milling, the types of equipment can be grouped by their method of size reduction. Plate mills have a rubbing action, hammer mills an impact or hitting action and roller mills a pressing action with some rubbing. The selection of the best mill depends in part on the type of food to be ground (wet/dry, hard/soft etc.) and in part on the size of particles that are required. Care is needed when milling dry foods to avoid excessive dust which is a health hazard and is potentially explosive.

Emulsification is the name given to the preparation of oil and water into a stable emulsion. This is done by high speed mixers, or beating the two liquids together with an emulsifying agent such as egg yolk, mustard or a synthetic emulsifier. At the larger scale this is done using a piece of equipment named an homogenizer, but homogenization is not possible on a small scale owing to the high capital costs.

Extraction and separation are important stages in many food processes. For example, cream can be separated from milk to leave behind skimmed milk as a by-product, using a manual or powered centrifuge. Components can be extracted from plant materials either for direct consumption (e.g. fruit juices) or for use in preparing other foods (e.g. sugar, pectin and vegetables oils). This

Table 2 Methods of size reduction

Method of size reduction	Examples of products
Chopping, cutting, slicing and dicing	
○ large to medium	Meat cubes, sliced fruit for bottling
○ medium to small	Biltong, cassava chips
○ small to granular	Minced meat, flaked nuts, shredded vegetables
Milling to powders or pastes	Spices, flours, fruit nectars, powdered sugar, starches, smooth pastes
Emulsification and homogenization	Mayonnaise, milk, essential oils, butter, ice cream

can be achieved either in two stages (e.g. grinding to produce a pulp, followed by separation in a press) or in a single stage in expellers and juicers which both rupture the cells and press out the liquid. Oil produced in this way is used directly in cooking, whereas fruit juice or pulp are the starting materials for the manufacture of soft drinks, preserves and wines. A wide range of hand-operated and small powered pulpers and presses is available.

Filtration is used either to clarify liquids by removing small particles (for example from water or wines, oils and syrups) or alternatively to separate liquids from the solid part of a food (for example fruit juices). Gravity filtration is a slow process but finds application in small-scale juice and oil processing and in water filters.

Heating

Heating is one of the most important methods used in food processing because:

○ It improves the eating quality of many foods.

○ It preserves food by destroying enzymes, micro-organisms, insects and parasites.

○ It destroys the anti-nutritional components of some foods.

○ It improves the digestibility of some foods.

○ It is relatively simple to control the process.

Another important effect of heating is to remove water by evaporation. This is the basis of drying and concentration by boiling.

In general, higher temperatures and longer periods of heating cause greater destruction of micro-organisms and enzymes, so preserving foods for longer times. However, these conditions also cause a greater loss of colours, flavours and vitamins. Foods are therefore more damaged by the severe heating used in canning and concentration than by the milder processes of blanching and pasteurization. There is therefore a 'trade-off' to be made, as the milder conditions cause fewer changes to the quality of foods but give a shorter shelf-life (see Table 3).

The time and temperature combination that is needed properly to heat a food is a complicated calculation. It is based on the number of micro-organisms present in a food, which varies from batch to batch of raw material. It is also influenced by the acidity of the food and the size of the pieces. A specific combination of temperature and time is calculated and this is used to process every batch of the same product. However, it is essential that each batch of incoming raw material has similarly low levels of micro-organisms and that proper selection, washing and sorting procedures are used to ensure this.

Different micro-organisms and enzymes have different resistances to heat, so a knowledge of this is needed to calculate the heating conditions required (e.g. for pasteurization, blanching or canning). In practice, the most heat-resistant enzyme or micro-organism in a given food is used to calculate process conditions and it is assumed that other less heat-resistant types are then also destroyed. As calculations are complicated, expert advice should be sought to complete them correctly.

Table 3 Effects of different heating times/temperatures on shelf-life of foods

Process	Example of time/temperature used:			Approximate shelf-life when properly packaged
	minutes	°C	°F	
Canning	20	121	250	> 6 months
Concentration	45	100	212	> 6 months
Baking/roasting	20	200	392	3 days (bread) 6 months (biscuits)
Frying	5	180	356	1 day (doughnut) 3 months (banana chips)
Pasteurization	30	63	145	3 days (milk) 6 months (fruit juice)
Blanching	1	100	212	a few hours unless processed further

The main types of heating used in food processing are shown in Table 3, and described in more detail below.

Blanching is used to destroy enzymes and some micro-organisms in vegetables and in a few types of fruits, but it is not intended to preserve foods. It is used as a pre-treatment before drying or freezing. This is because the highest temperature that a food reaches during drying or freezing is not enough to destroy enzymes. If the food is not blanched, enzymes can cause loss of flavour, colour and nutritional value during storage, and micro-organisms can survive and grow when the food is used.

In blanching, foods are heated rapidly in boiling water or steam, held for a known time and then cooled quickly to near room temperature. The times and temperatures are not severe and do not cause excessive softening or loss of flavour in the food. However, some minerals and water-soluble vitamins are lost, especially in hot water blanching. Sodium bicarbonate is sometimes added to blancher water to retain the colour of green vegetables and calcium chloride may be used to reduce softening.

Grains and flours have a relatively long shelflife. The purpose of **baking** is therefore not for preservation, but to change the eating quality of staple foodstuffs and to add variety to the diet. Baking and **roasting** are essentially the same processing stage as they both use hot air, but the term 'baking' is usually applied to flour-based foods or fruits, and 'roasting' to meats, nuts and vegetables.

During baking, food is heated by the hot air in an oven and also by the floor, walls and trays of the oven. Moisture at the surface of the food is evaporated by the hot air, and produces a dry crust in larger products such as bread and meat.

During storage, moisture moves through the food to the crust and softens it. This makes the food less acceptable and limits the shelf-life. Slower heating allows more moisture to escape from the surface of the food before it is sealed by the crust. This produces a dryer product as for example in biscuits. In general, baked goods provide plenty of scope for producers to use locally available ingredients to create a variety of value-added products.

Ovens can be either direct or indirect heating types: in direct heating, hot air and gases produced by burning fuels come into contact with the food. Gas is commonly used, but solid fuels are also found. In indirect ovens, heat from burning fuel is used to heat fresh air, which is then used to heat the baking chamber. Smoke and gases are passed through tubes in the baking chamber, or fuel is burned between a double wall and the smoke and gases leave through a chimney. Electric ovens are heated by plates or bars in the walls and base.

Frying is mainly used to alter the eating quality of a food. It also has a preservative effect as the heat destroys micro-organisms and enzymes and the surface of the food dries out. The shelf-life of fried foods is mostly determined by the moisture content after frying. Foods that have a moist interior (for example, doughnuts, fish and poultry products) have a relatively short shelf-life, owing to the movement of moisture into the crust during storage. In many developing countries these foods are not widely produced for distribution to retail stores, but are important as snackfoods/streetfoods or in catering outlets. They are fried until the centre is heated enough to destroy contaminating micro-organisms and to cook the food to the required amount. This is particularly important for meat products or other foods that may contain food poisoning bacteria.

Foods which need a crust and a moist interior are produced by high-temperature frying. Foods that need to be dry are fried at a lower temperature which also causes fewer changes to the surface colour and flavour (e.g. potato crisps, banana chips, maize snackfoods). These have a shelf-life of one to six months at ambient temperatures, provided correct packaging materials and storage conditions are used to maintain the quality over this period.

The time and temperature of processing are also important in frying. The time taken for a food to be completely fried depends on its type and thickness, the temperature of the oil, the method of frying (shallow or deep-fat frying) and the required change in colour or texture. The temperature used for frying depends mostly on economic considerations and the requirements of the product. At high temperatures, processing times are reduced and production rates are therefore increased. However, high temperatures also cause the oil to darken and thicken, form a blue haze and produce unpleasant flavours. This in turn means that oil must be changed more often and hence increases the costs.

Shallow frying is most suited to thin, flat foods (such as meat slices, flat breads, roti, poppadom, burgers and other types of pattie). The food is heated by the hot pan through a thin layer of oil. The thickness of the layer of oil varies owing to irregularities in the surface of the food. This, together with the action of bubbles of steam which lift the food off the hot pan, produces the irregular surface browning of shallow fried foods.

In deep-fat frying, the hot oil heats all surfaces of the food to the same extent to produce a uniform colour and appearance. This is suitable for foods of all shapes, but those with an irregular shape tend to trap more oil when removed from the fryer and so increase oil costs.

Both types of frying can take place using a simple pan heated by an open fire or other heat source. Alternatively, for deep-fat frying, an electric fryer fitted with a thermostatic control gives more control over heating for larger quantities of product.

Frying is unusual because the product of one food process (cooking oil) is used as the heating medium for another. The effect of heat on the oil influences the quality of the fried food as well as the direct effect of heat on the product. The oil therefore has a great impact on the taste, texture and keeping quality of the final product. Oils are subject to a type of deterioration known as *rancidity*. This produces disagreeable odours and flavours and makes the fried foods unpalatable. Some oils are more prone to rancidity than others and this is important when considering which oil to use.

In general, this technology is well-suited to small-scale production because it is relatively simple and it is usually well-known. It is profitable to add value to basic raw materials by processing them into snackfoods and the range of shapes, colours, flavours and sizes that can be produced is almost infinite. This allows producers with flair and imagination to develop their own individual products and their businesses.

Puffing Puffed grains and pulses are often used as ingredients in other foods or as snackfoods. During puffing, grains are exposed to a very high steam pressure which, when rapidly released, causes the grains to burst open. The equipment necessary for puffing involves the use of high pressures and the operator must take special care when handling the equipment in order to prevent accidents. An alternative is to mix moist grains with very hot sand or salt. The rapid rise in temperature puffs the grains and the sand or salt is then sieved out. Puffed grains and pulses may be further processed by roasting, coating or mixing with other ingredients.

Flaking Before being flaked, grains and pulses are softened by being partially cooked in steam. They are then pressed or rolled into flakes which are subsequently dried. Such partially cooked cereals may be used as quick cooking or ready-to-eat foods.

Pasteurization is used to preserve low-acid foods such as milk for several days or acidic foods such as bottled fruit juice for several months. It preserves foods by destroying enzymes and micro-organisms, but the mild heating causes few changes to the eating quality or nutritional value of a food. In low-acid foods the main purpose is to destroy food poisoning bacteria and some spoilage bacteria. In acidic foods, destruction of enzymes and spoilage micro-organisms is usually more important (for example, destroying pectic enzymes that would cause a layer of sediment to form in bottles of fruit juice during storage).

Products can be pasteurized in their bottles using hot water. The maximum temperature differences between a glass bottle and water are 20°C (68°F) for heating and 10°C (50°F) for cooling to avoid breaking the bottles. The filled bottles with their lids loosely closed are placed in a large pan of water with the water level around the shoulder of the bottle. This is then heated to boiling point.

Canning (or heat sterilization) uses heat to destroy all enzymes and micro-organisms that would otherwise spoil foods and as a result, canned foods have a shelf-life in excess of six months at room temperatures. However, the severe heat treatment during canning may produce substantial changes to nutritional and eating qualities of foods.

The amount of heating (both the temperature and time) needed to process a food safely will vary according to the type of food being canned and the size and shape of the can being used. In acidic foods micro-organisms such as yeasts and fungi or heat-resistant enzymes are used to establish processing times and temperatures. In low acid foods, the heat-resistant food poisoning bacterium *Clostridium botulinum* is used to set the processing conditions.

It is critical that the correct time/temperature combination is used when canning foods because if the food is not heated sufficiently there is a risk that micro-organisms will survive and grow inside the can. In low-acid foods (especially vegetables, meat, fish and milk) *Clostridium botulinum* can grow and cause severe food poisoning or death. It is therefore essential that the correct heating conditions are carefully established and maintained for every batch of food that is canned. This requires the skills of a qualified food technologist/ microbiologist.

If the food is overheated, the quality is reduced and it can become darkened, tasteless or burned and have a soft mushy texture which customers will find unpleasant.

When foods are heated in a sealed can the pressure outside the can must equal that inside, otherwise the can will explode. This is done by heating the cans in a strong metal vessel named a retort, using high pressure steam. In addition to a retort, the process also requires a steam generator and an air compressor. Each of these pieces of equipment needs regular maintenance by a skilled technician.

Assuming that cans are readily available, they are usually more expensive than other types of packaging materials. The insides of cans should be lacquered to prevent foods reacting with the metal during storage. Different types of lacquer are needed for different foods; fruit products, vegetables, meat and fish each require a different type. In addition a 'seamer' is needed to correctly fit the lid and regular checks are needed to make sure that the seams are properly formed, otherwise there is a strong risk of contamination of the food through faulty seams. This needs training and experience and requires the use of a seam micrometer to check the seam dimensions.

Because of the potential dangers from food poisoning with some types of food, it is necessary for a trained microbiologist routinely to examine samples of canned food that have been subjected to accelerated storage conditions. This also requires a supply of microbiological media and equipment.

Canning therefore requires a considerable capital investment, the need for trained and experienced staff, regular maintenance of the relatively sophisticated equipment, a supply of the correct types of can and comparatively high operating expenditure. As such, canning is a technology that is not recommended for small-scale producers, especially those on a first venture.

Concentration by boiling off much of the water in liquid foods is used to reduce their weight and volume which reduces storage, transport and distribution costs. The removal of water also increases the solids content and preserves the product (for example jam, molasses). Concentrated products have greater convenience for the customer (such as fruit drinks for dilution, tomato or garlic pastes) or for the manufacturer (e.g. liquid pectin, fruit or meat concentrates).

Many small-scale processors use domestic saucepans for processing. At a larger scale an evaporator consists of a hemispherical stainless steel pan heated directly by fire, gas or electricity or heated indirectly by steam passed through tubes or an external jacket.

During boiling, care must be taken to avoid localized overheating which is likely to lead to burning and colour changes. This is especially true during confectionery production when thick viscous liquids are being boiled. Boiling is carried out until the desired solids content is reached. There are various ways to test for this, but in confectionery or jam manufacture, it can be conveniently measured using a hand-held refractometer or a sugar thermometer.

Drying

The main purpose of drying is to preserve foods by removing the water that is needed for microbial growth and enzyme activity. It also reduces the weight and bulk of foods for cheaper transport and storage. Dried foods can have poorer nutritional and eating qualities than the corresponding fresh foods, so the correct design and operation of dryers is therefore needed to minimize changes to the food.

Sun-drying is traditionally carried out in places where in an average year the climate allows foods to be dried and stored without the risk of them becoming moist and spoiled. If drying is not traditionally done in an area it is usually because the climate is not suitable and the food does not dry fast enough to prevent spoilage. If drying is to be introduced to such areas it is necessary to use either solar or artificial dryers to assist the drying process, and also to package the dried food for storage. These measures increase the cost of the process and hence the cost of the product.

It is possible to identify different groups of products for which drying is an important method of preservation. For lower value, high volume crops such as cereals, the dryer should be large enough to cope with the high volumes of food that are dried in a short harvest period. Higher value, lower volume foods such as herbs, spices and other food ingredients offer a better opportunity for small-scale producers because there is more value added to the food by processing it. In addition, the lower volumes require a smaller dryer and hence a lower investment.

Drying is carried out using hot air or, less commonly, hot metal pans (the last stage in making gari is an example of drying using hot metal). During drying, water is removed quickly from the surface of a food by evaporation. Water from the inside of the food then moves slowly to the surface and evaporates. The speed at which water evaporates from the surface depends mostly on the properties of the drying air. For effective drying, air should be *hot, dry* and *moving*. These factors are inter-related and it is important that each is correct (for example, cold moving air or hot moist air are less effective). The level of dryness of air is termed 'humidity'—the lower the level of humidity, the dryer the air.

Hot, dry air must be blown over foods so that it can pick up water from the surface of the food and remove it. Faster moving air carries moisture away from the food more quickly than slow moving or stationary air. The speed can be increased by using fans or by heating the air to set up convection currents. However, not all foods need a high rate of drying. Some, for example fruits and fish, undergo 'case hardening' if the rate of drying is too high. When this happens, a layer of sugars and minerals forms on the surface of the food and seals it. This barrier stops further moisture from leaving the food and the food has a tough, dry skin but is wet inside. Further drying is not possible or very slow and during storage the moisture gradu-

ally moves to the surface and the food spoils. To prevent this, the rate of drying is reduced. The size of the pieces of food also has an important effect on the rate of drying. Smaller pieces dry faster than larger pieces.

Many fruits and some vegetables are pretreated with sulphur dioxide to keep the natural colour and to reduce the number of contaminating micro-organisms. Care is needed when using sulphur dioxide as it causes coughing and eye irritation. Foods are treated with sulphur dioxide either as a gas (in a sulphuring cabinet) or by dipping the food in a solution of sodium sulphite or sodium metabisulphite (termed sulphiting). The level of sulphur dioxide that is permitted in dried foods varies from country to country and local legislation should be consulted at a Bureau of Standards (see also pages 92–4).

In high concentrations both salt and sugar act as preservatives. Salt is used mostly to treat fish or meat before drying. Sugar also draws moisture out of a food and is used to produce candied or crystallized fruits. The food is then dried and when a solar dryer is used, the process is known as 'osmosol drying'.

Solar drying is popular with agencies and research stations, but there are only a few small-scale commercial solar dryers yet operating economically. There are a number of reasons for this:

○ There is insufficient control over drying conditions in a solar dryer to produce high value foods of consistently high quality. Solar dryers are subject to the same problems of availability of sunshine as sun-drying but have a higher capital cost. Fuel-fired dryers permit greater control over drying conditions and the higher capital and operating costs can be offset by better quality products and improved production control.

○ The loss of quality in traditional sun-drying is not necessarily reflected in lower prices. People may be willing to pay nearly the same amount for discoloured foods and there is therefore no incentive for producers to risk money in a dryer when there is not a great return. Similarly, some benefits of proper drying (for example absence of mould, and better milling characteristics of grains) cannot be easily assessed by customers and as such there is no increase in value of the food.

○ Dryers are only needed in villages if the weather is unsuitable for traditional methods. If these conditions are not very common, the dryer will not be needed. Often the dryer is not big enough to handle the amounts of crop involved.

There are, however, advantages to solar drying which can be summarized as follows:

○ The higher temperature, movement of air and lower humidity all increase the rate of drying compared with sun-drying.

○ Food is enclosed in the dryer and therefore protected from dust, insects, birds and animals.

○ The higher temperatures deter insects and the faster drying rate reduces the risk of spoilage by micro-organisms.

○ The higher drying rate also gives a higher throughput of food and hence a smaller drying area is needed.

○ The dryers are waterproof and so the food does not need to be moved when it rains.

○ Dryers can be constructed from locally available materials, and these are relatively low in cost compared with fuel-fired dryers.

Fuel-fired dryers give close control over the drying conditions and hence produce high quality products. They operate independently of the weather and have low labour costs. However, they are more expensive to buy and operate than other types of dryer. In some applications, where consistently high product quality is essential, it is therefore necessary to use artificial dryers. Combined solar and fuel-fired dryers use a solar collector to pre-heat the air and therefore reduce fuel consumption. These are finding wider use in many circumstances.

Salting is often combined with drying. Most spoilage bacteria cannot live in salty conditions and a concentration of 6–10 per cent salt in a food such as fish will prevent spoilage. However, a group of micro-organisms known as 'halophilic bacteria' are tolerant of salt and will spoil salted fish. Further removal of the water by drying is needed to inhibit these bacteria. Salting requires little equipment, but the method used is important. Traditional methods involve rubbing salt into

the flesh of the fish or placing alternate layers of fish and salt into a container. There may be a problem if the concentration of salt in the flesh is not sufficient to preserve the fish if it has not been uniformly applied. A better technique involves immersing the fish in brine (16 per cent salt). A lower concentration is used for pickles (see Pickling and fermentation below).

The preservative effect of the **smoking** process is partly due to drying, partly depositing natural chemicals from wood smoke onto the food, which inhibit bacteria, and partly due to the heat from the smoke.

Foods can be smoked in a variety of ways, but as a general principle the longer it is smoked the longer its shelf-life will be. Smoking can be either cold smoking, where the temperature is not high enough to cook the food, or hot smoking when the food is cooked. Hot smoking is often the preferred method because the process requires less control than cold smoking and the shelf-life of the hot smoked product is longer.

There are many types of kiln available in different parts of the world which are used for smoking. Although traditional kilns and ovens have low capital costs, they commonly have the disadvantage that they lack an effective air flow system, resulting in poor economy of fuelwood and lack of control over temperature and smoke density. Improved smokers are available and there are also improved techniques for fish processing which involve pre-salting so that the moisture content is reduced prior to smoking.

Pickling and fermentation

There are several types of pickles, depending on the process and the mixture of ingredients used. Sweet pickles, for example, contain fruit, spices, sugar and oil. Preservation is often by fermentation of sugars to acids although unfermented sweet pickles are also made. In sour pickles, vegetables may be fermented in a similar way or acids may be added. It is usual for salt to be added to the vegetables to inhibit the growth of spoilage bacteria until the fermentation has become established. In yet other types of pickle a higher salt concentration is used as the main preservative and there is only a limited fermentation. With so many different possible types of pickles it is necessary for a producer to assess local tastes and demand and then make a suitable product.

Preservation by acids, salt and/or sugar is the main method for pickles and fermented foods, although some are also pasteurized. The balance in the amount of acid, salt or sugar is critical to achieving an adequate shelf-life, and it is possible to calculate a value known as the 'preservation index'. This is used to assess whether the product is safe from food spoilage and food poisoning micro-organisms. The value can be calculated as follows:

$$\frac{\text{Total acidity} \times 100}{(100 - \text{Total solids})} = \text{Not less than 3.6}$$

If a producer does not have access to basic laboratory equipment the analysis can be done at a food testing laboratory which will be able to give advice on adjusting the recipe.

Fermentation is a process whereby beneficial bacteria are encouraged to grow. These bacteria increase the acidity or alcohol content of a food and therefore prevent the growth of spoilage and food poisoning bacteria. Fermentations have the following advantages:

○ The use of mild pH and temperatures, which retain and often improve the nutritional and eating qualities of the food.

○ The production of foods which have flavours or textures that cannot be obtained by other processes.

○ Low energy consumption and low capital and operating costs.

In some fermentations, especially those that involve low acid foods (for example milk and meat), a starter culture is added to produce large numbers of micro-organisms rapidly. This reduces fermentation times and slows the growth of spoilage and food poisoning bacteria. For example, in cultured milk products (such as yoghurt, curd and cheese) lactic acid is produced by added lactic acid producing bacteria. In some other fermentations, the natural micro-organisms are sufficient to produce acid quickly and prevent contamination by undesirable micro-organisms.

In most alcoholic fermentations, alcohol is the main product and this preserves the food. In dough fermentation, however, carbon dioxide is the main product which expands the dough to produce the characteristic texture in bread. Alcohol is evaporated during baking. The most common examples of alcoholic beverages are wines and beers. Beer is usually made from cereal whereas wine can be produced from either cereal or fruit.

The fermentation that produces wines and beers involves the conversion of sugars already present in the raw material, or added to it, into alcohol and carbon dioxide. Different varieties of the yeast *Saccharomyces cerevisiae* are used, and although it is possible to use any strain of brewer's yeast for fermentation it is necessary for a small producer to select one type that works well and continue to use it in order to produce a consistent product.

Both beer and wine can be distilled to produce spirits with an alcohol content of 30–50 per cent. Alcohol has a lower boiling point than water and distillation (vaporizing the alcohol and then condensing it) is used to concentrate the alcohol in spirit drinks. Distillation is carried out in a still which can be purchased or constructed using locally available materials. It must be remembered that distillation is illegal in many countries without an official permit.

Cooling and freezing

Cooling (or chilling) reduces the temperature of a food to below 10°C. It slows enzyme and microbiological activity and therefore extends the shelf-life of foods. However, it does not destroy enzymes or micro-organisms and only slows their growth. Foods therefore have a relatively short shelf-life. Refrigerators should lower the temperature of the product as quickly as possible through the critical warm zone (50–10°C/122–50°F) where maximum growth of micro-organisms occurs. To supply chilled foods successfully there must be sophisticated distribution systems which involve chill stores, refrigerated transport and chilled retail cabinets. Low acid chilled foods, which have a high risk of contamination by food poisoning bacteria, must be prepared and packaged under strictly controlled hygienic conditions and kept cool for the whole shelf-life. Chilling is not likely to be suitable for small-scale producers because of the cost and organization required to maintain chilled distribution.

During freezing a proportion of the water in a food changes to ice. Preservation is achieved by a combination of low temperatures, reduced water availability and, in some foods, pre-treatment by blanching. There are only small changes in nutritional or eating qualities but again, freezing only slows micro-organisms and does not destroy them. They can therefore grow again when the food is thawed. A substantial amount of energy is needed to freeze foods and there are similar problems of frozen transport, storage and distribution to those that are found with chilled foods. This makes freezing a costly process which is not generally suitable for small-scale processors.

Extrusion

Cold extrusion involves forcing food through a hole (or die) to produce strands or other shapes. Once the food has been extruded it is likely to undergo a series of further processes such as frying, boiling or drying. Extruded doughs include snack foods such as Bombay mix and a wide variety of pasta products and noodles. Noodles can be made from a range of flours including rice, wheat, maize and potato. The dough can be processed in one of two ways: rolled out into thin sheets and then cut into strands or extruded. The strands are then steamed and may either be eaten fresh or dried for later use. Some products require special pieces of equipment, but the majority are affordable by small-scale producers. The technical knowledge required for many cereal/pulse based products is quite basic, but consistent quality and a degree of flair and skill are both needed to produce a marketable product.

Hot extrusion uses sophisticated equipment named 'extruders' to make a wide range of expanded snackfoods, cereal and confectionery products. They are generally too expensive for small-scale enterprises.

Packaging

The main aims of packaging are to keep foods in good condition until they are consumed and to encourage customers to buy the product. Correct packaging extends the shelf-life of food, allowing it

to be distributed to more distant markets. Good packaging also attracts customers to buy a product in preference to a competitor's brands, and can develop an image of quality or value for money, encouraging people to buy the same product again.

In many parts of the world, foods are wrapped in simple materials such as re-used newsprint, leaves or papers. These are normally only used for foods that are eaten soon after purchase (such as snackfoods and bakery goods) and need little protection from extra packaging. Foods with a longer expected shelf-life have different needs and may require more sophisticated packaging to protect them against air, light, moisture, crushing, insects, or micro-organisms. For these foods, packaging should perform the following functions:

o It should provide a barrier against dirt, micro-organisms and other contaminants to keep the food clean.

o It should prevent losses (e.g. packages should be securely closed to prevent leakage).

o It should protect food against physical and chemical damage (such as bruising, crushing or the harmful effects of air and light).

o It should be convenient for handling and storage during distribution, sale and in the home.

o It should help the customer to identify the food and give instructions on how to use it correctly.

There are a number of problems that many producers face in packaging foods adequately. Packaging can represent a large part of the total cost of production in many cases. This may be due to the high cost of packaging or the higher unit cost when small quantities are ordered for small-scale production. A careful evaluation of the requirements of the food and the cost of alternative packs is needed in all cases.

The most commonly used packaging materials in many developing countries are described below.

Leaves, fibres and wood

Maize, vine, banana or plantain leaves are often used for wrapping small amounts of spices and salt or for steamed doughs and confectionery. These are satisfactory for products that are eaten soon after purchase, as these foods do not need long-term protection and the packaging is cheap and readily available.

Fibres from bamboo, banana, coconut, cotton, jute, raffia, sisal or yucca are made into strings which are then woven into sacks and bags. They are strong, biodegradable and to some extent re-usable. They also have resistance to tearing and are lightweight for handling and transportation. However, like leaves, they do not protect foods intended to have a long shelf-life.

Wooden boxes and crates have traditionally been used for a wide range of solid and liquid foods including fruits, vegetables, tea leaves and beer. Wooden containers are strong and rigid and can easily be stacked without being crushed. However, plastic containers are cheaper and have largely replaced wood in many applications. The use of wood continues for some wines and spirits because flavours from the wooden barrels im-prove the quality of the product.

Paper and films

Paper is an inexpensive packaging material that can be used to keep foods clean and offer limited pro-tection against moisture, light and micro-organisms. Some improvement in the protection offered by papers can be made by treating them with wax or impregnating them with varnish or resin. The barr-ier properties of paper can also be improved by laminating it with polythene or other films. News-print should be used only as a outer wrapper and not in direct contact with food as the ink is poisonous.

The use of plastic films mostly depends on what is available in a particular country. If films are available and their cost is relatively low, they have the following benefits:

○ Most form a good barrier against moisture and air.

○ Most are heat sealable to prevent leakage of contents.

○ They are easy to handle and convenient for the manufacturer, retailer and consumer.

○ They add little weight to the product and they fit closely to the product, thereby wasting little space during storage and distribution.

Flexible films include cellulose (for example, cel-lophane), polypropylene and polythene (also known as 'polyethylene') among the many hun-dreds of different materials available (Table 4).

Table 4 Properties of some common packaging films

Material	Properties
Cellulose	Plain cellulose is a glossy, transparent film which is odourless and tasteless. It is tough and puncture resistant, although it tears easily. Unless coated, it is not heat sealable and the dimensions and the permeability of the film vary with changes in humidity. It is used for foods that do not require a complete moisture or gas barrier.
Low density polythene	Heat sealable, inert, odour free and shrinks when heated. It is a good moisture barrier, but has relatively high gas permeability, sensitivity to oils and poor odour resistance. It is less expensive than most films and is therefore widely used.
High density polythene	Is stronger, thicker, less flexible and more brittle than low density polythene and has lower permeability to gases and moisture.
Polypropylene	Polypropylene is a clear glossy film with a high strength and puncture resistance. It has a moderate permeability to moisture, gases and odours, which is not affected by changes in humidity. It stretches, although less than polythene. It has good resistance to oil and therefore can be used successfully for packaging oily products.
Coated films	These are films coated with other plastics or aluminium to improve the barrier properties.
Laminated films	Laminated films are two or more films glued together. This improves the appearance, barrier properties or the strength of a package. Aluminium foil is used where a barrier to gases, water vapour, odour or light is required.

Table 5 Barrier properties of packaging materials

Resistance to: Type of packaging	Puncture/ crush etc.	Sunlight	Air	Water	Heat	Odour	Insects	Rodents	Micro- organisms
Metal cans	*	*	*	*	#	*	*	*	*
Glass (bottle, jar)	*	coloured	*	*	#	*	*	*	*
Paper bag		*					#		
Cardboard	#	*			#		#		
Wood (box)	*	*		#	*		#	#	
Pottery (sealed lid)	*	*	*	*		*	*	*	*
Foil		*	*	*	#	*	#		
Polythene			#	#		#	#		#
Plastic tub, sealed	*	*	*	*	#	*	*	#	#
Cellulose, uncoated			#	*		#	#		*
Cellulose, coated		*	*	*		*	#		*
Polypropylene			*	*		*	#		*
Polyester plain			*	*		*	#		*
,, metallized		*	*	*	#	*	#		*

* = High level of protection
# = Limited protection

Pottery and glass

Earthenware pots are widely used to store liquids and solid foods such as curd, yoghurt, beer, dried foods and honey. They can be sealed using corks, wooden lids, leaves, wax, plastic sheets or combinations of these. Unglazed earthenware is porous and is suitable for products that need cooling (such as curd). Glazed pots are needed for storing liquids (oils, wines) as they are moisture-proof and also light-proof. All sealed pots protect the food against micro-organisms, insects and rodents.

Glass has a number of advantages as a packaging material: it can withstand heat treatments such as pasteurization and sterilization; it does not react with foods; it is rigid and protects the food from crushing and bruising; it is impervious to moisture, gases, odours and micro-organisms; it is reusable, resealable and recyclable; it is transparent, allowing products to be displayed; and coloured glass protects foods from light.

There are also a number of disadvantages in using glass. It is heavier than most other packaging materials and this incurs higher transport costs; it is easy to break, especially if heated or cooled too quickly; and serious dangers can arise from glass splinters in the food.

Metal cans

Cans have a number of advantages over other types of containers: they totally protect foods against insects, micro-organisms, light, gases, moisture etc., and they are tamperproof and convenient for presentation. However, they are more costly than most other packs and their weight means higher transport costs than most other materials, except glass and pottery.

Table 5 summarizes the barrier properties of a range of packaging materials.

Food packaging should contain information about the ingredients, net weight, and the name and address of the manufacturer [IT/MM]

7. Storage

All processed foods, whether packaged or not, should be stored under carefully controlled conditions. As the producer has spent the time and money on their production, losses at this stage are the most expensive. In general, they should be kept as cool as possible, away from direct sunlight and off the ground away from dust and animals. Insects and rodents can be a particular problem in food stores, and measures such as insect netting on windows and doorways, sealing any holes in the building against rats, and rat guards on drains should be used.

Ideally, foods should be stored in a room that has no gaps between the walls and roof, has an overhanging roof to shade the walls from sunlight and has a ceiling to prevent dust falling from the roof and to help insulate against heat. It should have a sealed concrete floor and racks or pallets to keep the food at least 45cm (18 inches) off the floor. Processed foods that are to be distributed to shops are usually packaged and may be collected into larger boxes named 'shipping containers'. These give added protection against insects, rats, crushing and changes in temperature.

It should also be remembered that storage of packaging materials before they are filled with food requires the same attention to correct storage conditions as those described for the foodstuffs.

8. Quality assurance

The aim of quality assurance is to ensure that every batch of food that is produced has a satisfactory and uniform quality. This does not necessarily mean that it is the highest quality possible, but that it reaches the standard that customers are willing to pay for. The important point is that once a quality standard has been decided on and has been found acceptable to customers it should be maintained for every batch produced.

The quality of food is highly subjective and what is acceptable to one customer is unacceptable to another. However, there are some basic considerations that can be kept in mind. First the food should have a microbiological quality that will not harm the customers by giving them food poisoning. This depends on:

○ Selecting good quality raw materials.

○ Processing under correct conditions of temperature/times etc.

○ Ensuring high standards of personal hygiene by operators and environmental hygiene in the processing rooms.

○ Using correct packaging and storage conditions.

○ Selling the product within the expected shelf-life.

Quality assurance procedures should therefore be seen as an essential contribution to the success and profitability of a small business and not as an unnecessary cost.

The main types of quality control procedures involve the training of operators to look out for defective foods or ingredients and remove them from the process. A bonus scheme for operators may provide an incentive, provided it is properly administered.

The number and type of tests that must be performed on foods depends on the type of product and the level of quality control that the producer wants to enforce. However, in general, tests should be low cost, simple to perform and quickly give the information that is needed. Too much information is confusing and too little may result in a wrong decision, so the nature of the tests and the frequency with which they are carried out needs to be considered carefully before production starts. Advice from a food technologist is frequently needed to establish suitable quality assurance procedures (see Further reading).

PART TWO

PRODUCTS

1. CEREAL AND LEGUME PRODUCTS

There is a huge variety of cereal and legume products, and the selection below, from Africa, Asia and Latin America (source of product details shown in *italics*), is included to give examples of different groups of products.

Whole and split grains and beans   32

Pre-packed whole grains (*Africa*)
Rice (brown and white) (*South Asia*)
Parboiled rice (*South Asia*)
Kincheye (split cereals) (*Africa*)
Kikk (split legumes) (*North Africa*)

Cooked grains and beans   40

Roasted whole fava (broad) beans (*West Africa*)
Gebse kolo (roasted barley) (*North Africa*)

Germinated grains   44

Malted grains (*South Asia*)

Flours   46

Cereal flour (maize and sorghum) (*Southern Africa*)
Soy/composite flour (*South Asia*)
Shiro (spiced flour from legumes) (*Africa*)

Doughs and porridges   50

Kenkey (fermented maize dough) (*West Africa*)
Egbo (maize paste) (*West Africa*)
Ogi (fermented maize paste) (*West Africa*)

Breads and pancakes   56

Injera (fermented flat bread) (*North Africa*)
Fermented sweet bread (*Latin America*)
Chapati (pancakes) (*East Africa*)

Biscuits and cakes   62

Biscuits (*Latin America*)
Rich fruit cake (*Latin America*)

Snackfoods   66

Dabbo qolo (wheat flour snack) (*North Africa*)
Fresh maize tortilla (*Latin America*)
Maize tamales (*Latin America*)
Popcorn (*Latin America*)
Popped sorghum (*Southern Africa*)

Millet is one of several cereal grains that can be dried and packaged whole, or made into injera, togwa or beer [IT/JB]

Whole and split grains and beans

Pre-packed whole grains

Product description

The cereal grains maize, sorghum and millet (kurakkan) all undergo similar processes of drying and packaging. This produces a stable packaged product which, when purchased, is prepared and cooked before consumption. These staple foods are eaten as the main part of the diet (in the form of doughs, porridges, gruels or breads), and can also be further processed into a variety of foods such as snacks and beverages.

Packaged rice is dealt with separately because the raw material (paddy) undergoes a milling operation and may also be further processed before packaging. Sorghum and millet grains may also have their outer layers removed by a pearling operation to produce whitish whole grains, which are then packaged for retail. This, however, is not a common traditional method.

Principles of preservation and processing

The preservation principles are the removal of moisture by drying* to a moisture content sufficiently low to inhibit enzyme and microbial activity during storage, and the maintenance of correct moisture content by suitable packaging and storage conditions.

* (In some areas maize cobs are smoked for up to eight weeks rather than dried. Smoking reduces the moisture content of the grains and also helps to inhibit insect damage.)

Preparation and processing methods involve first checking the moisture content of the grain and, if necessary, drying further to the correct moisture content. This is followed by cleaning and sorting the grain, sieving and packaging.

Note Drying is usually carried out at or near the fields of production. The separation of the grain from the rest of the plant, as well as its drying to a suitable moisture content for storage, are part of the harvesting operation. Maize, however, may be dried and stored on the cob. In this case, a shelling operation is also required as part of the processing.

Process	Notes
Dried grains	Moisture content of grains should be between 12 and 13 per cent. Check using methods described below. If too wet, grain is sun-dried to a maximum of 13 per cent moisture content.
Maize	Maize stored as cobs requires shelling.
Shell	Maize shelling is most efficient at 13–14 per cent moisture content. If moisture content of grain is too high, sun-dry under hygienic conditions.
Sort	Remove stones, damaged and discoloured grains by hand.
Clean	Winnow to remove chaff and dust.
Sieve	Sieve to produce uniform-sized grains.
Pack	Pack in convenient quantities, usually 250g; 500g; 1kg; 5kg and larger. Smaller quantities can be packaged in plastic bags and heat-sealed, while larger quantities are filled into jute sacks.
Store	Store in a cool, dry, ventilated place, protected from insects, rodents and birds.

Hygiene

As long as the raw material has been adequately dried and stored, there is little risk of microbial contamination during this process. Normal hygienic handling throughout processing is therefore sufficient.

Raw material

Grains should be free of debris (husk, soil/dust, stones, etc.) and free of insect damage. They should be whole, as broken grains are more susceptible to insect infestation and mould growth.

To minimize the risk of mould damage, grains should have a moisture content of 12 to 13 per cent. Depending on the end use of the grain, a minimum moisture content is also important. For

Cereal and legume products

example, if maize is to be milled, grains dried below 12 per cent moisture may require conditioning with water to bring them to 13 per cent. Also, if grains are too dry, or have been dried at extreme temperatures, there may be increased breakages.

A traditional method for checking the moisture content of dried grains is to apply pressure to the grain with the teeth or thumbnail. The greater the resistance, the drier the grain. With the correct moisture content the grain will become brittle (crack) when bitten.

Process control

The quality of the product depends upon its freedom from defects (mould and insect damage, broken grains), and on uniformity of size and colour.

The main control points are to clean the grains carefully, to sort them, and to sieve them effectively.

Note If washing is necessary to clean grains, adequate drying must also be carried out to achieve the correct moisture content.

Maize shelling If shelling is necessary, this operation is most efficient when the grain has a moisture content of 13 to 14 per cent, and is inefficient if it is between 17 and 25 per cent. Various hand-powered devices include rotary hand shellers or free-standing shellers with outputs varying from 8 to 15kg/h for the former and 14–100kg/h for the latter.

It should be noted that smoked maize grains can be quite dark in colour, and depending on the temperature and length of smoking they can also become quite hard.

Packaging and storage

Use clean dry bags or sacks to package standard quantities of grains. (Control the fill-weights using scales.) In humid conditions, moisture-proof packaging in strong plastic bags (which are heat sealed) is necessary to maintain the low moisture content of the product. For large quantities, natural fibre sacks are sufficient providing the product is stored under cool, dry and clean conditions. Stored grains must be protected from rodents, birds and insects.

Equipment
Winnower
Sieve
Scales
Heat sealer

Rice (brown and white)

Product description

Rice is a widely consumed, important staple food. Whole grain rice is also a variable product, according to the genetic variety and the processing methods. For example, in Sri Lanka alone, more than 15 varieties of rice are retailed to local consumers. These dried and packaged products have a shelf-life of several months/years when properly stored.

The two main processes produce uncooked rice, which may be brown or white; and parboiled (partially cooked) rice. In both cases, whether the final product is brown or white rice depends upon the extent of the hulling/milling operation. Rice can also be further processed and used as an ingredient for other local food products (fried and roasted snackfoods such as rice doughnut, fermented foods such as rice beer and in weaning foods).

The first process—rice which is not pre-cooked—is considered here. Parboiled rice is described separately.

Principles of preservation and processing

The principles of preservation are primarily the removal of moisture, by drying to a moisture content sufficiently low to inhibit enzyme and microbial activity during storage and, in the production of white rice, removal of the oil-rich bran layers by dehusking, which extends the shelf-life of the rice.

Hygiene

Because the rice does not undergo any pre-cooking, the food is dry throughout processing and there is very low risk of microbial contamination. Normal hygienic food handling practices are sufficient.

Raw material

Paddy should be harvested when fully mature and the harvest should be carefully timed. A delay in harvest often exposes the grain to becoming alternately wet and dry, and this leads to the development of stresses in the kernels, causing shattering, especially later on when the grain is milled. Shattering may also occur if the grains become overheated during drying (when exposed for too long to hot sun, for instance).

The grain should be sorted to remove stones, insects etc. and cleaned by winnowing to remove dust, stalk and leaves. The grain must be properly stored in well-ventilated rooms to prevent absorption of moisture which causes mould growth and discoloration. It should also be protected against rodent infestation, insects and birds.

Process control

The main control points are:

○ A moisture content of 12–14 per cent to optimize dehusking and keeping qualities.

○ The holding time in the dehusking and polishing machines is optimized to reduce breakage of grains and to minimize the percentage of unhusked grains in the final product. It also determines the extent of dehusking and thus the type of product—white rice is dehusked to a greater degree than brown rice.

Packaging and storage

The main control points are:

○ The use of clean, dry sacks or bags to avoid contamination and moistening of the grain. If the normal climatic conditions allow the grain to remain dry in the store it may be packaged in jute or sisal sacks. If it is transported to a more humid area it may be necessary to pack it

Process	Notes
Store	Store paddy in a well-ventilated room. Keep sacks off the floor on pallets and protect against rodents. The store should be safe from entry by animals, insects and birds.
Sort	Remove stones, insects etc. by hand, winnow to remove dust, stalk, leaves etc.
Dehusk/ polish	Dehusking/polishing machines can be manually operated, or diesel or electric-powered.
Pack	In paper/plastic sacks, or for smaller quantities, plastic or paper bags.
Store	In a well-ventilated room. Protect from insects and rodents. Shelf-life up to two years, depending on packaging and storage conditions.

Cereal and legume products

in polythene sacks. Retail bags include paper packets for short-term storage or heat-sealed polythene bags for longer storage.

○ The control of fill-weights of packages using scales.

○ Correct storage conditions to prevent moisture uptake by the grain and contamination by insects and rodents.

Rice can be used to make noodles or, parboiled, made into kalu dodol; see index for full range of rice products [IT/Neil Cooper]

Parboiled rice

Product description

Parboiling is a centuries-old technique popular throughout India and Pakistan. The product differs according to local custom, and there is no single standardized method of parboiling rice. In some areas a strong flavour, odour, and/or a yellow colour to the rice are desirable qualities, whereas in other areas these may be unacceptable. Steeping the paddy for long periods of time allows fermentation and imparts flavour and colour to the rice. In other areas, the paddy is not soaked but simply boiled until the husks burst before drying. This method only partially gelatinizes the starch, so that the grains are not fully hardened.

Parboiled rice has many advantages over raw milled rice. The process of parboiling hardens the grain, thus reducing breakages during dehusking and making grains less liable to insect attack during storage. The nutritional value of the rice increases owing to migration of nutrients from the outer bran layers into the grain, which are therefore not lost subsequently on dehusking. Conversely, oil in the grain migrates out, leaving the product with a reduced oil content and reduced liability to rancidity, thus extending its shelf-life.

Principles of preservation and processing

The principles of preservation are to heat the grain to destroy natural enzyme activity (the heating process also removes the greater part of the oil in the grain increasing the shelf-life of the rice), and to remove moisture to prevent the growth of moulds during storage.

There are many 'improved' methods of parboiling to prevent off-odours, off-flavours, and discoloration developing. These methods make various adjustments to the time, temperature and pressure for both soaking and steaming operations. However, the process below illustrates a traditional method which can be adapted.

Hygiene

The heating during processing destroys most contaminating micro-organisms, but normal hygienic food handling practices should be used to prevent recontamination before the product is dried.

Process	Notes
Paddy store	Store in a well-ventilated room. Keep sacks off the floor on pallets and protect against rodents. The store should be safe from entry by animals, insects and birds.
Sort	Remove stones, insects etc. by hand, winnow to remove dust, stalk, leaves.
Steep (soak)	Hot soak in water (60–80°C/140–176°F) for 1–3 days.*
Steam	Steam for 20 minutes at 100°C/212°F.
Dry	Sun-dry carefully to avoid extreme high temperatures or wet weather, until moisture content is 12–14 per cent.
Dehusk/ polish	Dehusking/polishing machines can be manually operated, or diesel or electric-powered.
Pack	In paper/plastic sacks, or for the smaller quantities, plastic or paper bags.
Store	In a well-ventilated room. Protect from insects and rodents. Shelf-life up to two years, depending on packaging and storage conditions.

Note In traditional parboiling methods the length of soaking is variable, but is often between one and three days with an initial water temperature of 60–80°C. If a constant temperature is maintained throughout soaking time, it can be reduced to between three and six hours. This is often the case in methods which limit the development of off-flavours.

Raw material

Paddy should be harvested when fully mature and the harvest should be carefully timed. A delay in harvest often exposes the grain to becoming alternately wet and dry, and this leads to the development of stresses in the kernels causing shattering, especially later on when the grain is dehusked. Shattering may also occur if the grains become overheated during drying (when exposed for too long to hot sun, for instance).

The grain should be sorted to remove stones, insects etc. and cleaned by winnowing to remove dust, stalk and leaves. The grain must be properly stored in well-ventilated rooms to prevent absorption of moisture which causes mould growth and

Cereal and legume products

discoloration. It should also be protected against rodent infestation, insects and birds.

Process control

The main control points for parboiled rice are:

○ Soaking the grain at a fixed temperature for a set period of time to produce the type of product desired. Parboiled rice differs in its flavour, odour and colour according to the steeping and steaming operations.

○ Steaming for the correct time and temperature in order to halt fermentation, especially if the product has been soaking for some time.

○ Drying the grain to 12–14 per cent moisture content to prevent microbial contamination and to make dehusking easier.

○ The holding time in the dehusking and polishing machines is optimized to reduce breakage of grains, and to minimize the percentage of unhusked grains in the final product. The degree of dehusking also determines whether or not the final product is white or brown rice.

Packaging and storage

The main points are:

○ The use of clean, dry sacks or bags to avoid contamination and moistening of the grain. If the normal climatic conditions allow the grain to remain dry in the store it may be packaged in jute or sisal sacks. If it is transported to a more humid district it may be necessary to pack it in polythene sacks. Retail bags include paper packets for short-term storage or heat-sealed polythene bags for longer storage.

○ The control of fill-weights of packages using scales.

○ Correct storage conditions to prevent moisture uptake by the grain and contamination by insects and rodents.

Equipment
Winnower
Destoner (optional)
Parboiler
Dehusking mill
Polishing mill (may be necessary if white rice is required)
Scales
Bag sewing machine or heat-sealer

Kincheye (split cereals)

Product description

Split grains of hulled barley, hard wheat or corn, which are used as a breakfast meal by cooking to a porridge with water and eaten with butter or milk.

Principles of preservation and processing

Removal of moisture from the product inhibits microbial growth and prevents recontamination during storage.

The grains are cleaned and sorted, then dehusked before splitting and packing.

Process	Notes
Raw material |	Hard wheat with large seeds or barley with small and round grain is selected.
Clean and sort |	By hand and winnow to remove impurities.
Dehusk ↓	*Barley* grains are soaked in lukewarm water and then dehusked with a pestle and mortar. *Wheat and corn* grains are also hulled using a mortar and pestle, to scrape off the husk, and then winnowed.
Dry ↓	The cleaned raw material is sun-dried until the grains become brittle upon pressing between front teeth.
Mill (split) |	Grains are split using hand-operated or powered grinders.
Clean and grade |	The splits from the grinders are sifted with straw sifters or wire screens to remove foreign particles and remaining bran (husk).
Pack	The product is packed in 0.5kg and 1kg plastic bags and heat-sealed.

Hygiene

As long as the raw material has been adequately dried and stored, there is little risk of microbial contamination during this process. Normal hygienic handling throughout processing is therefore sufficient.

Raw material

Grains should be free of debris (husk, soil/dust and stones) and free of insect damage.

To minimize the risk of mould damage, grains should have a moisture content between 12 and 13 per cent.

A traditional method for checking the moisture content of dried grains is to apply pressure to the grain with the teeth or thumbnail. The greater the resistance, the drier the grain. At the correct moisture content the grain will become brittle (crack) upon biting.

Process control

The main control points are to clean and sort the grains effectively, and to sift the grains thoroughly.

Note If washing is necessary to clean grains, adequate sun-drying must then be carried out to achieve the correct moisture content.

Packaging and storage

Use clean dry bags or sacks. The final product must be uniform and marked 'wheat' or 'barley' as appropriate.

In humid conditions, moisture-proof packaging in strong plastic bags (which are heat-sealed) is necessary to maintain the low moisture content of the product. For large quantities, natural fibre sacks are sufficient, providing the product is stored under cool, dry and clean conditions. Storage areas must also be protected from rodents, birds and insects. The quantities in the packs should be standardized using scales.

Equipment

Sifter—made of straw or wire mesh
Winnowing tray—made of straw
Pestle and mortar (wooden)
Grinder (hand-operated or powered)
Scales

Cereal and legume products

Kikk (split legumes)

Product description

Kikk is split dried peas, chickpeas, broad beans, lentils or vetch. It is widely available in supermarkets, local food shops and open markets either packed in plastic bags of 500g or 1000g, or in 100kg sacks. Kikk is also prepared in the home and is commonly used to make 'wet' (a traditional sauce that goes with injera, a fermented bread-type product).

Principles of preservation and processing

Removal of moisture from the product inhibits microbial growth and prevents recontamination during storage.

The legumes must be cleaned and graded before splitting and packing.

Process	Notes
Raw material	Dried peas, chick peas, broad beans, lentils or vetch.
Clean	Remove any foreign material, especially stones, either manually or with a cleaning machine.
Sieve/ grade	Graded into uniform sizes to facilitate splitting.
Split	The graded legumes are split using a stone grinder.
Dehusk	During splitting the husks come away and are then removed by hand or by winnowing.
Pack	The product is packed in plastic bags (500–1000g) and sold in food stores, or in 100kg sacks and delivered to retailers.

Hygiene

As long as the raw material has been adequately dried and stored, there is little risk of microbial contamination during this process. Normal hygienic handling throughout processing is, therefore, sufficient.

Raw material

Legumes should be free of debris (husk, soil/dust, stones, etc.) and free of insect damage.

To minimize the risk of mould damage, legumes should have a moisture content not exceeding 10 per cent.

Process control

The quality of the product depends upon its freedom from defects (mould and insect damage, crushed seeds), and on uniformity of size, colour, and pack fill weight.

The main control points are to clean effectively and sort the legumes; legumes must be graded into uniform sizes as otherwise, during splitting, small seeds will pass through without being split or large seeds will be crushed to powder.

Note If washing is necessary to clean the legumes, adequate sun-drying must then be carried out to achieve the correct moisture content.

Packaging and storage

Use clean dry bags or sacks to contain standard amounts, checking the weights with scales. In humid conditions, moisture-proof packaging in strong plastic bags (which are heat-sealed) is necessary to maintain the low moisture content of the product. This type of packaging will extend the shelf-life of the product, providing correct storage conditions are maintained. For large quantities, natural fibre sacks are sufficient providing the product is stored under cool, dry and clean conditions. Storage areas must also be protected from rodents, birds and insects.

Equipment
Sieve
Stone mill
Plastic bag sealer
Scales

Cooked grains and beans

Roasted whole fava (broad) beans

Product description

Roasted fava beans are generally consumed as a snack. Alternatively they may be used as raw material for the preparation of gruel or 'atole'. Fava beans are a relatively good protein source.

Principles of preservation and processing

Roasting causes inactivation of enzymes and micro-organisms and the heat reduce moisture content inhibits microbial growth during storage.

The fava beans are cleaned and roasted on an iron or clay griddle or in a mechanically rotating roaster, at 200°C/390°F for about 20 minutes, until brown in colour. They are then cooled before packaging.

Process	Notes
Raw material	Dry, whole, fava beans.
Clean	Remove stones, broken and spoiled kernels and foreign matter by hand. Winnow to separate light kernels, leaves and dust.
Roast	Place beans on a pre-heated griddle or in a rotating roaster for 20 minutes at 200°C/390°F.
Cool	Cool to room temperature.
Pack	Pack in paper or polythene bags.
Store	Store in a cool, dry place.

Hygiene

The risk of food poisoning and food spoilage is minimized by adhering to good hygienic practices with respect to food handlers, equipment and premises. Spoilage and contaminating micro-organisms are controlled by the high temperatures used.

Raw material

The use of whole, mature, good quality, dry fava beans is necessary, free from infestation and well cleaned.

Process control

Control over the time taken and temperature of the roasting operation is important. Care must be taken not to burn the seeds during roasting. The continuous moving of the product during the roasting operation is necessary to ensure uniform processing. The product must be cool before packing it in polythene bags to prevent condensation and mould growth.

Packaging and storage

Polythene bags are commonly used. Providing the product is cooled before packaging this product is very stable, because of its low moisture content and protective outer layer. Simple paper bags may also be used as packaging in areas of low humidity.

Equipment
Roaster (surface or mechanically rotating)
Scales

Note This process is used for many types of beans and grains (such as toasted maize, roasted grain). In some cases the beans or grain may be roasted, using sand preheated to 250°C/482°F, until golden in colour and crisp in texture. They are removed from the sand using a perforated spoon which allows the sand to pass back through the holes. In some countries the beans are spiced and/or salted before packaging.

Miscellaneous beans and pulses [Panos/Adrian Evans]

Gebse kolo (roasted barley)

Product description

Roasted barley is commonly used as a snackfood. The product can be made from different varieties of barley, but barley with large round seeds and with easily removed bran is preferred. The roasted barley, without bran, has a light brownish appearance, with a good taste and flavour. Nowadays it has become a popular snack even in international hotels. The product is marketed on the streets and in bars by measuring it with tea cups, or delivered to hotels/grocery stores in bags of about 200g each.

Principles of preservation and processing

The principles of preservation are the removal of moisture from the product, in order to inhibit microbial growth and prevent recontamination during storage, and the destruction of enzymes and micro-organisms by heat.

The processing method involves conditioning and dehusking barley before it is roasted.

Hygiene

The risk of food poisoning and food spoilage is minimized by adhering to good hygienic practices with respect to food handlers, equipment and premises. Spoilage and contaminating micro-organisms are controlled by the high temperatures used in processing as well as the low moisture content of the product.

Raw material

Grains should be ripe, fully mature, dry, clean and free from mould growth. Removal of contaminants is essential—that is, they should be free from debris, soil, foreign particles and discoloured and broken grains. The moisture content of the grains should be 13–14 per cent. Spoiled grains impart an unpleasant flavour and colour to the product, in addition to increasing the risk of microbial contamination.

Process control

The main control points are as follows:

○ Conditioning of grain to maximize efficiency of hulling.

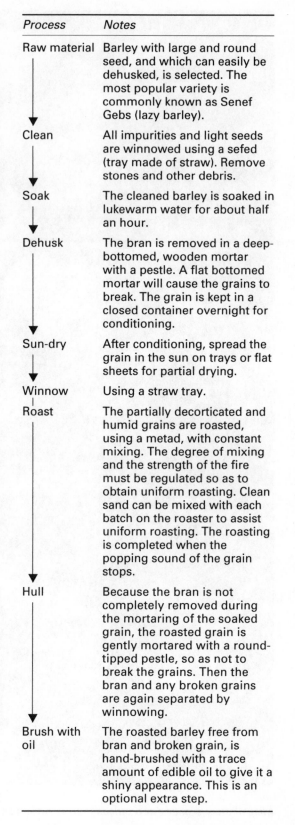

Process	Notes
Raw material	Barley with large and round seed, and which can easily be dehusked, is selected. The most popular variety is commonly known as Senef Gebs (lazy barley).
Clean	All impurities and light seeds are winnowed using a sefed (tray made of straw). Remove stones and other debris.
Soak	The cleaned barley is soaked in lukewarm water for about half an hour.
Dehusk	The bran is removed in a deep-bottomed, wooden mortar with a pestle. A flat bottomed mortar will cause the grains to break. The grain is kept in a closed container overnight for conditioning.
Sun-dry	After conditioning, spread the grain in the sun on trays or flat sheets for partial drying.
Winnow	Using a straw tray.
Roast	The partially decorticated and humid grains are roasted, using a metad, with constant mixing. The degree of mixing and the strength of the fire must be regulated so as to obtain uniform roasting. Clean sand can be mixed with each batch on the roaster to assist uniform roasting. The roasting is completed when the popping sound of the grain stops.
Hull	Because the bran is not completely removed during the mortaring of the soaked grain, the roasted grain is gently mortared with a round-tipped pestle, so as not to break the grains. Then the bran and any broken grains are again separated by winnowing.
Brush with oil	The roasted barley free from bran and broken grain, is hand-brushed with a trace amount of edible oil to give it a shiny appearance. This is an optional extra step.

○ Control of the time and temperature of the roasting operation for product uniformity and development of flavour, colour and texture characteristics.

○ Special care is taken to remove bran, debris and discoloured and broken grains (especially if the product is to be delivered to international hotels or sold in grocery stores).

○ Cooling of product to room temperature before packaging.

Packaging and storage

Condensation and mould growth are minimized by ensuring the product is at room temperature before packaging, and packaging it in dry moisture-proof containers such as heat-sealed polythene bags. The store room should be clean, cool, well-ventilated and dry. Storing on raised platforms and packaging the product also helps prevent damage from insects and other animal pests.

Equipment
Straw tray (sefed)
Wooden mortar and pestle
Metad
Scales

Germinated grains

Malted grains

Product description

Germinated (sprouted or malted) grains are used in beer making. An enzyme (amylase) converts carbohydrates in the grain into simple sugars which are then converted to alcohol by yeast during beer fermentation (page 88). The quality of the malted grain depends on the amylase activity which in turn depends on the germination time and conditions, and the quality (age, maturity and condition) of the grains.

Process	Notes
Raw material	Wheat, barley or rice grains.
Store	Grain dried to 10–14 per cent moisture are ready to store in a waterproof, dry and well-ventilated room. Protect from insects, rodents and birds.
Clean	Remove dirt and sand by sieving; and lighter particles by winnowing.
Soak	Soak clean grain in potable water for approximately 48 hours at room temperature, (until maximum swelling of grains is achieved). Soaking time depends on temperature.
Drain and rinse	Drain the water and rinse the grain with clean water.
Germinate	Place grain on a material that will allow air to circulate (such as gauze, cloth or mesh). Cover with cloth or leaves to retain moisture. Leave at room temperature until sprouts are 0.5–1.0cm/½in long.
Wash	Wash the germinated seeds with clean running water.
Dry	Sun-dry until fully dried to 8 per cent moisture content.
Pack	In gunny sacks, plastic sacks.
Store	In a cool, dry store, protected against insects, rodents and birds.

Principles of preservation and processing

The principle of preservation is the removal of water by drying to about 8 per cent moisture content. At this moisture content amylase does not function during storage and microbial growth is inhibited. The enzyme begins to act when the malted grain is rehydrated during brewing. The processing method involves storing moistened grains under carefully controlled conditions to induce germination and then drying the germinated grains.

Hygiene

Drying inhibits the growth of almost all micro-organisms in the malted grain, but does not destroy them. Contamination by micro-organisms during processing results in them regrowing during beer fermentation to spoil the brew. High quality water used in processing and hygienic handling of moist grains are both essential to prevent contamination of the product. During storage the most important risk is from moulds which contaminate the product if proper storage conditions are not maintained. Follow good hygienic practices with respect to food handlers, equipment and premises.

Raw material

The grains must be mature, dry and free from physical damage.

Process control

○ Cleaning is done by winnowing to remove dust, light seeds and other foreign matter.

○ Time of soaking—grain should be soaked until maximum swelling is achieved (for example, the moisture content of barley grains should reach 42–46 per cent in order to germinate). If soaking time is reduced, germination is retarded, and if soaking time is too long (or poorly drained), the grains may become contaminated and rot.

○ After soaking, grain must be properly drained and aerated in order to keep the plant alive and avoid contamination during germination.

○ Germination time—the grain should be allowed to germinate fully to obtain maximum amylase activity.

Cereal and legume products

○ After germination, washing the germinated grains is essential to minimize microbial contamination, and to avoid affecting the fermentation of the beverages (develop sourness).

○ Rapid sun-drying to 8 per cent moisture content is necessary to inhibit enzyme and microbial activity before the product spoils.

The most important factor determining quality is the amylase activity, but it is rarely necessary to measure this on a small scale. The grains should be intact, free from mould and with an intact protruding shoot (the radicle). In this condition the amylase activity is usually adequate for brewing.

Packaging and storage

The most important factor is control of moisture content, and suitable packaging materials include plastic sacks or containers if there is a risk of moisture uptake from the air. If the climate is sufficiently dry and there is little temperature variation in the store, sisal or jute sacks may also be used.

The store room should be dry, cool and with adequate ventilation to prevent the growth of moulds. The absorption of moisture by the dry malted grains would also lead to a reduction in amylase activity.

Equipment
No special equipment needed

Flours

Cereal flour (maize and sorghum)

Product description

Cereal flours, especially from maize and sorghum, are staple foods which have a high domestic demand. They are also used for the small-scale production of bakery products, snackfoods and as ingredients in other foods. The flours are fine and white (although incorporation of different quantities of bran alter the colour to pale brown). Under correct storage conditions the flours have a shelf-life of up to two years.

Principles of preservation and processing

The principle of preservation for flours is to reduce the moisture content to a level at which microbial and enzyme activity is inhibited. The process involves sorting, cleaning, conditioning and dehusking the grains, grinding to a flour, and removing the bran.

Process	Notes
Raw material	Dried maize or sorghum seed.
Clean	Sort by hand to remove leaves, stones etc.—winnow using a winnowing basket.
Condition	Add cold water to soften the maize.
Dehusk	Use dehusking machine.
Soak	Soak grains for three to four days in water.
Dry	Sun-dry for three to five hours.
Grind	Use grinding mill.
Dry	Sun-dry the flour for one to two hours.
Sieve	Use a fine sieve, e.g. 1mm aperture.
Pack	Use sealed plastic bags.
Store	In a cool, dry place.

Hygiene

As both the raw material and flour are in a dry state there is little risk of transmitting food poisoning bacteria. Good hygiene practices and careful storage are generally sufficient.

Raw material

Grains should be fully ripe, intact and free from mould, soils or other contaminants.

Process control

○ Adequate conditioning of the grain to ensure that the correct amount of moisture has been absorbed to give good milling characteristics (i.e. the grains break down to a fine flour in the mill without shattering into pieces or clogging the mill). This is achieved when grains soften but are not wet when squeezed.

○ The type of mill, speed and setting adjustment all affect the extraction rate and hence the quality of the flour obtained.

○ Sieve apertures determine the fineness of the flour.

○ Adequate drying of flour to ensure that the expected shelf-life is achieved.

Product control

The main quality factors are colour and texture (fineness) of the flour. These are determined by the extent of conditioning, milling specifications, and the extent of bran removal by sieving.

Packaging and storage

If the flour is produced in an area of low humidity, it may be stored in hessian or jute sacks. If it is produced in or transported to a region of higher humidity it may be necessary to package it in plastic sacks. In either case the store should be cool and protected against birds, insects and rodents.

> **Equipment**
> Winnowing basket
> Dehusker
> Grinding mill
> Scales
> Sieve
> Heat-sealer or bag stitchers

Cereal and legume products

Shiro (spiced flour from legumes)

Product description

Shiro is a flour made of pre-cooked and spiced peas, broad beans or chickpeas. Its main use is to make a stew known as 'shiro wet'.

Principles of preservation and processing

Heat treatment inhibits the growth of micro-organisms and enzymes, and careful storage of the flour prevents recontamination. Spices are mixed with the base material in appropriate proportions to give the taste associated with the product, and the mixture is then ground to a fine flour.

Process	Notes
Raw material	Peas, broad beans or chickpeas.
Clean	Foreign materials, undersized seeds and other grains are removed using a mechanical sifter or manually.
Roast	Roast the peas, broad beans or chickpeas at about 150°C/300°F for not more than 10 minutes.
Hull, winnow	Remove the husk by splitting the seed in a stone mill and winnow the husk away.
Mix	Add about 0.3 per cent each of bishops weed and basil, 0.5 per cent cardamon, 0.7 per cent fenugreek and 0.2 per cent coriander and mix well.
Grind	Grind the mixture into a fine flour with a stone mill.
Pack	The flour can be stored in large, tightly covered bins before it is packed and sealed in plastic bags.
Store	In a dry place.

Hygiene

Peas, chickpeas and broad beans must be cleaned well before they are roasted. Roasting, hulling, mixing and grinding equipment must be cleaned in regular intervals and dry when used. Good hygiene practices should be followed by food handlers.

Raw material

Good quality materials must be used, free of foreign matter and undersized seeds.

Process control

○ Time and temperature control of the roasting operation, to prevent off-flavours developing in the product.

○ Peas, chickpeas or broad beans must be mixed with the right proportion of spices to give the characteristic taste.

○ Shiro should be fine flour; grinding time and sieve apertures determine the fineness.

Packaging and storage

Shiro can last for a fairly long period if it is stored in a dry place, and packaged in plastic bags it will keep for over a year.

> **Equipment**
> Mechanical sifter
> Roaster
> Mixer
> Grinding mill
> Plastic sealer

Note Metin shiro is another pea flour, made with garlic, ginger, onion, rue seeds, red pepper, basil seeds, coriander, bishops weed, cardamom and salt. Most often it is used to prepare a special type of shiro wet known as Bozena shiro.

Soy/composite flour

Product description

Soy flour is a fine creamy flour which is combined with maize flour or other cereal flours to increase the protein content and balance the amino acid composition of the composite flours. In this form it is used as a breakfast porridge and weaning food.

Principles of preservation and processing

Preservation is mostly achieved by the low moisture content of the flour which inhibits enzyme activity and microbial growth. A secondary benefit of mixing flours to form a composite flour is that the fat content of the mixed flour is lower than that of pure soy flour and the rate of deterioration due to rancidity is reduced.

Process	Notes
Clean	Remove husks/pebbles and other debris using a winnower or winnowing baskets.
Boil	Immerse beans in lime water (1 per cent calcium hydroxide). Water should be approx three times the volume of solids.
Peel	Drain and rinse beans, then peel off the seed coats by rubbing in the palm of hands.
Dry	Sun-dry on raised platforms.
Grind	Grind using a mortar and pestle or a mill.
Sieve	Use fine (1mm) sieve.
Mix	Mix 20:80 soybean flour:cereal flour.
Pack	In polythene bags using a heat sealer and scales.
Store	In a cool, dry place.

Hygiene

The raw material and product remain dry throughout the process and hygiene problems are therefore less than for wet foods. However, normal hygiene rules for safe food handling should be observed and hygienic handling of flour is important to prevent recontamination.

Raw material

Beans should be free of husk, soils and other debris and free of insect damage. They should be stored in a cool, dry room on raised pallets and protected from insects, birds and rodents.

Process control

○ Boiling is essential to remove the beany flavour/odour, to destroy micro-organisms, to destroy a trypsin inhibitor in the beans which would reduce the nutritional value of the flour, and to assist in removal of the seed coat.

○ Drying to a low moisture content is a further control point to allow production of a free-flowing flour during grinding, without clogging the mill.

○ The sieve aperture determines the fineness of the flour, and this should be similar to that of the other cereal flours with which it is to be mixed, to allow thorough and uniform mixing.

○ The proportions of each flour in the composite mixture should be weighed out carefully.

Packaging and storage

The flour is hygroscopic and should therefore be packaged in moisture-proof containers (e.g. strong polythene bags) and fully sealed. Care is necessary to prevent the flour from contaminating the heat seal of a plastic bag and making it ineffective. The packages should be filled carefully to standard weights.

Equipment
Grinding mill
Sieve
Scales

Cereal and legume products

Soybeans can be made into flour or milk [IT/PMM]

Doughs and porridges

Kenkey

Product description

Kenkey is a widely consumed traditional staple food in Ghana. There are several similar staple dough-like products that can be made from maize (such as banku, abolo, tuo zaafi and kunu), which vary only slightly in the processing methods used. Kenkey is prepared from fermented maize dough and usually wrapped with dried corn husks, dried plantain or other leaves. The final product is round-ish in shape, light cream to whitish in colour with a solid, soft, sticky texture and slightly sour taste.

Kenkey is used as a main meal constituent, usually eaten with fresh pepper sauce (freshly ground pepper, tomatoes, onions and salt to taste) with fried fish or with stew or soup.

Two main types of kenkey exist. The Ga-type is usually wrapped with corn-husks and part of the maize dough is exposed. Salt is added to this dough. The Fanti-type is completely wrapped with dried plantain leaves and salt is not added to the maize dough. The Ga-type is also slightly more sour (because there is a longer fermentation of the dough) than the Fanti-type.

Principles of preservation and processing

The main principle of preservation is the inhibition of contaminating micro-organisms and enzymes by heat treatment. The kenkey is wrapped and sealed in leaves prior to cooking, thus providing some protection from recontamination.

This is a moist product and it is usually consumed soon after preparation or is retailed for direct consumption as part of a meal. For this latter purpose it is traditionally wrapped well in polythene and kept covered inside pots, which protects it from recontamination.

The process of making kenkey is a lengthy one and involves preparing a fermented dough from maize. This dough is cooked to gelatinize the starch and to form a thick consistency which can be moulded into the desired shape, wrapped and boiled or steamed.

Hygiene

The risk of food poisoning and food spoilage is minimized by adhering to good hygienic practices

Process	Notes
Dried maize grain	Dried grains (removed from cobs) can be used at a moisture content of 12–15 per cent. (Semi-dried grains of 18–20 per cent moisture content have also been used.)
Clean and wash	To remove foreign matter and spoiled grains.
Soak	Soak grains in water. (Dry grains may be soaked between one and three days. Semi-dried grains usually soaked overnight.) Remove any remaining spoiled grains and pieces of corn cob at this stage.
Drain and mill	Grains are milled once using mills such as the Premier 2A to produce a fine-textured maize meal with visible bran particles.
Mix with water	Maize meal is mixed with small quantities of water at a time to produce a firm but soft dough.
Ferment	The prepared dough is kept in covered containers and allowed to ferment under normal ambient conditions for one to two days.
Heat	Mix portions of the fermented maize dough with water to produce a slurry. This is cooked in large cast iron pots while stirring with a wooden ladle until the consistency of the slurry thickens (this is *aflata*). The process may take about one hour. Salt may be added at this stage.
Mix raw and fermented maize dough	Mix the *aflata* with raw uncooked fermented maize dough in proportions ranging between 1:1 and 2:1 (*aflata*:raw uncooked maize dough), in large wooden tubs or aluminium bowls.
Mould and wrap	Mould the mixture into round balls and wrap with corn husks or dried plantain leaves (carefully selected and pre-wetted). In the case of corn husks, the top (pointed ends) of the husk are twisted together after wrapping and inserted into the dough mixture. The space created is then filled with some dough mixture. The end product is a smooth, rounded ball covered with husk.

Heat ↓	The kenkey balls are packed in large cast iron pots, placed on a fire. To begin with, the base of the pot is lined with corn husks or dried plantain leaves to prevent charring of the kenkey balls. After packing, enough water is added to the pot to cover the kenkey balls completely. The pot is covered with a thick polythene sheet, and sometimes a hessian sack. Finally, a metal or wooden tray is placed over the sack and the kenkey is cooked for one to two hours, depending on the quantity of balls.
Pack	Pack while hot into large, thick polythene bags contained in large aluminium bowls or traditional baskets. In addition, a couple of layers of white clean cloth and polythene sheets may be placed to cover the product, to keep it hot for a longer period while on sale.

with respect to food handlers, equipment and premises, and the use of potable water. In addition, the wrapping materials, such as corn husks or dried plantain leaves, must be thoroughly washed to remove any dirt and insects.

Spoilage and contaminating micro-organisms are controlled by the heat treatment, but it is essential that the cooked product be handled hygienically with clean hands, since it is a moist product and no further heat processing is carried out before consumption.

Raw material

Grains must be free from infestation and any spoiled grains. The quality of the maize grain used affects the quality of kenkey produced. Semi-dried maize (with about 18–20 per cent or more moisture content) produces kenkey with a tough and brittle texture. The taste may also be slightly sweet. Dry maize (about 10–13 per cent moisture) produces the desired soft and sticky kenkey.

Process control

○ A soft and sticky texture and slightly sour product is preferred. The texture is dependent upon many factors, such as:

– how fine the soaked grains are milled (the finer the flour, the softer the kenkey);
– the initial moisture content of the dried grains;
– the ratio of *aflata* to raw uncooked fermented maize dough, for example, a 3:1 or 2:1 ratio of *aflata* to raw maize dough may be more desirable than a 1:1 or 1:2 ratio.

○ Control over fermentation time is important. The maize dough must be prepared with clean water and properly covered during fermentation to avoid contamination. Over-fermented maize dough (where fermentation has lasted beyond three days) produces sour and strongly off-flavoured kenkey.

○ Placing some padding (plantain leaves or corn husks) at the bottom of the cooking pot prevents charring of kenkey balls during cooking.

○ Completed cooking time is judged when the top-most layer of kenkey is cooked. This is done by removing one, splitting it open and tasting it.

Packaging and storage

The day's production should, ideally, be sold by the end of each day.

However, kenkey is stable under tropical ambient temperatures for periods of two to three days, providing it is wrapped well with the leaves and handled hygienically after the final cooking operation. Kenkey is traditionally protected by wrapping carefully in leaves (so that the product is completely covered). This provides a good seal, and protects it to a certain extent from recontamination.

The product is usually contained in a thick polythene bag and carried in large aluminium bowls. To keep the product hot for sale, extra insulation is placed over the top of the container.

Kenkey which is a day old is preferred by most people and the quality is in the main unchanged. Beyond two days, there is a definite flavour change. The product gets slightly more sour to taste and mould may be seen.

Equipment
Maize mill

Maize products include flour, egbo, ogi, tortilla, tamales, and popcorn [IT/PH]

Egbo

Product description

Egbo is a thick, bland, white paste made from dehusked white maize. It is a staple food often eaten with a stew made from ground red pepper and onion, palm oil and crayfish (optional). Egbo is consumed when freshly prepared.

Principles of preservation and processing

This product is not kept long-term. It is consumed or sold for immediate consumption. Cooking the maize inactivates enzymes and contaminating micro-organisms. The moist quality of the product limits its shelf-life and it must be kept hygienically covered to prevent recontamination.

The process consists of cooking dehusked clean whole maize grains in water and salt in traditional pots, and mashing to a thick paste before serving for consumption.

Hygiene

The risk of food poisoning and food spoilage is minimized by adhering to good hygienic practices with respect to food handlers, equipment and premises, and by the use of potable water.

Raw material

The maize grains should be mature, free from infestation and of the correct moisture content (13–14 per cent) having been stored well.

Process control

The main quality control points in the process are:

○ The dehusking operation must be thorough to ensure husks are removed, giving a good quality white product.

○ The cooking operation must be carefully managed so that the maize can be easily mashed into a thick paste of the correct consistency.

Packaging and storage

Egbo is served hot in the earthenware cooking pot. It is eaten with a special stew or with plain groundnut or melon oil according to preference. It is usually eaten alone as a breakfast meal or as a mid-day snack.

Egbo keeps for a short while, providing the pot is covered to protect it from insects and is served under hygienic conditions, paying particular attention to utensils and handlers.

Process	Notes
Maize ↓	The maize grains are cleaned of spoiled grains and foreign material and sorted.
Dehusk ↓	The grains are dehusked either mechanically using a pearler or manually using a pestle and mortar.
Cook ↓	The dehusked grains are then cooked using a special narrow-mouth earthenware pot on a fire overnight, until they become very soft. Salt is added to taste.
Mash ↓	They are then mashed to a thick paste. Some producers then add cooked (but not too soft, *nor* broken/mashed) whole peanuts (groundnuts).
Pack	The egbo is sold warm in earthenware pots placed on a tray with the pepper stew *or* with plain groundnut oil, according to preference.

> **Equipment**
> Maize huller/pearler or pestle and mortar
> Traditional earthenware pot (narrow neck)

Ogi

Product description

Ogi is a thick paste made from maize or guinea corn. Ogi has a bland or sour taste and assumes the colour of the variety of the grain. It is traditionally kept under water for better preservation, the water being changed daily. It is a popular product, much in demand and eaten as a breakfast cereal. It is sold from big covered bowls or trays.

Principles of preservation and processing

The product is preserved by the production of acids by micro-organisms during the controlled fermentation. The acids produced have a relatively low preservative effect, but keeping the ogi cool under water results in a longer shelf-life.

The process involves soaking the cleaned grains, allowing a natural fermentation to take place, wet milling the grains and then sieving to produce a finer texture.

Hygiene

Since there is no heating involved at any point during processing, in order to avoid any risk of food poisoning bacteria, good hygiene is of critical importance.

The risk of food poisoning and food spoilage is minimized by adhering to good hygienic practices with respect to food handlers, equipment and premises, and the use of potable water.

Raw material

The maize grains should be mature, free from infestation and of the correct moisture content (13–14 per cent) having been stored and sorted well. The variety of the grains selected depends on the type/colour of ogi to be made.

Process control

The main quality control points in the process are:

○ Temperature of fermentation (26–30°C/79–86°F) to ensure fermentation is completed in two to three days.

○ Time of fermentation (experience and skill are needed to know when the taste is just right).

○ Extent of milling and size of sieve: some like ogi to have a very smooth texture and a muslin cloth is used for sieving, while others prefer it coarser. The residual kernel skins are usually fed to poultry.

○ Changing the water in which the ogi is stored on a daily basis.

Packaging and storage

The ogi is kept under water. However, those who have refrigerators may drain the water, squeeze the ogi to reduce the water content and finally store it under refrigeration.

The traditional method of storage and of changing the water is age-old and helps to

Process	Notes
Prepare raw material ↓	Whole grain (corn/maize or guinea corn) is cleaned and winnowed to remove foreign matter and spoiled grains.
Wash ↓	Wash the grains to remove other impurities and dust adhering to the grain surface.
Ferment ↓	Soak the grains in clean water almost double the weight of the grain, for 48–72 hours at room temperature in a vessel with a cover. This softens the kernels in preparation for milling, and allows some fermentation to occur.
Drain, rinse ↓	The liquor is drained off, the grains are rinsed in fresh clean water.
Mill ↓	The grains are milled wet to a fine slurry with as little water as possible.
Sieve ↓	The finely milled grain is diluted with water and sieved to remove the outer skins (sieve mesh size varies from 0.0394 to 0.0234 inches depending on taste). It is better not to use too much water, or the resultant paste becomes too dilute.
Store	The ogi is stored under water in a clay or plastic pot with its lid on, and taken out for sale as needed. The water is changed regularly to prevent further fermentation which could result in a sour taste, and to avoid contamination.

Cereal and legume products

prevent further fermentation. It also helps to keep the ogi free of mould.

In addition, traditional unglazed pots are used to keep the product cool by water evaporation from the outside of the pot.

So long as the paste water is changed daily for clean fresh water, ogi can keep for four weeks.

> **Equipment**
> No special equipment necessary

Breads and pancakes

Injera

Product description

Injera is a traditional fermented bread. It is large, flat, round, and uniformly thin and measures about 60cm in diameter. The top has uniformly spaced honeycomb-like eyes, each measuring about 4–5mm in diameter and the base has a smooth surface. Injera looks whitish cream, reddish brown or brown depending on the type of cereal flour used. It tastes slightly sour and is eaten with a kind of Ethiopian stew known as 'wet'. ('Wet' can be made from meat, pulses, vegetables or a mixture of them including red pepper, onion, butter or oil and spices.) The product is supplied in bulk to hotels and institutions while individual consumers can purchase pieces in the open market or in traditional food shops.

Principles of preservation and processing

The process of griddling or 'dry' frying causes the destruction of enzymes and micro-organisms in the food by heating, thus preventing spoilage and potential food poisoning. The removal of moisture by heat, particularly from the surface of the bread, inhibits mould growth during storage.

The process of fermentation produces a low pH which restricts the growth of potentially harmful bacteria.

In general, the shelf-life of this product is short (about three days), and depends on adequate storage conditions (particularly to prevent surface mould growth).

The method of processing involves preparing and mixing the ingredients to a dough, which is fermented and subsequently thinned to a batter. The batter is then poured onto a hot griddle in a thin layer to cook, developing its colour, flavour and texture.

Hygiene

Good hygienic practices should be carried out with respect to food handlers, raw materials, equipment and premises. In particular, the fermenting vat should be well cleaned after each batch of injera making. Potable water should be used. The injera

Process	Notes
Raw material	Tef (*Eragrostigs tef [Zucc] Trotter*) is an indigenous cereal for making injera. Other cereals which may be used are sorghum, millet, barley, wheat or a combination of cereals.
Clean	All impurities are removed by hand and winnowed in the case of sorghum, millet, barley and wheat. Tef is simply winnowed and sifted through a fine sieve.
Hull	Sorghum, barley and wheat are usually dampened and pounded traditionally in a wooden mortar and pestle to remove the bran. Mechanical hullers are also available.
Grind	The sifted tef is ground through a stone mill.
Mixing and first fermentation	Mix one part of flour, two parts of water and about 16 per cent ersho (a starter saved from previously fermented dough) by weight of the flour. Mix very well and leave it to ferment for three days.
Thin and heat	Discard the surface water formed on the top of the dough. For every 1kg of original flour, take about 200ml of the fermented mixture and add twice as much water, mix and bring to a boil (traditionally it is known as 'absit' making). It should be cooled to about 46°C/115°F before it is mixed into the main part of the dough. Thin the main dough by adding water equal to the original weight of the flour.
Batter-making and second fermentation	Add the absit to the thinned dough and mix well (known as batter making). Leave the batter for about 30 minutes to rise (the second fermentation), before baking commences. A small portion of the batter is saved to serve as a starter (ersho) for the next batch.
Griddle	Injera is griddled by pouring about two-thirds of a litre of the batter onto the hot greased electrical 'metad' (injera griddle made of clay) using a circular motion from the outside towards the centre. It is cooked in about 2–3 minutes. Rapeseed oil is used to grease the metad between each one.
Store	Several layers of injera can be stored in a 'messob' (traditional straw basket) with a tight cover for three days in a cool, dry, ventilated place.

Cereal and legume products

must not be handled with wet hands as surface moisture will facilitate mould growth.

Raw material

Cereal flours should be sifted to remove foreign materials, debris and any other contaminants, and to remove bran and produce a uniform flour particle size. The quality of the starter material (ersho) must be good enough to ferment the dough within three days.

Process control

○ Accurate weighing of ingredients and thorough mixing to maintain the quality of the final product—the ratio of the flour, water and starter should be optimal to produce a fermented injera of the required taste.

○ The 'absit' should not be cooled below 46°C/115°F before it is mixed into the remaining dough in order to facilitate the second fermentation. Thorough mixing is required to obtain a uniform batter.

○ Temperature control of the metad is important. It should be hot enough so that each piece of injera is baked within 2–3 minutes, thus producing a uniformly eyed, soft and unburnt injera. Correct temperature of the griddling process ensures optimum texture, colour and flavour of the product.

Packaging and storage

Good storage control is necessary to prevent mould growth, which is a significant risk in this product. Contamination by moulds is less important in cool highland regions than in warm lowland regions. To prevent mould growth the product should be properly cooled and dry before packing. Any surface moisture will encourage contamination. The straw baskets used to store injera should have tight covers, and be kept in a ventilated, cool, dry place, raised off the floor. Packaging also protects to some extent against insects, animals and soils. When empty, the baskets should be regularly cleaned and stored dry, raised off the floor in a dry place.

Equipment
Mortar and pestle
Winnowing basket
Traditional sieve
Electrical metad
Stone mill

Fermented sweet bread

Product description

This type of bread resembles a leavened biscuit with a soft texture and dark brown toasted crust. It is very popular and can be prepared in several ways. It stores very well under ambient conditions for a week or two.

Principles of preservation and processing

The process of baking causes the destruction of enzymes and micro-organisms in the food, thus preventing spoilage and potential food poisoning. The removal of moisture from the surface of the bread inhibits mould growth during storage.

Process	Notes
Raw materials	Soft wheat flour; sugar; fat; water; yeast; eggs; baking powder; salt.
Mix	1. Mix together the flour and water. 2. Mix in the sugar, fat, yeast, baking powder, salt and eggs to form the dough.
Rest	After thorough mixing, the dough is covered with a damp cloth or oiled polythene and left to rest for 20 minutes.
Roll form	Divide the dough equally into appropriate sized pieces, depending on final product size desired. Form each piece to a round shape and place on a tray.
Fermentation	Cover dough pieces with a damp cloth to prevent drying out. (The dough pieces may be coated with a layer of fat and sprinkled with flour.) Leave for three hours at a temperature of 20–24°C/68–72°F.
Bake	Bake at 180°C/350°F for about 25 minutes. For very large loaves, lower the temperature and bake for longer. The surface should be a dark brown colour when baking is complete.
Cool	Remove from oven and cool sufficiently before packaging.
Pack	Pack in paper or polythene bags depending on length of storage time before sale or consumption.

The process of fermentation produces a low pH which restricts the growth of potentially harmful micro-organisms. The high proportion of sugar may also restrict some micro-organisms.

In general the shelf-life of this product is one or two weeks, and this depends on adequate storage conditions (particularly to avoid surface mould growth).

The method of processing involves preparing a dough by mixing together all ingredients thoroughly; dividing and shaping the dough into uniform pieces before leaving it to rise. The risen pieces are baked to set the structure and develop characteristic texture, flavour and colour of the product.

Hygiene

Good hygienic practices should be carried out with respect to food handlers, raw materials, equipment and premises. Use potable water to prevent contamination. Containers used to ferment the dough, and the storage baskets, must be cleaned well before each batch.

Raw material

Ingredients

45.5kg/100lb soft wheat flour
11 litres/19 pints water
11.35kg/25lb sugar
8.4kg/18.5lb lard (pork fat, or hydrogenated vegetable oil)
1.35kg/3lb dried yeast
1.35kg/3lb baking powder
454g/1lb common salt
400 eggs (approx 9kg/20.5lb)

The flour must be free from foreign matter, soils and other contaminants (such as weevils). Good quality active yeast must be used in order to ferment the dough to the desired level within the required time.

Process control

○ Flour, water and yeast should be in the right proportions to produce a fermented product of the required texture. Accurate weighing of ingredients is an important control point, because small variations can cause significant differences in the final product.

Cereal and legume products

○ Thorough mixing and kneading of the dough will result in a uniform product especially in shape and texture.

○ Temperature and time control of the baking process are important to ensure the colour, texture and flavour qualities of the product.

Packaging and storage

Good packaging and storage control are necessary to prevent mould growth, which is a key problem with this product. To prevent it, the product should be properly cooled before packing, taking care to adhere to hygienic measures. Any surface moisture will encourage contamination (if packed hot in polythene, moisture will condense inside as the product cools, providing conditions for mould contamination). For this product, polythene bags and paper bags are the most commonly used, which also provide protection against some insects and soil contamination. In large quantities they may be packed in cardboard boxes. Store in a ventilated, cool, dry place, raised off the floor.

Equipment
Dough mixer
Bread forming tables and moulds
Baking trays and oven
Heat sealer (if polythene bags are used)
Scales

Chapati (pancakes)

Product description

The chapati is a round, flat, unleavened bread made from wheat dough. It has a soft brown/white mottled crust and a white honeycombed inside. It is used as part of a main meal or as a snack and it is similar to the roti (India), the kisra (Sudan), and the tortilla (Latin America). In East Africa the Indian name 'chapati' is used.

Principles of preservation and processing

The principles of preservation for chapati are to destroy enzymes and contaminating micro-organisms by heat during frying, and to remove water from the crust to inhibit moulds.

The expected shelf-life is three to five days. The method of processing involves mixing ingredients to form a uniform dough, and 'dry' frying in oil to set the structure of the dough and develop the characteristic flavour, aroma and colour of the product.

Hygiene

Heat during the frying process kills almost all micro-organisms in the dough. The most important risk is from moulds which recontaminate the baked product if proper storage conditions are not maintained. However, it is necessary to use good hygiene practices and potable water when preparing and handling dough to avoid excessive contamination and/or food poisoning bacteria which might survive frying.

Raw material

Chapatis can be made from white, brown or wholemeal flour. White flour is finely ground, but it is more common to use brown flour of 85 per cent extraction rate. It should be free of insects and other contamination. The formula can be varied to taste, but for production all ingredients should be weighed accurately as even a small variation can cause large differences in the final product.

Process control

The main quality control points are:

○ Weighing the ingredients and mixing/kneading to obtain a uniform dough.

○ The thickness of the rolled dough.

○ The frying time and temperature which control the development of flavour, colour and the correct texture in the crumb and crust. Control over the oil temperature and frying time is therefore essential.

Packaging and storage

The main problem during storage is mould growth, and chapatis should be stored in a dry, well-ventilated and cool place. When left in the open air, chapatis dry out to form a hard, unacceptable product. Packaging is used to prevent contamination by dirt and insects. A suitable

Process	Notes
Mix	Ingredients mixed into a smooth mixture (at 37–40°C/98–104°F). Proportion 2:1 flour to milk (or water). If eggs are used less water will be required. Salt to taste; fat is optional.
Knead	Knead to produce a smooth and elastic dough within 8–10 minutes by hand.
Relax (rest)	Shape the dough into smooth balls, cover with a clean piece of damp cloth. Rest for 10 minutes.
Divide	Divide dough into portions (1kg/2.2lb flour will produce a minimum of 10–12 chapatis). Form into balls and cover with clean damp cloth.
Roll	Roll each piece on a floured surface using a rolling pin. Grease the surface of the dough with a little oil, form the dough into a ball, then roll again to a round piece 15cm/6in diameter and 2–3mm thick (diameter may be varied depending on size of frying pan).
Fry	Grease a frying pan with a little oil and fry until surface is brown.
Cool	To room temperature.
Pack	In plastic bags.
Store	Shelf-life 2–5 days depending on storage conditions and packaging. Store in a cool, dry place away from sunlight.

Cereal and legume products

packaging material is a polythene bag which is usually tied in a knot instead of heat sealing. Chapatis should not be packaged hot into plastic bags as moisture vapour will condense on the inside of the bag, wet the product and cause mould growth. The weight of each chapati is determined by the weight of the dough pieces and this should be made uniform from batch to batch.

Equipment
Electric mixer (optional)
Rolling pins
Scales
Frying pan
Cooling racks

Biscuits and cakes

Biscuits

Product description

Biscuits are a baked product, usually produced from wheat flour in a large variety of shapes, sizes, textures and flavours. They are a dry product, usually with a golden brown crust and a crisp, pale brown crumb.

For rapid baking, the thickness of the biscuits is usually not more than 3–4mm. They may be coloured with food dyes, and dried fruit or nuts may also be incorporated. The shelf-life is several months under correct storage conditions. Biscuits comprise a diverse range of products and are eaten as snacks.

Principles of preservation and processing

There are two principles of preservation: heat destruction of enzymes and micro-organisms during baking, and the removal of water during baking which inhibits spoilage micro-organisms during storage.

Process	Notes
Flour	Cake flour (from soft wheat).
Sieve	Sieve using a fine sieve—1mm aperture.
Mix	Mix flour, margarine, baking powder and salt together by hand or with an electric mixer.
Mix	In a separate container mix the egg with the sugar and milk or water.
Knead	Add the liquid mix to the flour-based mixture and use a small mixing machine or hands to form a dough.
Roll	Using a rolling stick/pin and board, roll thinly (5mm).
Cut	Cut to any required size, e.g. round or square shape—use a hand-cutter.
Bake	Bake at 200–250°C/390–480°F for between 5 and 20 minutes until golden brown.
Cool	Cool on a wire rack to room temperature.
Pack	Pack in sealed plastic packets.
Store	Store in a dry and cool place.

The method of processing involves mixing ingredients to form a dough, rolling and forming into the desired shape, and then baking.

Hygiene

Heat during baking destroys most contaminating bacteria and the dryness of the finished product restricts recontamination during storage. Good hygienic practices should be followed during preparation of the dough to prevent contamination. Hygienic practices apply to food handlers, equipment, premises and the use of potable water.

Raw material

Ingredients

250g/10oz soft wheat flour
65g/2½oz margarine
7g/¼oz baking powder
Pinch of salt
1 egg
20g/¾oz sugar
15g/½oz milk or water

The main quality factors are the colour and fineness of the flour and freedom from soils, mould, insects, weevils and so on.

Process control

The main control points are:

○ Accurate weighing and thorough mixing of ingredients, as even a small variation can cause large differences in the final product.

○ The time and temperature of baking, which controls the final colour, texture, flavour and crispness of the product.

Product control

The main quality factors are colour, size/shape, aroma, texture and flavour of the product, and freedom from blemishes, contamination and soils. Each of these is determined by the amounts and types of ingredients, control over mixing and baking stages and correct storage.

Packaging and storage

The product should be properly cooled before packaging into a moisture-proof wrapper in order to prevent water vapour condensing onto the inside of the pack, moistening the biscuits and promoting mould growth. As biscuits are a hygroscopic product (that is, they will readily absorb moisture from the air), they should be stored in a moisture-proof container. The packaging also prevents contamination by soils, insects and so on. The product should be stored in a cool, dry place away from sunlight, which accelerates rancidity.

Packaging

Some biscuits, especially those that contain a high proportion of fat or those with cream fillings, require a more complex type of packaging than simple polythene. This may be a major limitation for a small-scale processor and it is strongly advised that the availability and cost of packaging is investigated first if it is proposed to produce these types of biscuits. In all cases the package should be moisture-proof, greaseproof and preferably light-proof.

Equipment
Mixer (optional)
Cutter
Rolling pin
Oven
Heat sealer
Scales
Thermometer
Clock

Rich fruit cake

Product description

This type of cake contains a mixture of dried fruit incorporated into the sponge. The richness of the cake depends on the amount of fruit added and can vary enormously from lightly fruited cakes to heavily fruited cakes. The latter are often the type made for special occasions (for example, a wedding cake), as they can be expensive. In these cases they are covered with icing and decorated. When cooked, fruit cake is firm to the touch and dark in colour, with pieces of fruit scattered throughout the whole cake. It is very sweet to taste, and can be round, square or rectangular in shape.

Principles of preservation and processing

The principles of preservation are that heat and the removal of water act to destroy microbial activity. High levels of sugar in the product and relatively low moisture content act to inhibit any subsequent growth of micro-organisms. Cooking also inactivates all the enzymes present in the cake. Any spoilage is limited to mould growth and this can be controlled by storing the cake in an airtight container in a cool place.

The method of processing is by the sugar-batter method and the fruit is mixed into the batter last before being filled into baking tins. Because it is rich (contains a lot of sugar), this type of cake is cooked at a low temperature for a long time.

Note The dried fruit may be prepared by small food producers using small industrial dryers. Crystallization of the fruit can also be done easily on a small scale.

Hygiene

Because this cake is rich in sugar it is very difficult for most micro-organisms to grow. Heat during baking destroys most contaminating bacteria and the relatively dry crust restricts recontamination during storage. Good hygienic practices should be enforced during preparation of the cake. These practices apply to food handlers, equipment, premises, and the use of potable water.

Process	Notes
Weigh raw materials ↓	See list. Prepare a 25cm/10in round or 23cm/9in square cake tin by lining with a double thickness of grease proof paper.
Mix ↓	Cream the fat and sugar together in a mixing bowl to a light foam, pale in colour. Add the treacle carefully.
Beat ↓	Beat the eggs together and slowly incorporate into the fat/sugar batter. If using a mechanical mixer, turn to a higher speed and pour the egg in a steady stream into the side of the bowl until all has been incorporated. If mixing by hand, add the beaten egg in several small portions, beating well after each addition.
Sieve and fold ↓	Sieve the flour separately (1mm aperture of sieve). Fold the flour and dried spices into the batter mixture as gently as possible. If using a mechanical mixer, turn speed to a minimum. The final batter should be smooth and free of lumps.
Mix ↓	Mix in all fruit and nuts carefully until evenly distributed.
Fill ↓	Spread the mixture into the prepared baking tin.
Bake ↓	Bake at 177°C/350°F for 90 minutes in a pre-heated oven.
Cool	Cool on a raised rack.
Package ↓	In an airtight container or seal in plastic bags.
Store	Store in a clean, cool, dry, ventilated place. The shelf-life is a few months.

Raw material

Ingredients for one cake

250g/10oz butter, softened	(11%)
250g/10oz soft brown sugar	(11%)
6 eggs	(14%)
30ml/1.5 tablespoons black treacle	(1%)
275g/11oz plain flour	(12%)
Grated rind of 1 lemon	
7.5ml/1.5 teaspoon mixed spice	(0.3%)
2.5ml/1.5 teaspoon nutmeg	(0.3%)

100g/4oz glazed cherries	(4%)
100g/4oz mixed cut peel	(4%)
400g/1lb currants	(18%)
250g/10oz sultanas	(11%)
150g/6oz raisins	(7%)
100g/4oz chopped nuts	(4%)

The main quality factors are the colour and fineness of the flour and freedom from soils, mould, insects, weevils, etc. All ingredients should be of good quality and should have been stored under correct conditions.

Process control

The main control points are:

O Accurate weighing of ingredients, as even a small variation can cause large differences in the final product.

O Mixing—beating of the fat/sugar mixture to the correct consistency is important to trap sufficient air; beating eggs and sieving flour also incorporates air. Careful addition of the fine flour is important, so as to minimize interference with the incorporated air. The amount of air incorporated into the mixture determines the size of the final cake and the openness of the crumb structure.

O Time and temperature of baking, which control the colour, texture, flavour and moistness of the product. A rich fruit cake is baked at low temperature for a long time. If the temperature is too high the product will burn at the crust before the crumb is cooked. If it is too low the crumb will dry out before the crust colour is formed. To prevent any crust burning in a fruit cake, line the edges of the tin with greaseproof paper. The oven door should not be opened during baking.

Product control

The main quality factors are colour, size/shape, aroma, texture and flavour of the product, and freedom from blemishes, contamination and soils. Each is determined by the amounts and types of ingredients, control over mixing and baking stages and correct storage.

Packaging and storage

The product should be properly cooled before packaging into a moisture-proof bag in order to prevent water vapour condensing onto the inside of the pack, moistening the surface of the cake and promoting mould growth. The pack also prevents contamination by soils, insects, and so on. The product should be stored in a cool, dry place away from sunlight, which would accelerate rancidity of the fats in the cake.

Equipment
Food mixer (optional)
Scales
Wire rack
Sieve
Greaseproof paper
Cake tin
Oven
Thermometer

Snackfoods

Dabbo qolo (wheat flour snackfood)

Product description

Dabbo qolo is an Ethiopian fried spiced and/or sweetened snackfood, made from wheat flour. It resembles a flattened peanut, but its size and shape can vary. Normally, the smallest is about the size of pea while the largest could be as big as a broad bean. It has a crunchy texture and a golden brown colour. It can be served with coffee or tea between meals. It is commonly used by travellers on a long journey. In traditional shops it is sold in small measures (the Ethiopian coffee cup, for example).

Principles of preservation and processing

The principles of preservation are the removal of most of the moisture from the product, which inhibits microbial growth and prevents re-contamination during storage; and the destruction of enzymes and micro-organisms by heat.

The processing method involves making a dough and shaping it into small 'pea-sized' pieces which are then fried.

Hygiene

The risk of food poisoning and food spoilage is minimized by adhering to good hygienic practices with respect to food handlers, equipment and premises. Thus, containers for making the dough, the frying pan and scissors must be cleaned before making each batch of dabbo qolo. Spoilage and contaminating micro-organisms are controlled by the high temperatures used in processing as well as the low moisture content of the product, thus reducing any risk of contamination to a minimum.

Raw material

Flour should be good quality (free from insects and other foreign materials). It must be sifted and berberrie should be fine and with a strong spice flavour.

Process	Notes
Flour	Sifted stone-milled wheat flour.
Dough making	Mix together in a large bowl one part of flour, then add 7 per cent berberrie, 10 per cent oil and 1 per cent salt by weight of the flour. Add small amounts of water in stages to form a stiff dough. Knead well for five minutes to form a ball.
Roll and cut	Tear pieces (about a spoonful) of the dough and roll between slightly oiled palms to form a long strip. The strip should be about the thickness of a pencil. Cut the strips into small pieces, about the size of a pea, with scissors.
Fry	Heat in about 5cm (2 inches) of oil in a pan. Fry for about five minutes until golden brown, turning them several times.
Cool	Drain off excess oil and cool to room temperature.
Store	Fried dabbo qolo can be stored in tin containers or plastic bags for several days, or even months in dry areas.

Note This product can be either fried in frying pans as described or roasted on a slightly greased electrical metad.

Process control

○ All ingredients must be well mixed and kneaded to produce the required dough characteristics.

○ Size and shape: the diameter of the dough strip must not be larger than pencil size and should be cut into uniformly sized pieces.

○ The temperature and time control of the frying operation are vital to produce a uniform product.

○ The product should be cooled to room temperature before packaging.

Packaging and storage

Dabbo qolo can be kept for a fairly long period if it is stored correctly. The main risk is moisture uptake, which causes the softening of the product and provides the conditions for growth of moulds. Moisture absorption is minimized by ensuring the product is at room temperature before packaging it in dry, moisture-proof containers such as heat-sealed polythene bags. The store room should be clean, cool, well-ventilated and dry. Storing on raised platforms and packaging the product also helps prevent physical damage from insects and other animal pests.

Equipment
Mixing bowl
Scissors
Electrical metad or a frying pan

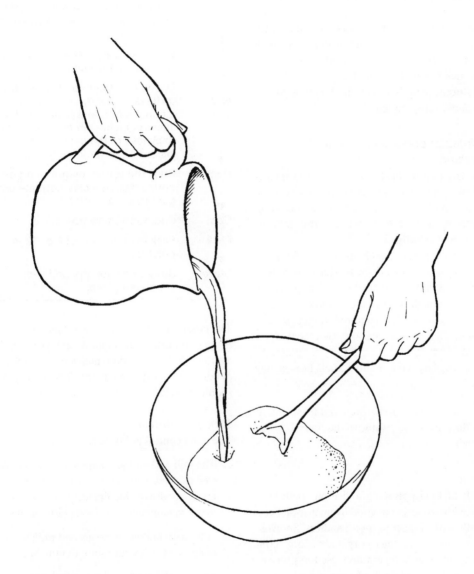

Add small amounts of water to make a stiff dough

Fresh maize tortilla

Product description

The tortilla is a type of pancake which is the staple in some Latin American countries such as Mexico and the Central American region. It is consumed with every meal (instead of bread) and is also the basis of a variety of snackfoods. Tortillas with bean purée, with meat, with sausage or with cheese are usually prepared as 'sandwiches'. Fresh tortillas need to be consumed in a day or two; if longer storage periods are required they should be stored under refrigeration.

Principles of preservation and processing

The destruction by heat of enzymes and micro-organisms is the main principle of preservation. The griddling process also reduces the moisture, mainly at the surface of the product, thus inhibiting microbial growth.

The method of processing involves cooking the maize in lime (calcium hydroxide) to soften it, removing hulls and milling to a paste or dough. This dough is pressed by hand or machine to a disc shape of the required thickness and diameter. These pancakes are then heated on both sides by griddling on a clay hotplate. In general, tortillas have a short shelf-life—a day or two.

Note Tortillas can also be prepared from instant tortilla flour by adding water to the flour to make the dough.

Hygiene

The risk of food poisoning and food spoilage is minimized by adhering to good hygienic practices, especially with respect to food handlers. Spoilage and contaminating micro-organisms are controlled by the high temperatures used in processing, thus reducing any risk of contamination to a minimum. However, the product should be handled carefully to avoid recontamination.

Raw material

Ingredients

4.5kg/10lb whole, clean common maize
70g/2½oz of lime powder (calcium hydroxide)

Process	Notes
Boil	Boil maize grain in water plus lime for one hour. Ensure the level of water covers the grain.
Wash	Wash the grains by agitating them in running water to remove the hulls, and the excess lime in the water. Drain to produce clean, hulled grains.
Mill	Wet-mill using a stone or disc mill. A dough is formed.
Divide and shape	Divide the dough and shape the tortillas by hand, or by pressing in a hand-press, to a pancake of about 10cm (4 inches) in diameter. The thickness of the pancake differs according to regional traditions.
Heat	Cook the tortilla by griddling on both sides on a clay hotplate until golden in colour (about 1 minute).
Cool	Cool to room temperature.
Pack	Pack in quantities of 6 or 12 in polythene bags.
Store	Store in a cool, dry and well-ventilated place.

The grain used should be of good quality. The use of high-moisture or mouldy grains should be avoided. Yellow or white maize may be used, depending on local availability. The lime powder should be dried.

Process control

The main control points are:

○ The mill and all the equipment used should be well cleaned. Also, if the tortillas are formed by hand, good hygienic practices are necessary to avoid contamination by food poisoning bacteria.

○ Adequate hulling of grains and milling to produce a consistent and smooth dough.

○ Shaping the dough to uniform pieces.

○ Time and temperature of griddling to produce characteristic texture and colour of the product.

○ Cooling the tortillas before packaging.

Packaging and storage

Tortillas are usually eaten fresh and not packaged, but if they are to be stored for more than a day the

Cereal and legume products

most commonly used packaging material is polythene bags. Care should be taken to pack the tortillas *after* they cool down to prevent any condensation of moisture inside the bag, which would provide conditions for mould growth. The product should be stored under refrigeration if they are to be consumed after two days.

Equipment

Mill (stone or disc mill)
Clay hot surface (*comal*)
Machine to form tortillas (optional)
Heat sealer (optional)

Maize tamales

Product description

Cooked maize is prepared with cooked meat (pork, chicken or turkey are added) along with other ingredients, such as tomatoes, chilli or pepper. It is usually consumed during weekends and holidays, either in its 'red' or 'black' version. The colour of the tamale depends on the condiments or other additives used. Black tamale is in general a sweet product which might include prunes and raisins in its formulation, while red tamale (below) is a salted type of product typically prepared with olives and capers. Since many formulations exist for these products, a typical one is presented here. This type of product needs to be stored under refrigeration if consumed in two or three days or in a freezer if longer periods of storage are desired.

Principles of preservation and processing

The main principle of preservation is the heat destruction of enzymes and micro-organisms. There are two main heating stages: boiling the maize, and boiling the tamale. For food safety the final processing is the most important, especially as meat is used in this product.

The method of processing involves cooking the maize in lime (calcium hydroxide) to soften it, removing hulls and grinding to a dough. Fat is incorporated into the dough (along with other ingredients), and small amounts are spread in banana leaves. Meat and a prepared sauce are added, the leaves are wrapped and tied and the product is steamed. It is usually eaten warm.

Red tamale

Hygiene

The risk of food poisoning and food spoilage is minimized by adhering to good hygienic practices, and the use of potable water. Spoilage and contaminating micro-organisms are controlled by the high temperatures used in processing, but there is a high risk of recontamination during handling and storage of the product.

Process	Notes
Raw grains	Maize and rice
Clean	Separately clean the rice and maize. Soak the rice overnight (8–12 hours), drain and put aside.
Boil	Boil maize with lime until soft and outer hull becomes loose.
Wash	Drain maize and wash by agitating in running water to remove hulls and excess lime.
Grind	Grind the cooked maize and the soaked rice to form a dough. Put to one side.
Prepare other ingredients	(a) Chop cleaned tomatoes, sweet pepper and chilli peppers, remove seeds and boil for 8 minutes. Grind together and mix in annatto paste. (b) Roast the sesame seeds, whole peppers and cinnamon. Mix with bitter pumpkin seeds and grind together.
Mix	Mix together (a) and (b) to give a red sauce, sieve and fry in 170g/6oz of the fat, and add salt to taste. If too runny, thicken with a little of the prepared maize/rice dough.
Sieve dough	Add enough water to the previously prepared maize/rice dough to soften it, mix and sieve the dough.
Mix	Mix in 454kg/1lb of the lard to the maize/rice dough thoroughly to give a uniform product. Mix in salt to taste.
Heat	Heat the softened dough, stirring continuously until it thickens to the consistency of a puree.
Fill	Spread small amounts of maize/rice purée (227g/8oz weight) in clean banana leaves (30cm by 20cm or 12in by 8in). Add 28g/1oz of raw meat and top with 56g/2oz of the red sauce. Finish with olives and capers.
Wrap	Wrap the leaf around the filling. Secure with a tie.
Steam	Steam in small amount of water for two hours in a covered pot. Top up with water as necessary to prevent drying out.
Serve/ store	If not consumed immediately, store under refrigeration for two to three days, or freeze for longer periods.

Cereal and legume products

Raw material

Ingredients

1.8kg/4lb whole, dry, clean, common white maize
227g/8oz dry, polished, clean rice
40 tomatoes (approx 2.7kg/6lb)
454g/1lb ground cherry tomatoes
8 sweet peppers
7 chilli peppers (dry)
14g/½oz annatto paste
113g/4oz roasted seeds of bitter pumpkin (*pepitoria*)
56g/2oz sesame seeds
14g/½oz whole large pepper (*pimienta gorda*)
7g/¼oz cinnamon
624g/1lb 6oz lard (pork fat or hydrogenated vegetable oil)
1.4kg/3lb meat (pork, chicken or turkey)
14g/½oz lime powder (calcium hydroxide)
10 plantain or banana leaves (as packaging material)

Grains should be ripe, fully mature, dry and free from mould growth. The moisture content of the grains should be 13–14 per cent. Spoiled grains impart an unpleasant flavour and colour to the product, in addition to increasing the risk of food poisoning. The banana leaves used should be very well washed, ensuring that they are free from any insecticide or pesticide.

Process control

○ Adequate hulling and milling to produce a smooth dough.

○ Weighing the ingredients and thorough mixing to obtain uniformity.

○ Hygienic handling of product while filling leaves, securing leaf wraps to avoid product loss.

○ Time and temperature control of steaming stage—the main problem here is to prevent the product drying out, because of the length of steaming required.

Packaging and storage

The final steaming stage sterilizes the product in its own packaging. Providing the leaves are secure and the product is hygienically handled, recontamination is minimal. However, because of its high moisture content, it is necessary to store below 5°C/41°F or frozen, if it is not consumed on the same day as preparation. This product can be retailed by packaging quantities of 6 or 12 in polythene bags. The packs are stored under refrigeration or frozen.

Suitable packaging material The banana or plantain leaves are the most commonly used packaging materials. In special cases, when these products are scarce, aluminium foil may be used.

Equipment
Sieve
Mill (stone or disc mill)
Scales

Note Simpler formulations of similar tamale products exist, such as the Mexican canned tamales, and also more complex (with more ingredients) products can be found, such as the Nicaraguan 'nacatamale'.

Popcorn

Product description

An exploded grain of a special variety of maize, called popcorn maize, is consumed as a snackfood. It has a delightful texture, being crisp yet tender, with a delicate flavour. Popcorn can be further flavoured with salt or cheese.

Principles of preservation and processing

The main principle of preservation has two results: the high temperature reached causes the removal of most of the moisture from the product, which inhibits microbial growth and prevents re-contamination during storage, and also causes the heat destruction of micro-organisms and enzymes.

The method of processing involves heating the grains in a closed container until the moisture inside the grain vaporizes and expands the kernel causing it to 'pop' or explode. The principle is that the pericarp (outer layer) of the maize acts as a pressure vessel, allowing water in the kernel to be superheated until pressure ruptures the pericarp allowing the endosperm (starchy interior of the grain) to expand.

Process	Notes
Raw material ↓	Clean popcorn maize grains (already shelled and dried for storage).
Heat ↓	Heat grains (in a dry state) in a closed container (popcorn-making machine)* until 'popping' sound indicates that the grains have expanded and the product is ready. This occurs at approx. 177°C/350°F.
Mix ↓	Mix in salt (or other flavours) to taste.
Cool ↓	Remove the product from the vessel and allow to cool in a clean, dry place.
Pack ↓	Pack in moisture-proof packaging material.
Store	Store in a cool, dry, ventilated place.

* *Note* In some regions, the maize is heated in hot sand or in a little oil inside a closed container

to attain the required temperature for explosion of the grain. In other places special vessels are used, such as a rotating mechanical popcorn-making machine.

Hygiene

The risk of food poisoning and food spoilage is minimized by adhering to good hygienic practices. Spoilage and contaminating micro-organisms are controlled by the high temperatures used in processing as well as the low moisture content of the product.

Raw material

Grains should be ripe, fully mature, dry and free from mould growth. The moisture content of the grains should be 13–14 per cent. Spoiled grains impart an unpleasant flavour and colour to the product, in addition to increasing the risk from food poisoning.

Process control

The control points are as follows:

○ The pan should be preheated before loading the grains as the best results are obtained with abrupt changes in grain temperature.

○ The product should be cooled rapidly after popping to prevent overcooking or excessive drying. The cooling process is important to prevent moisture vapour condensing inside the bag when the product is packaged, which would otherwise encourage mould growth.

Packaging and storage

Moisture uptake causes softening and mould growth. This is a dry, hygroscopic product and moisture absorption is minimized by packaging it in moisture-proof containers such as heat-sealed polypropylene bags. The store room should be clean, cool, well-ventilated and dry. Shelf-life is one month at room temperature.

Equipment
Popcorn-making machine or suitable pan
Heat sealer
Scales

Cereal and legume products

Popped sorghum

Product description

Popped sorghum is a crisp, white, expanded product about 0.5cm in size, made from sorghum grains in a similar way to popcorn. It has a sweet taste with the aroma of sorghum. When processed and packaged correctly it has a shelf-life of approximately one month. It is used as a snackfood and is sold in restaurants and bars.

Principles of preservation and processing

The principles of preservation are the destruction of enzymes and contaminating micro-organisms in the raw material by heat, and the removal of most of the moisture from the product, preventing re-contamination during storage.

The process involves a rapid heating of moist sorghum grains to a high temperature. The rapidly increasing vapour pressure inside the grain causes it to burst or 'pop'.

Process	Notes
Raw material	Sorghum grains
Clean	Use a winnowing basket to remove light grains, leaves and dust. Remove stones, broken grains and unwanted materials by hand.
Soak	Soak in water to soften the bran for three minutes, and drain.
Pop	Pop the grain for two minutes in covered pans heated to 250°C/450°F.
Cool	Cool the popped grains on mats for five minutes, until they reach room temperature.
Separate	Remove unpopped grains by hand.
Pack	Package in airtight and moisture-proof polythene bags.
Store	Store in a cool, dry place.

Hygiene

The risk of food poisoning and food spoilage is minimized by adhering to good hygienic practices with respect to food handlers, equipment and premises, and by the use of potable water. Spoilage and contaminating micro-organisms are controlled by the high temperatures used in processing as well as the low moisture content of the product, thus reducing any risk of contamination to a minimum.

Raw material

Grains should be ripe, fully mature, dry and free from mould growth. The moisture content of the grains should be 13–14 per cent. Spoiled grains impart an unpleasant flavour and colour to the product, in addition to increasing the risk from aflatoxin poisoning.

Process control

The control points are:

○ The soaking time should be standardized at three minutes to optimize water uptake. Excessive water uptake results in delayed popping, whereas a low water uptake results in the product becoming charred during popping.

○ The pan should be preheated to approximately 250°C before loading the grains as the best results are achieved with the abrupt change in grain temperature.

○ The product should be cooled rapidly after popping to prevent overcooking or excessive drying. The cooling process is important to prevent moisture vapour condensing inside the bag when the product is packaged, which would encourage mould growth.

Packaging and storage

Moisture uptake causes softening, mould growth and the development of rancidity. This is a dry, hygroscopic product and moisture absorption is minimized by packaging it in dry, moisture-proof containers such as heat-sealed polythene bags. The store room should be clean, cool, well ventilated and dry.

> Equipment
> Covered pan
> Heat sealer
> Scales

Confectionery

Muscat

Product description

Muscat is prepared by concentrating a mixture of wheat starch, sugar and oil, adding pieces of cashew nuts, colour and essence. It appears oily and shiny and is usually yellow in colour. The product has a sticky texture. It is sold as large or small cakes, or very small cut pieces (approx. 2in by 2in or 5cm by 5cm) wrapped in oiled paper or polythene. The maximum shelf-life of the product is about 10–15 days, providing it is processed and packaged well.

Principles of preservation and processing

The principles of preservation are the destruction of enzymes and micro-organisms by heat, and the high sugar content which preserves the product by inhibiting microbial growth and preventing recontamination during storage.

Semolina (wheat flour grains) is placed on a piece of filter cloth, tied securely, and soaked in water. The process of soaking semolina initiates gluten development, and continued washing separates the starch from the gluten. Heating the starch with water and oil causes gelatinization of the starch granules. The process also inactivates enzymes and micro-organisms. Further heating removes water until a concentrated mixture develops which sets on cooling. Nuts and cardamom are mixed in to give it its distinct flavour.

Hygiene

The risk of food poisoning and food spoilage is minimized by adhering to good hygienic practices, especially with respect to food handlers. Spoilage and contaminating micro-organisms are controlled by the high temperatures used in processing, and to a certain extent by the high sugar content of the product, thus reducing the risk of recontamination.

Raw material

Ingredients
454g/1lb semolina
2 litres/3½ pints water

Process	Notes
Semolina ↓	Wrap semolina in muslin (filter) cloth and tie securely.
Wet ↓	Soak in water, agitating and pressing periodically to allow all starch to flow out through the cloth.
Wash/ rinse ↓	Wash out all the starch completely and retain the starch water for cooking.
Mix and concentrate ↓	Mix in sugar to starch water while heating. Stir until dissolved. Continue to heat and add cooking oil, small amounts at a time, stirring well until transparent in appearance. Add cashew nuts, cardamom, essence and colour and mix well.
Pour ↓	Pour onto an oiled, paper-lined tray and spread to the required thickness.
Cool ↓	Cool to room temperature.
Cut ↓	Cut into desired size and shape when cool.
Pack ↓	Wrap under hygienic conditions in moisture-proof, flexible packaging.
Store	Store in an airtight container, in a cool, dry and well-ventilated place.

1.8kg/4lb sugar
0.75 litres/1¼ pints cooking oil
Cashew nuts)
Cardamom)
Vanilla essence) to taste
Food colouring)

Semolina should be dry and free from insects and mould growth. All other ingredients should be of good quality, free from rancidity or mould growth.

Process control

Important control points are:

○ Weighing of ingredients and mixing: all ingredients must be well-mixed to achieve a uniform quality.

○ Temperature and time heating to produce a consistent product, in terms of colour and texture.

○ The product should be cooled to room temperature before packaging.

Packaging and storage

Muscat is heat-sealed in oiled paper or polythene. Freshly made muscat is traditionally stored as cakes in trays, covered to keep away flies. The wrapped or sealed product can be placed in larger boxes. For maximum shelf-life, the store room should be clean, cool, well-ventilated and dry. Storing the packaged product on raised platforms also helps to prevent damage from pests.

Note Instead of vegetable oil, any other good oil could be substituted. Some manufacturers also add ghee to the preparation. It should be possible to use other flours, or any other starch source (gluten-free flour needs no soaking or washing).

Kalu dodol

Product description
This is a popular confection, eaten as a snack or prepared for special occasions. It is available in a rolled form, wrapped in a leaf of the areca nut. This product is dark brown or black in colour, tastes sweet and has a shiny appearance and fleshy, gel-like texture. It is also available as small cubes wrapped in polythene. The product is stable when correctly stored for three to four weeks.

Principles of preservation and processing
Kalu dodol is made by heating a mixture of rice flour, jaggery (raw lump sugar) and coconut milk, with spices and pieces of cashew nut to form a jelly-like toffee.

Hygiene
The risk of food poisoning and food spoilage is minimized by adhering to good hygienic practices. Spoilage and contaminating micro-organisms are controlled by the high temperatures used in processing, and to a certain extent by the high sugar content of the product, thus reducing the risk of recontamination.

Raw material

Ingredients
250g/10oz parboiled rice
800g/1lb 12oz jaggery
Milk from three coconuts
20–30 cashew nuts
Cumin seeds
Cloves
10g/⅓oz salt

Parboiled rice should be dry and free from insects and mould growth. Spoiled grains impart an unpleasant flavour and colour to the product, in addition to increasing the risk from microbial contamination. All other ingredients should be of good quality.

Process control
Important control points are:

○ Sieving the flour to obtain uniform particle size.

○ Weighing of ingredients and mixing: all ingredients must be well-mixed to attain a consistent quality.

○ Temperature and time of the heating operation to produce a consistent product in terms of colour and texture.

○ If packaging in polythene, the product should be cooled to room temperature before packaging.

Packaging and storage
In the traditional packaging method, wrapping the product tightly in the leaf and leaving it to hang allows excess oil to drip away thus reducing rancidity during storage. The product keeps well in airtight packs such as polypropylene. Several such

Process	Notes
Raw material	Parboiled rice.
Clean	Sort by hand to remove leaves, debris and spoiled grains. Wash and destone.
Soak and drain	Soak the grain for five to six hours in water and drain.
Pound	Pound or mill to form a flour.
Sieve	Sieve flour to a fine particle size.
Heat and mix	Rice flour is added a little at a time to a warmed mixture of melted jaggery and coconut milk, stirring continously over heat.
Heat	Heat the mixture, stirring constantly until it thickens. Add salt and additional coconut milk (from two coconuts). Stir constantly, removing the top layer of oil as it collects.
Mix	Add chopped cashew nuts, cumin seeds and cloves just before the end-point is reached (i.e. just before the mixture has thickened fully) and mix well.
Portion and pack	Place a spoonful in the washed areca nut leaf, roll tightly and leave to hang. Alternatively, the mixture can be poured onto a baking sheet and left to cool before cutting into cubes and packaging in polythene.
Store	Store in a cool, dry place, protected from insects.

packs can be placed in boxes and stored. Storing the product in a cool, dry place in airtight containers delays rancidity.

Alternatively, kalu dodol is retailed freshly made, straight from the tray. If sold like this, it should be covered to protect from insects.

Equipment
Destoner
Pounder/mill
Sifter
Strainer
Coconut scraper
Weighing scale
Polythene sealer

Wheat flour nuecados

Product description
This is a fried, sweet snack produced from wheat flour which can be consumed either as a snack or as a dessert.

Principles of preservation and processing
The principles of preservation are the destruction of enzymes and micro-organisms by heat, and the high sugar content acts to preserve the product by inhibiting microbial growth and preventing recontamination during storage.

The process involves making a dough, forming small round pieces from the dough, frying them and coating them in a fondant. Pieces of nuecados are stuck together in groups of three or four before cooling and packaging.

Process	Notes
Prepare ↓	Sieve the flour; extract the juice from the oranges; beat the eggs.
Mix ↓	Mix thoroughly together the flour, egg yolks, eggs, salt and orange juice.
Dough formation	Knead to a soft dough.
Mould ↓	Pinch off small (10g/½oz) pieces and mould to a round shape.
Fry ↓	Fry the pieces in hot oil, pre-heated to frying temperatures (160–175°C/320–350°F), until golden brown in colour.
Drain ↓	Remove from oil and drain away excess.
Coat ↓	Brush the fried nuecados with egg white and coat with sugar fondant*. While still sticky, join the nuecados together in clumps of three or four.
Dry and cool	Leave to air-dry naturally on wire racks or a clean surface.
Pack ↓	Pack in moisture-proof bags and heat seal.
Store	In a cool, dry place.

* *Preparing the sugar fondant*
Dissolve the sugar in water and boil at 116°C/240°F before beating the syrup to form crystals. It is ready when it appears opaque white.

Hygiene
The risk of food poisoning and food spoilage is minimized by adhering to good hygienic practices. Spoilage and contaminating micro-organisms are controlled by the high temperatures used in processing.

Raw material

Ingredients
4.54kg/10lb soft wheat flour
80 egg yolks
40 whole eggs
28g/1oz common salt
10 fresh oranges
2.27kg/5lb hydrogenated vegetable oil
4.54kg/10lb sugar

Wheat flour should have the correct moisture content and be free from contaminants such as insects, pests and other foreign particles. All raw materials should be fresh and of good quality, free from blemishes and stored correctly.

Process control
Important control points are:

○ Weighing of ingredients and mixing: all ingredients must be well mixed to attain a uniform dough quality.

○ Controlling size and shape of dough pieces to standardize product.

○ Temperature and time control over:

    (a) the frying operation to produce uniform colour (golden brown), texture (crisp) and flavour.

    (b) the sugar boiling operation, to develop correct texture of fondant.

○ The product should be cooled to room temperature before packaging.

Packaging and storage
Protect from moisture uptake, as this product is hygroscopic. Polypropylene bags are often used. However, any heat-sealable, impermeable packaging material would be appropriate.

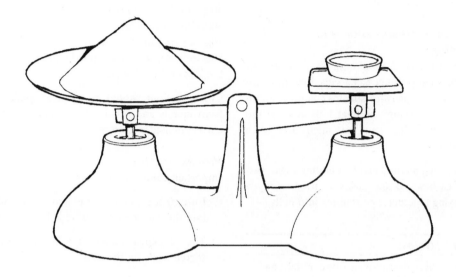

Weigh ingredients carefully to ensure a uniform dough quality

Chickpea ladoo

Product description

Although there are several types of ladoos made in India, chickpea ladoo is the easiest to make and has a long shelf-life. Ladoo is a sweet with a nutty flavour and a floury texture. It is yellow in colour and the size of a small lime.

Principles of preservation and processing

Ladoo is preserved in a number of different ways. The final product has a very low moisture content. Hence, micro-organisms cannot grow on it. During processing, the heat kills most of the dangerous bacteria, and the sugar acts as a preservative.

The processing method involves adding sugar, cardamom, cashew nut and raisins to fried chickpea flour, mixing together, and shaping into balls.

Process	Notes
Prepare raw materials	Weigh butter or ghee; chickpea flour (sieved); icing sugar; cardamom powder; chopped cashew nuts; chopped raisins.
Heat	Melt butter/ghee.
Fry	Fry chickpea flour, temperature up to 95°C/200°F, stirring constantly.
Cool	Remove from heat and cool to approximately 40–45°C/100–115°F.
Mix	Mix in the ground sugar (e.g. icing sugar) thoroughly, followed by the cardamom, chopped cashew nuts and chopped raisins.
Shape	Shape into balls by hand.
Pack	In polythene bags when cool.
Store	In airtight tins or on raised platforms.

Hygiene

Since ladoo is handled extensively after the heat treatment has been applied, strict enforcement of personal hygiene is necessary.

Raw material

Ingredients

400g/1lb butter or ghee
400g/1lb chickpea flour
800g/2lb icing sugar
10g/⅓oz cardamom powder
80g/3oz cashew nuts, chopped
50g/2oz raisins, chopped

Chickpea flour should be of good quality (free from insects and other foreign materials and of correct moisture content).

Process control

Important control points are:

○ Butter/ghee should be melted thoroughly before the chickpea flour is added.

○ The chickpea batter should be constantly stirred while on the heat.

○ The ingredients should be thoroughly mixed to attain uniform quality.

○ Temperature control should be exercised over heating chickpea flour to develop characteristic flavour and colour.

Packaging and storage

If retailing fresh, cover ladoo to prevent contamination by insects. If packaging, cool to room temperature first.

Ladoo can be packed in polythene bags and sealed in airtight tins and stored for several weeks.

For maximum shelf-life the store room should be clean, cool, well-ventilated and dry. Storing the packaged product on raised platforms also helps prevent damage from pests.

Equipment
Weighing scales

Semolina and noodles

Rice noodles

Product description
Rice noodles are hard, crisp, dry white tubes approximately 3mm in diameter and 15cm long, made from rice flour. They are used as part of a main meal or as a snackfood.

Principles of preservation and processing
The principle of preservation is the removal of most of the moisture from the product by drying, to prevent recontamination during storage. The process also allows conversion of rice flour to a more acceptable product.

Process	Notes
Polished rice	Rice which has been put through a polisher to remove its outer layers.
Mill/ grind	Mill to a fine flour using manual or powered grinding machine.
Sieve	Sift to obtain fine flour.
Mix	Gradually mix in just enough hot water to form a stiff porridge/ dough.
Extrude	Extrude using hand-operated extruder with 2–3mm diameter die.
Dry	The long extruded noodles are dried in shade for six hours.
Cut	Select for size and colour and cut into pieces up to 15cm in length.
Pack	Pack in a dry, moisture-proof bags.
Store	Store in cool, dry place.

Hygiene
The low moisture content of the product reduces the risk of spoilage and/or food poisoning by contaminating bacteria. Potable water and normal hygienic food handling practices should be used.

Raw material
Rice grains should be sorted to remove broken or mouldy pieces and should be free from soils or other contamination.

Process control
The smoothness of the noodle dough depends on the fineness of the flour and it is therefore sieved through a 0.5mm sieve to remove larger particles. Hot water is added slowly and stirred gently to make a smooth, stiff dough. Drying takes place in the shade to avoid rapid removal of water which would cause cracking or splitting of the noodles. When fully dried, the noodles will break when bent.

Packaging and storage
Moisture uptake causes softening, mould growth and the development of rancidity. This is a dry, hygroscopic product and moisture absorption is minimized by packaging it in dry, moisture-proof containers such as polypropylene or cellophane bags and heat-sealing. The store room should be clean, cool and dry.

Equipment
Mill
Extruder
Heat sealer
Scales

Semolina halva

Product description

Semolina halva is a widely consumed sweet all over the South Asia region. Semolina halva is sweet to taste, has a soft texture, is golden yellow in colour and is presented in rectangular pieces.

Principles of preservation and processing

Halva is preserved by a number of different mechanisms: the heat process kills most of the bacteria and the added sugar acts as a preservative. The cooking process then concentrates all the ingredients and therefore removes water from the product. This restricts the growth of bacteria.

The processing method involves mixing fried semolina, sugar, cardamom, fried cashew nuts, salt and raisins into boiled milk over heat, until the mixture thickens. It is spread onto trays, cooled and cut into pieces before packaging and retailing.

Process	Notes
Heat semolina ↓	Melt butter, add semolina and gently fry to a golden brown, set aside.
Boil milk ↓	Boil milk and reduce heat.
Mix ↓	Add the fried semolina and all the other ingredients and mix over heat (95°C/200°F), stirring constantly. When it thickens, remove from heat.
Spread ↓	Spread onto greased trays 2–3cm thick.
Cool ↓	Cool to room temperature.
Cut ↓	Cut into rectangular shapes 4cm by 6cm.
Pack ↓	In moisture-proof bags inside a box.
Store	In a clean, cool, dry place.

Hygiene

Spoilage and contaminating micro-organisms are controlled by the high temperatures used in processing, and to a certain extent by the sugar content of the product, thus reducing the risk of recontamination.

Raw material

Ingredients

200g/8oz semolina
100g/4oz butter
200g/8oz sugar
50g/2oz cashew nuts (fried)
150g/5oz raisins
400ml/¾ pint milk
3g salt
5g cardamom

The semolina should be a fine grade and free from insects and stones.

All other ingredients should be of good quality—the milk and butter used should be fresh, otherwise the final product will have an off-flavour.

Process control

The main process control points are:

○ Make sure that the butter is melted before you add the semolina. Ensure regular stirring at this stage to avoid burning.

○ Remove from heat once the mixture is thickening (i.e. after adding sugar and salt) to avoid it becoming too stiff. Constant stirring is necessary at this stage.

Packaging and storage

Semolina halva can be packed in polythene bags and placed in a box. Under these conditions it will keep for a few days.

> **Equipment**
> No special equipment required

Wheat grains can be malted, or ground into a flour which is an ingredient in chapati, biscuits and cake, and the semolina can be made into muscat or halva [Panos/Sean Sprague]

Beverages (alcoholic and non-alcoholic)

Soy milk

Product description

Soy milk is a creamy white liquid extracted from soybeans and used as a dairy milk substitute. It can be sweetened with 5 per cent sugar and consumed directly, or it can be flavoured with coffee, vanilla or fruit juices. It is also used with dairy milk by mixing in a ratio of one part dairy milk to four parts soy milk.

Principles of preservation and processing

Preservation is achieved by heat inactivation of enzymes and micro-organisms. Recontamination of this liquid product is prevented by hermetically sealed packages. The process involves grinding soaked beans to a purée, then boiling with water and pressing to extract the milk.

Process	Notes
Raw material	Soybeans.
↓	
Clean	Remove any foreign material, spoiled grains and debris by hand and wash with water.
↓	
Soak	10 hours soaking in 10 per cent sodium bicarbonate solution or 18–24 hours in cold water.
↓	
Wash	Twice with cold water.
↓	
Grind	Grind to a smooth paste or purée in a mortar and pestle, grain mill or a blender.
↓	
Boil	The paste is boiled with water (6 litres water/kg of beans) for 20 minutes to extract the milk.
↓	
Press	Use a pressing sack or bag and squeeze to extract the liquid 'milk' (or use a manual press: two pressings are usual).
↓	
Boil	Bring milk to boil rapidly and boil for six minutes. Stir continuously.
↓	
Cool	To room temperature.
↓	
Pack	In sterilized bottles or plastic pouches.

Hygiene

The extracted soy milk is a low acid product that is highly susceptible to spoilage and transfer of food poisoning bacteria to consumers. Hygienic practices therefore play an important role in determining the quality of the final product. Strict hygiene should be enforced when handling the extracted milk, and especially after boiling when the risk of recontamination is highest.

The main hygienic requirements are:

○ Thoroughly clean and sterilize (with chlorine solution or boiling water) all equipment and utensils used to handle the milk (e.g. filter bags, fillers) before and after processing (any aluminium equipment should *not* be cleaned with chlorine solution).

○ Strict enforcement of personal hygiene measures.

Raw material

Beans should be free of husk, soils and other debris and free of insect damage. They should be stored in a cool, dry room on raised pallets and protected from insects, birds and rodents.

Process control

The main control points are:

○ To soak the beans for an adequate time to allow proper grinding. If the beans are too hard through inadequate soaking, the yield of milk will be reduced and the product will have a stronger, 'beany' flavour.

○ Careful filtering of the milk through a fine mesh bag to remove solid particles in the milk. Solids will settle out on storage and reduce the value of the product.

○ The time and temperature of boiling should be controlled to adequately pasteurize the milk and to destroy micro-organisms and antinutritional factors in the milk. Continuous stirring should be used to prevent the product from burning onto the pan.

Packaging and storage

During packaging the most important quality control check is to ensure that the filling equipment, bottles and caps are thoroughly cleaned and sterilized to prevent recontamination of the heat-treated milk. This is especially important if the bottles are reused. Bottle fill weights should be accurately controlled. An alternative bottling method is to fill bottles with the freshly extracted milk and heat the filled bottles with loose caps in water at 100°C/212°F for one hour. Tighten cap and cool. Repeat 24 hours later. Store in a cool, dry place.

> **Equipment**
> Grinding mill
> Press and pressing bags
> Bottle cleaner/sterilizer
> Bottle filler
> Capping machine

Togwa

Product description

Togwa is a non-alcoholic beverage which is used as a refreshing, energy-rich drink. It is made from sorghum, millet or rice and the colour of the product is determined by the raw materials used. All versions are slightly hazy, sweeter and more viscous than beer. Togwa has little or no alcohol to inhibit microbial growth during storage and the shelf-life is therefore only a few days under proper storage conditions.

Principles of preservation and processing

Preservation is achieved by the destruction of enzymes and contaminating micro-organisms by heat. The process involves germinating the grains, which are then milled to a flour before mixing with water, and heating, maturing and filtering.

Hygiene

Although the raw materials are sterilized by boiling, the wort is an excellent substrate for microbial growth. It is therefore essential that all equipment is thoroughly sterilized to prevent contaminating bacteria from spoiling the togwa after it has been boiled. This can be done by cleaning with boiling water or with chlorine solution.

Raw material

Grains should be harvested when fully mature to maximize the carbohydrate content, and properly germinated to maximize amylase activity. Dried grains should be properly stored to prevent moisture pickup which would allow mould growth and reduce amylase activity.

Process control

The main control points are:

○ Correct germination of grains and thorough drying.

○ Proper grinding of the cereals to increase the surface area and maximize amylase activity.

○ Adequate time and temperature of boiling to convert carbohydrates to sugars.

The main quality factors of the final product are colour, flavour and the clarity of the drink. The colour and flavour are determined mostly by the extent of boiling of the mash. The clarity of the final product is determined by the success of filtration.

Packaging and storage

Packaging is only required to contain the product for its relatively short shelf-life and to prevent contamination by dust, insects and so on. Cleaned glass or plastic bottles, gourds etc. are sufficient. The product should be stored in a cool place away from direct sunlight.

Process	Notes
Raw material	Dried grains.
Winnow	Spoiled light grains, foreign particles and dust are removed using a winnowing basket.
Wash	Wash thoroughly using cold water.
Dry	Sun-dry for 10–12 hours.
Germinate	Germination is carried out in dark conditions. Banana leaves or a large sheet of cloth can be used to cover grains.
Grind	Grind to a fine flour to pass through a 1mm sieve. Grinding can be done by hand or powered mill.
Dry	To a dry flour, 2–5 hours in the sun.
Heat	Boil in water for 30 minutes to produce a gruel or wort.
Cool	Stirring is important to assist cooling and to avoid the formation of a hard top layer.
Heat	Heating should be carried out steadily to just below boiling point.
Mature	Leave overnight to mature.
Filter	Through clean cloth.
Pack	In plastic containers.
Store	In a cool, dark place.

Equipment
No special equipment is required.

Cereal and legume products

Sorghum can be used to make alcoholic and non-alcoholic drinks, packaged whole, or made into a flour [IT/PMM]

Beer

Product description

Beer is a fermented beverage and can be made from sorghum, finger millet or rice. The colour of the product varies from whitish (rice beer) to reddish brown (sorghum and millet beer). The flavour reflects the raw material used and it has a sweet, alcoholic taste. The shelf-life of the product is relatively short usually up to two weeks, as it is not pasteurized after fermentation. It is possible, however, to extend the shelf-life to several months by bottling and pasteurization.

Process	Notes
Dried grains	Sorghum, finger millet or rice.
Winnow	Husks and dust removed, using a winnowing basket.
Wash	Washing removes foreign matter.
Germinate	For rice beer, paddy is used for germination to produce malt.
Dry	Sun-dry for one or two days.
Grind	Grinding should give a fine flour to pass though a 1mm sieve. Grind by hand or use powered milling machines.
Mix	Add the malted flour to water and mix.
Heat	Boil for 3–5 hours.
Cool	Cooling is important to allow the starter (yeast) to act. Room temperature is recommended.
Mix	Add starter (2–10 per cent by weight).
Ferment	Fermentation time depends on climate, type of starter and cereal. In hot climates one or two days are needed, but in colder climates it will take more than three days.
Filter	To remove solids and produce a clear product.
Pack	In gourds or bottles.
Store	In a cool place out of sunlight.

Principles of preservation and processing

Preservation is achieved by the inactivation of enzymes and contaminating micro-organisms during boiling and by the relatively high levels of alcohol which inhibit the growth of many spoilage micro-organisms.

The process involves preparation of the malted grain 'mash' and fermentation by yeasts to produce the alcohol.

Hygiene

Although the raw materials are sterilized by boiling, the wort is an excellent substrate for microbial growth. It is therefore essential that all equipment is thoroughly sterilized to prevent contaminating bacteria from competing with the added yeast and producing acid instead of alcohol. This can be done by cleaning with boiling water or with chlorine solution. Care is necessary to wash the equipment free of residual chlorine as this would interfere with the action of the yeast.

Raw material

Grains should be harvested when fully mature to maximize the carbohydrate content, and properly germinated to maximize amylase activity. Dried grains should be of the correct moisture content and should be properly stored to prevent moisture pickup which would allow mould growth and reduce amylase activity.

Process control

The main control points are:

○ Correct germination of grains and thorough drying.

○ Proper grinding of the cereals to increase the surface area and maximize amylase activity.

○ Adequate time and temperature of boiling process to hydrolyse carbohydrates to sugars and thus make them more available for yeast action.

○ Preparation of an active yeast inoculum and addition of the correct amount to the wort.

○ Cooling the wort to an optimum temperature for yeast action. Too low and the fermentation time is extended and may spoil before the alcohol level is increased, too high and the yeast would be destroyed (yeast is inactivated at about 45°C/113°F).

○ Proper filtration to produce a clear product.

The main quality factors of the final product are colour, flavour and clarity of the beer. The colour and flavour are determined mostly by the extent of boiling of the mash and the flavour is also determined by the extent of yeast activity. The clarity of the final product is determined by the success of filtration.

Packaging and storage

Packaging is required to contain the product for its relatively short shelf-life and to prevent contamination by dust, insects and so on. Cleaned glass or plastic bottles, gourds etc. are sufficient. For a longer shelf-life it is possible to pasteurize the bottled beer at 80–90°C/176–194°F for 30 minutes. The product should be stored in a cool place away from direct sunlight.

Equipment
No special equipment is required.

2. FRUIT PRODUCTS

Because of their low prices during the harvest season and a high demand for the wide variety of products that can be made from fruits, they are often a good raw material on which to base a small food business. In addition, most fruits are acidic and therefore have a lower risk of causing food poisoning. Although care should always be taken with food handling and hygiene, fruit processing is often a safer option than other products for inexperienced food processors.

Dried fruit products

Dried fruits

Product description

These are dried pieces of fruit for confectionery or for use in baked goods or other food preparations. They have a soft, rubbery texture and a sweet taste with the characteristic flavour and colour of the fruit which has been used. Dried fruit can be made from most fruits including mango, guava, banana, grapes, papaya (pawpaw), pineapple and passion-fruit.

Principles of preservation and processing

Preservation relies on the removal of moisture by soaking in sugar syrup and by drying. An acid dip or sulphur dioxide may also be used to reduce the number of contaminating micro-organisms.

Raw material

Fruits should be harvested at the correct stage of maturity. If they are overripe they are easily damaged and may be difficult to dry; underripe and they have a poor flavour, colour and appearance. Harvesting should be done as carefully as possible to prevent spoilage, bruising and loss of quality during transport. Specially designed, low-cost boxes can protect the fruit. It should not be piled on the ground or in vehicles.

Process control

The size of fruit pieces affects the time needed for pre-treatments such as sulphuring or dipping, and drying. Pieces should have a uniform size. In both initial and later drying stages the size of the pieces is important. In the first stage smaller pieces have a greater surface area for water to evaporate from. In the second stage the smaller the pieces the less distance the moisture must move to reach the surface of the food.

The rate of drying should be controlled as not all foods need a high rate of drying. Some fruits undergo 'case-hardening' if the rate of drying is too high. Red fruits or those that are expected to become brown after drying (for example dates and grapes) should not be treated with sulphur dioxide. In other fruits the pre-treatment protects the colour of the fruit.

Process	Notes
Fruit	Harvest at the correct stage of maturity.
Wash	Use clean water to remove stones, leaves, or soils.
Sort/grade	To produce a uniform dried product, foods are sorted for colour, size, shape and maturity. Sorting is done by hand.
Peel	Peeling increases the rate of drying (because peel prevents moisture leaving the food). It is usually done by hand using sharp stainless steel knives, but small peeling machines are available for fruits.
Cut/slice/core	To reduce the size of pieces to 0.5–1.0cm cubes and allow faster sulphuring and drying. Usually by hand, but small-scale equipment is available.
Acid dip or sulphur dioxide	Optional, to reduce browning during drying. Sulphur dioxide should not be used for red fruits as the colour is bleached. Care is needed as it causes coughing and eye irritation. Dip in lemon juice or citric acid for 5–10 minutes, or treat with sulphur dioxide by (a) sulphuring or (b) sulphite dip. Burning sulphur is used at 350–400g/100kg fruit (or 2–3 tablespoons/kg fruit) in a sulphuring cabinet. Exact amount depends on type of fruit. Sulphite dip is used as 0.2–0.8 per cent sodium (or potassium) metabisulphite solution.
Mix with sugar syrup	Boil in 60–70 per cent sugar for 10–15 minutes and then soak for up to 18 hours. Up to half the water in the fruit is removed and therefore production rate increases in the dryer. Gives good colour retention in food and a sweeter, blander product. However, lower acid levels may lead to spoilage if the food is not properly dried and packaged.
Dry	Rate depends on temperature, generally 50–60°C/120–140°F, humidity and speed of air, type of dryer and size of food pieces.
Pack	In moisture-proof packs.
Store	In a cool, dry place, away from sunlight.

Note The use of sulphur dioxide is controlled by law in some countries.

Packaging and storage

Dried fruits should be stored in moisture-proof plastic, plastic-lined paperboard boxes or glass jars. They should be stored in a cool, dry place, away from sunlight.

> **Equipment**
> Wash tank
> Boiling pans (optional)
> Sulphuring cabinet (optional)
> Dryer (optional)
> Heat sealer

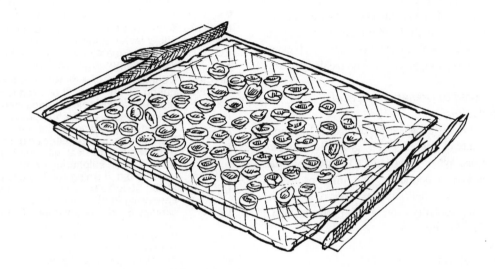

Apricots make good and nutritious dried fruits

Fruit leathers

Product description

These are dried sheets of fruit pulp which can be rolled in plastic sheets for intermediate storage and cut into different shapes as confectionery or for use in baked goods or other food preparations. Layers of different coloured leathers can be pressed together to form a confectionery 'sandwich'. They have a soft rubbery texture, and a sweet taste with the characteristic flavour and colour of the fruit used. Leathers can be made from most fruits, including mango, guava, banana, papaya (pawpaw), pineapple and passion-fruit.

Principles of preservation and processing

Preservation is achieved by drying. A low moisture content prevents the growth of micro-organisms. When the product is carefully dried and packed in containers that offer protection from moisture, light, insects and rodents and stored in a cool, dry room, these products have a shelf-life of many months.

Raw material

Fruit should be harvested at the correct stage of maturity. If they are overripe they are easily damaged and may be difficult to dry; underripe and they have a poor flavour, colour and appearance. Bananas should be harvested before they are fully ripe and with the skin slightly green. Harvesting should be done as carefully as possible to prevent spoilage, bruising and loss of quality during transport. Specially designed, low-cost boxes can protect the fruit. It should not be piled on the ground or in vehicles.

Process control

The size of fruit pieces affects the time needed for pre-treatments such as sulphuring or dipping in syrup. The thickness of the pulp layer affects the rate of drying. Sulphur dioxide is used to protect the colour of the product.

Packaging and storage

Leathers should be stored in moisture-proof plastic until further processing. The pieces are later packed in moisture-proof polypropylene bags

Process	Notes
Fruit ↓	Harvested at the correct stage of maturity.
Wash ↓	Use clean water to remove stones, leaves, or soils.
Sort/grade ↓	To produce a uniform dried product. Foods are sorted by hand for colour, size, shape and maturity.
Peel ↓	Peeling increases the rate of drying (because peel prevents moisture leaving the food). It is usually done by hand using sharp stainless steel knives, or small peeling machines.
Cut/slice/ core ↓	To reduce the size of pieces and allow faster sulphuring/drying. Usually done by hand, but small-scale equipment is available.
Acid dip or sulphur dioxide ↓	Optional to reduce browning during drying. Neither should be used for red fruits as the colour is bleached. Care is needed as sulphur dioxide causes coughing and eye irritation. Dip in lemon juice or citric acid for 5–10 minutes, or treat with sulphur dioxide by (a) sulphuring or (b) sulphite dip. Burning sulphur used at 350–400g/100kg fruit (or 2–3 tablespoons/kg fruit) in sulphuring cabinet. Exact amount depends on type of fruit. Sulphite dip used at 0.2–0.8 per cent sodium or potassium metabisulphite solution (0.3–0.45g per litre of water).
Mix with sugar syrup ↓	Boil in 60–70 per cent sugar for 10–15 minutes and then soak for up to 18 hours. Up to half the water in the fruit is removed and therefore drying rate increases. Gives good colour retention in food and a sweeter, blander product, but lower acid levels may lead to spoilage if the food is not properly dried and packaged.
Pulp ↓	Small-scale pulpers or liquidizers are available. Spread pulp on polythene sheets, aluminium foil or greased paper for drying.
Dry ↓	Rate depends on temperature (generally 38–60°C/100–140°F), humidity and speed of air, type of dryer and size of food pieces.
Pack ↓	Roll in polythene sheets and seal the ends.
Store ↓	In a cool, dry place, away from sunlight.
Cut ↓	Into small pieces with a knife or cutter.
Coat with sugar ↓	Sprinkle pieces with ground sugar.
Pack ↓	In retail packs of 20–100g.
Store	In a cool, dry place, away from sunlight.

(polythene is not an adequate barrier to moisture and the product will keep for only a few weeks in this material). They are stored in a cool, dry place, out of sunlight.

```
Equipment
Wash tank
Boiling pans
Pulper
Sulphuring cabinet (optional)
Dryer (optional)
Heat sealer
```

Note Fruit leathers are known by different names in different countries. For example in Latin America a product named 'guava rings' is made by a similar process, but the dried sheet is cut into strips of about 1cm by 10cm and 0.5cm thick, and then formed into rings.

Papain

Product description

Papain is the white latex-like substance that is obtained from green papaya (pawpaw) fruits. It is a proteolytic enzyme (it breaks down proteins) and is used as a meat tenderizer. When dried it has a shelf-life of many months.

Principles of preservation and processing

Shallow, longitudinal scratches are made in the early morning to the skins of fully formed but unripe papaya fruits. The latex drips out and is collected in containers. New scratches can be made every three to five days as long as the fruit remains green. The latex coagulates naturally within four to six hours, but this can be accelerated to about ten minutes by stirring it. The coagulated latex is spread thinly on trays and dried in the sun or in dryers at 40°C to 5–8 per cent moisture. Drying prevents deterioration by microorganisms. This is raw latex which is suitable as a meat tenderizer. It is further purified on a large scale for numerous other industrial uses.

Raw material

There are no special control points, except the selection of mature green fruits without infection.

Process	Notes
Papaya ▼	Mature, unripe fruits are used.
Cut ↓	Make longitudinal scratches down the fruit.
Collect ↓	Collect the dripping latex in containers placed below.
Stir	Stir to coagulate the latex.
Dry ↓	Arrange in thin sheets on trays at 40°C/104°F in a dryer or in the sun to 5–8 per cent moisture.
Pack	In moisture-proof bags.
Store	In a cool, dry place away from sunlight.

Process control

Drying temperatures should not exceed 40°C to avoid damaging the enzymes in the latex and therefore reducing their activity. It is fully dried when it forms a free-flowing powder.

Packaging and storage

The product readily absorbs moisture and should be stored in moisture-proof plastic bags. It should be stored in a cool, dry place away from sunlight.

Equipment
Drying trays
Collecting cups
Heat sealer

Papaya (pawpaw) is extremely versatile: the fruits can be dried, made into fruit leather, toffee, or juice, and latex from unripe fruits can be used to make a meat tenderizer [Panos/Dominic Sansoni]

Pulps, pastes and sauces

Tomato paste

Product description

This is a thick, bright red paste which is used to prepare many traditional sauces and soups and as a flavouring, colouring and thickener. It can be sold from bulk containers, in jars, polythene bags or cans and has a shelf-life of several months.

Principles of preservation and processing

Heat is used to blanch the tomatoes and to concentrate tomato pulp to a thick paste. The heat also destroys enzymes and contaminating microorganisms. The relatively low moisture content and high acidity of the final product prevents recontamination to some extent, but the opened container should be used within a few days or kept under refrigeration if sodium benzoate preservative is not used. In this case preservation is mainly due to the packaging used.

Raw material

The fruits for processing and storage should be carefully selected to be sufficiently ripe or even overripe, provided there is no mould growth or rotting.

Process control

The main points of control are:

○ Blanching time/temperature to soften the skins for peeling and to destroy enzymes and microorganisms.

○ Pulping, to ensure no skin or seeds in the final product.

○ Control of acidity to ensure that it is below pH 4.0.

○ Correct addition of preservative (controlled by law in many countries).

○ Control of solids content at 30 per cent.

○ Pasteurization time and temperature to ensure that the product will remain stable without fermenting.

Process	Notes
Sort ↓	Remove any mouldy or rotten tomatoes.
Wash ↓	Wash in 8 litres clean water per 10kg tomatoes.
Blanch ↓	Blanch in a waterbath at 80°C/145°F for five minutes.
Pulp ↓	Pulp in a pulper-finisher fitted with a 1mm sized sieve.
Mix with lemon juice ↓	This stage depends on the acidity of the pulp. If it is pH 4.0 or below, no lemon juice is needed. If the pH is above 4.0, lemon juice should be added until the pH falls below 4.0.
Mix with sodium benzoate ↓	Add 0.3g sodium benzoate per 10kg of pulp to preserve the product after the bottle/can has been opened.
Concentrate ↓	Traditionally, this is done in an open pan over a fire. Heating must be done slowly with constant stirring to prevent the pulp from burning. With care the bright red colour can be retained in the final product. Heating is continued until a paste with 30 per cent solids is obtained. This can be measured by refractometer or judged by an experienced processor.
Separate juice ↓	An improved method is to place the pulp in a white cotton sack and hang it up for one hour to allow the water to drain out. The pulp loses half of its weight.
Add salt ↓	Add 2.5 per cent salt by weight of concentrate and mix thoroughly.
Separate salted juice ↓	Re-hang the sack for one hour until pulp is one-third of its original weight.
Fill ↓	Fill into bottles or cans.
Seal ↓	Seal containers.
Heat ↓	Pasteurize at 90°C/195°F for 45 minutes.
Cool ↓	Cool to room temperature.
Store	Store in a cool place, away from sunlight.

Packaging and storage

The product should be protected from air, moisture and other forms of contamination. Glass bottles or metal cans are best but if these are not obtainable or too expensive, sealed polypropylene bags can be used. Cans that are lacquered on the inside to resist the acids in the product should be used. Other types of can will rust due to the low pH of the food.

Equipment
Boiling pans
Pulper
Cotton sack
Filler
Weighing scales
Bottle or can sealer or heat sealer
Pasteurizer
Thermometer
Refractometer
pH meter or papers

Tomato sauce (or ketchup)

Product description

This is a red sauce made from fresh tomatoes. It is a thick sauce with a sweet taste and tomato flavour, commonly used in cooking or as a table relish. It has a shelf-life of more than one year in glass bottles or jars when the container is unopened.

Raw material

Ingredients
20kg tomatoes
1.5kg sugar

450g onions, finely chopped
3.5g mace
9g cinnamon
11.25g cumin
11.25g cardamom
11.25g ground black pepper
5g ground white pepper
5g ground ginger
330g salt
800g vinegar

Tomatoes should be fully ripe, sound and of the correct processing varieties with a high solids content. Spices must be clean, mature and not infected with mould.

Process	Notes
Sort tomatoes	Select good quality, fully ripe, red fruits without infection, mould or rot.
Wash	Wash in clean water.
Heat	Blanch in hot water for three to five minutes until the skin is loosened.
Cool	Cool immediately in cold water.
Peel	Remove skin and core.
Pulp	Chop and pulp by hand, with a grinder or using a pulper-finisher depending on the scale of operation.
Mix ingredients	Add 500g sugar, the onions, and the spices tied loosely in a muslin bag: mace, cinnamon, cumin, cardamom, black pepper powder, ground white pepper, ground ginger.
Heat	Heat to below boiling point in a pan with continuous stirring until it has reduced to half the original volume.
Separate	Remove the spice bag.
Mix sugar, salt and vinegar	Add 1kg sugar, the salt, and the vinegar; continue heating for 5–10 minutes.
Fill	Hot-fill into pre-sterilized bottles or jars at not less than 80°C/145°F.
Seal	Close the lids/caps tightly.
Cool	Cool to room temperature.
Store	Store away from sunlight in a cool place.

Process control

○ The ratio of ingredients must be carefully monitored and controlled according to the formulation for each batch to produce the desired taste, consistency and flavour each time.

○ The product must be stirred continuously during heating to prevent burning.

○ The end of boiling should be determined by checking the soluble solids content with a refractometer (10–12 per cent solids).

Packaging and storage

The sauce can be kept for more than a year without losing the flavour and taste, but it can lose its colour if exposed to direct sunlight. It should therefore be stored in a cool, dark place or in boxes.

Equipment
Pulper
Boiling pans
Refractometer
Thermometer
Wash tank
Bottle filler
Capper
Scales
Bottle sterilizer

Note Product variations can use other spices including cayenne pepper, onion powder, cloves, pimento and mustard, according to local tastes. Tomato chilli sauce is a similar product in which 2.5g of chilli powder is added per 10kg tomato pulp before processing.

Other spices which may be used include whole mace (3.5g), broken cinnamon sticks (9g), cumin, black pepper and cardamom (11.25g each), white pepper (5g) and ground ginger (5g), all tied loosely in a muslin bag and boiled with 10kg of tomato pulp.

Tomatoes have a longer shelf-life if made into a paste or sauce [IT/ZUL]

Awaze (chilli sauce)

Product description

Awaze is a red sauce made from the dried fruit of the chilli plant with added spices, water or tej (a traditional alcoholic drink in northern Africa). It is a thick sauce or paste with a similar consistency to tomato ketchup, commonly packed in bottles or jars and served with raw, grilled or fried meat. It has a shelf-life of more than one year when the jar is unopened.

Principles of preservation and processing

Unlike tomato sauce, awaze is not acidified with vinegar and preservation is therefore dependent on the heat treatment, the high solids content, and the antimicrobial properties of the spices.

Raw material

Chillies and spices must be clean, mature and not infected with mould. The chillies must have a good red colour and be a variety that is not too hot.

Process control

The ratio of chilli to the added spices must be carefully monitored and controlled for each batch to produce a consistent taste and flavour over time. The pasteurization temperature and time need to be controlled to ensure that enzymes and contaminating micro-organisms are destroyed and produce the expected shelf-life.

Packaging and storage

Awaze can be kept for more than a year without losing the flavour and taste, but it can lose its colour if exposed to direct sunlight. It should therefore be stored in a cool, dark place or in boxes.

Note Similar products are made in many regions, often with the addition of tomato pulp, green chillies or other fruits. Berberrie fruits can be used when available.

Process	Notes
Sort	Good quality red chilli pods are selected.
Clean chilli	Stems, seeds and other impurities are removed.
Clean spices	Impurities from ginger, garlic, onion, cloves, basil, bishops weed, rue seeds, cardamom and cinnamon are removed by winnowing and hand sorting.
Wash	Cleaned chillies are rinsed with cold water to remove dust.
Dry	Sun-dry for three to four days.
First mixture	The chillies and spices are chopped and mixed in the following proportions: 20 per cent fresh ginger, 37 per cent fresh garlic and onion each, 4 per cent fresh basil and 2 per cent of rue seeds by weight of chilli.
Dry	Sun-dry for three to four days.
Second mixture	A mixture of 4 per cent each of cloves, dry basil and cinnamon, 3 per cent bishops weed and 13 per cent cardamom by weight of chilli.
Heat	Heat on a hotplate for three to five minutes at 150°C/300°F until heated thoroughly.
Mix	Mix the first and second mixtures.
Mix	Add 10 per cent salt by the weight of chilli to the mixture.
Mill	Grind to a fine powder with a stone mill.
Sieve	Sift the awaze powder through a fine sieve (1mm diameter).
Mix	Mix with water or tej to the required thick consistency.
Fill	Fill into bottles or jars.
Seal	Close the lids/caps tightly.
Pasteurize	In boiling water for 15 minutes.
Cool	Cool to room temperature.
Store	Store away from sunlight in a cool place.

Equipment

Stone mill
Electric metad or hotplate
Wash tank
Drying mats
Bottle filler
Capper
Pasteurizing waterbath
Scales

Chilli sauce is a popular product in many countries

Confectionery

Fruit toffee

Product description

This is a sweet confectionery made by concentrating a mixture of fruit pulp (such as banana, mango, guava, papaya/pawpaw), sugar, milk powder and fat. It is light brown and has a sweet, fruity taste, combined with a mild milky flavour. The texture is soft and smooth. It is sold in small pieces (2cm × 2cm × 1cm) individually or as packs containing several pieces, and has a shelf-life of three to four months under cool, dry storage conditions.

Principles of preservation and processing

Ingredients are boiled until the mixture becomes viscous, and it is then poured onto a tray as a 1cm thick sheet and cooled. Boiling the mixture destroys micro-organisms and concentrates the sugar solution. Heat is also used to partially invert the sugar and therefore control the consistency of the product.

Preservation is due to the heat and low moisture content of the product. Packaging protects against moisture pick-up from the air and prevents further contamination.

Raw material

Ingredients

1kg/2lb fruit pulp
100g/4oz glucose syrup
160g/6oz milk powder
100g/4oz hydrogenated fat

Fruits should be fully ripe without mould; milk powder and fat should not have off-flavours or rancidity.

Process control

The sugar solution should be filtered to remove impurities in the sugar. Controlled heating of the mixture to 116°C/240°F is essential to give a mass of the correct consistency. If the temperature is too low the product will be more like a fudge, whereas if it is too high it will become a hard crystalline product like a boiled sweet. Heating

Process	Notes
Sort fruit	Select good quality, fully ripe fruits without infection, mould or rot.
Wash	Wash in clean water.
Pulp	Pulp manually or with a powered pulper. Remove all skin and seeds. Peeled banana can be steamed for five minutes instead of pulping.
Heat	Heat until the pulp has reduced to one third of its original volume, stirring continuously.
Mix ingredients	To the fruit pulp add sugar, glucose syrup, milk powder and hydrogenated fat with constant stirring.
Heat	Continue heating with constant stirring until the mixture reaches exactly 124°C/255°F (soft ball consistency).
Pour	Pour onto metal trays in a layer 1cm thick. Alternatively, the mass can be spread onto an oiled table and stretched into long strands.
Cut	The sheet is marked and cut while cooling. Pieces are separated to speed up cooling. If strands are formed, they are then cut into pieces with a knife.
Cool	Cool to room temperature.
Pack	Pack in moisture-proof plastic bags or glass jars.
Store	Store in a cool, dry place.

the mixture also develops the required colour and flavour.

Packaging and storage

Fruit toffee is hygroscopic (it will absorb moisture from the air) and it is therefore packaged in moisture-proof bags or glass jars. Polythene is a poor moisture barrier and the product will keep for only a few days in this material, especially in humid areas. Packs should be stored in a cool, dry place, away from sunlight.

Note A large number of products can be made using this method depending on the types of fruit available, and different shapes, sizes and colours can produce a wide product range.

As with other confectionery products, toffees are sometimes criticized by health and dental authorities because of their high sugar content.

Non-alcoholic beverages

Fruit juices and nectars

Product description

Fruit juices are pure, filtered juices with nothing added. Nectars are similarly fruit pulps with nothing added and containing at least 30 per cent fruit solids. Juices can be made from almost any fully ripened fruit, but common types include pineapple, orange, grapefruit, passion-fruit and mango. A common nectar is made from guava. Here, orange is used as an example of juice manufacture. A pure, bright orange juice, sweet and acidic with the characteristic taste of oranges, can be packed in glass or plastic bottles, or in laminated paperboard cartons, for consumption as a drink.

Principles of preservation and processing

Fruit juices and nectars rely for their preservation on pasteurization and packaging in hermetically sealed bottles or other containers. They are drunk immediately after opening.

Heat is used to destroy enzymes and micro-organisms, and the acidity of the product together with the packaging prevents recontamination. Sodium benzoate preservative is used in some places, but this is not necessary if the product is consumed completely soon after opening. Unopened bottles have a shelf-life of a year or more.

Raw material

Fruits should be fully ripe and free of mould or discoloration.

Process control

The pulping, filtering and heating stages of the process should be monitored and controlled as described to achieve a consistent product quality. As the product is acidic there is little risk of food poisoning, but normal hygienic practices should be enforced. It is normal for a sediment to form in the bottom of the bottle, but if this is excessive a finer filter should be used.

Process	Notes
Sort	Discard any mouldy or underripe fruit.
Wash	Wash in clean water.
Cut	Cut fruits in half.
Press	Use hand-operated juice extractors or 'reamers'.
Separate pulp	Press through filters by hand to remove pieces of pulp.
Fill	Use pre-sterilized bottles.
Seal	Seal bottles to keep contents fresh.
Heat	Pasteurize in a boiling waterbath for 8–10 minutes.
Cool	To room temperature.
Store	Store in a cool place, away from sunlight.

Packaging and storage

The product depends on the package for its preservation and the bottles and caps should be carefully checked to ensure that they are sound and well-sealed.

Equipment
Juice extractor
Filter
Boiling waterbath
Capper
Filler

Note Juices should not contain syrup or other ingredients. They can be made from almost any fruit by pressing out the juice, or by pulping the fruit and filtering out the juice. Other common products include juices from pineapple, mango, papaya (pawpaw), melon, passion-fruit, lime, tomato, grape and apple. If the pulp is not filtered it is known as a 'nectar' and the most common of these is guava nectar.

Fruit squashes and cordials

Product description

These are drinks containing at least 25 per cent fruit pulp from a single fruit or a mixture of fruits, mixed with sugar syrup. They are diluted with water before consumption. They have the characteristic colour and flavour of the fruits used and a sweet taste. Squashes may contain fruit pulp and be cloudy, whereas cordials are crystal clear. They are sold from bulk containers or in glass bottles and have a shelf-life of six months or more if bottled.

Principles of preservation and processing

Fruit pulp and sugar syrup are mixed in the correct proportions, pasteurized and then hot-filled into pre-sterilized glass bottles. Heating the juice inactivates enzymes and destroys micro-organisms. The increased solids content (around 15–20 per cent sugar), the high acidity, the sodium benzoate preservative (if used), and packaging (if bottled) prevent recontamination by micro-organisms.

Raw material

Fruits should be fresh, fully ripe and not fermenting or mouldy. Other quality factors such as minor skin damage are less important for this product, and as such it is a good way of using excess fruit that cannot otherwise be sold.

Process control

Heating juice should be done carefully to avoid burning as this will affect both the colour and flavour of the product. Pasteurization should be at the correct temperature for the correct time in order to inactivate pectic enzymes and thus prevent a layer of sediment forming in the bottom of the bottle.

Packaging and storage

Squashes and cordials can keep for up to one year under ambient conditions, provided they are protected from light and heat. Airtight and moisture-proof glass bottles are used.

Process	Notes
Fruit ↓	Any soft fruit or citrus fruit can be used.
Sort ↓	Remove mouldy fruit; surface damage is acceptable and overripe fruits may be used.
Wash	Wash in clean water.
Peel ↓	Peel by hand or with a small peeling machine. Wear gloves if peeling manually, especially when using pineapple as it will damage the skin.
Pulp	Use a fruit press, pestle and mortar, pulper or liquidizer.
Filter ↓	Strain through clean muslin cloth to remove seeds and extraneous materials.
Mix with syrup ↓	Heat a 50 per cent sugar syrup to 90°C/194°F and add to the juice to give 25 per cent juice in the final product.
Heat ↓	Pasteurize at 90°C/194°F for 10–15 minutes.
Fill ↓	Hot fill into pre-sterilized bottles and seal.
Cool	To room temperature.
Store	In a cool, dry place.

Equipment
Pulper
Filter cloth
Boiling pan
Bottle sealer
Refractometer (optional)
Thermometer
Bottle filler
Scales

Fruit syrup

Product description

A thick, viscous liquid treacle, light or dark brown with a sweet, fruity flavour, is made by concentrating unfermented fruit juice from a number of different fruits. It is sold in glass bottles and has a shelf-life of a year or more. It can be eaten as a sweet or used instead of sugar.

Principles of preservation and processing

Boiling the juice inactivates enzymes and destroys micro-organisms and also provides the required viscosity and flavour. The high solids content (around 80 per cent sugar) prevents recontamination by micro-organisms. The syrup is concentrated by evaporating the water over an open fire. This treacle-like, viscous liquid is then hot-filled into pre-sterilized glass bottles.

Raw material

Fruits should be fresh and not fermenting or mouldy. Other quality factors are less important for this product and it is a good way of using excess fruit that cannot otherwise be sold.

Process control

Boiling should be done slowly to evaporate the water without burning the product especially during the later stages when the thick treacle is formed.

Process	Notes
Fruit ↓	Any soft fruit or citrus fruit can be used.
Sort ↓	Remove mouldy fruit; surface damage is acceptable and overripe fruits may be used.
Clean ↓	Wash in clean water.
Peel ↓	Peel by hand or with a small peeling machine. Wear gloves if peeling manually, especially when using pineapple as it will damage the skin.
Pulp ↓	Use a fruit press, pestle and mortar, pulper or liquidizer.
Filter ↓	Strain through clean muslin cloth to remove seeds and extraneous materials.
Heat ↓	Concentrate slowly over a low heat with regular stirring until a treacle is formed (78–80 per cent sugar by refractometer).
Fill ↓	Hot fill into pre-sterilized bottles and seal.
Cool ↓	To room temperature.
Store	In a cool, dry place.

Packaging and storage

Fruit syrup can keep for up to one year under ambient conditions, provided it is protected from moisture. Airtight and moisture-proof glass bottles are used.

Equipment
Filter cloth
Boiling pan
Bottle sealer
Refractometer (optional)

Cocoa

Product description

A fine brown powder with the characteristic taste of cocoa is used in the confectionery industry or, when de-fatted, as a beverage or ingredient in bakery products. The product has a shelf-life of several months.

The process and the principles of preservation

Seeds (beans) of the cocoa plant (*Theobroma cacao*) are cured, dried and roasted. The purpose of curing is to promote the breakdown of the fleshy fruit tissue by micro-organisms and enzymes in the fruit. The process also develops flavour in the beans.

Drying reduces the moisture content, preserves the beans and also contributes to the development of colour and flavour.

Packaging and storage

Cocoa powder is hygroscopic (picks up moisture from the air) and should be protected, especially in humid climates. Lidded tins may be used, but a cheaper alternative is sealed polypropylene bags.

The seeds keep well (for several months) if stored in a cool, dry place. Both seeds and powder contain a high proportion of fat and they should therefore be stored away from heat, light and moisture to reduce the development of rancidity.

Equipment
Plate mill
0.5mm aperture sieve
Roaster

Process	Notes
Raw material	Cocoa pods.
Sort	Select beans that are fully mature and free of mould or rot.
Ferment	Place in cemented tanks for several days until the flesh becomes soft and the seeds can be removed.
Separate pulp	By hand.
Wash	In clean water.
Dry	Sun-dry for four to five days to a moisture content of about 12 per cent.
Package	Use gunny bags or smaller plastic bags.
Store	In a cool, dry place, away from sunlight.
Roast	In a roaster for 30–60 minutes at 150°C/300°F.
Grind	Use two or more passes through a plate mill.
Sieve	Use a 0.5mm aperture.
Pack	In moisture-proof plastic bags.
Store	In a cool place, away from sunlight.

Note This is whole cocoa powder, and extraction of cocoa butter to make de-fatted cocoa is not usually done on a small scale.

Coffee

Product description

A fine, dark brown powder made from roasted coffee beans, brewed with boiling water and consumed as a drink, often with sugar and milk. The powder is sold in packets of various sizes (from 10g to 1kg) or in jars or cans. It is stable for several months if well packed in moisture-proof containers.

The process and the principles of preservation

Ripened coffee fruits (orange to red in colour) are harvested and the pulp is allowed to rot and drain away. The seeds (beans) are sun-dried on woven containers for several days until the skin becomes black and wrinkled and is easily removed by hand. The seeds are further dried for a few more days until they become very hard. They are then winnowed and stored for use. For roasting, a pot is pre-heated to about 250°C (480°F) and the seeds are placed in it and roasted until they become dark brown or black (moisture content about 2.5 per cent). The roasted grains are then pounded or milled and packed immediately.

Sun-drying removes water from the beans and prevents microbial, enzymic and chemical reactions to preserve the beans. Roasting causes a further loss of water, destroys enzymes and micro-organisms, and develops the characteristic coffee flavour.

Raw material

Fruits should be fully ripened and red. Select fruits that are not damaged by insects or mould. The quality of the final product is determined in part by the variety of coffee beans that are used.

Process control

The quality of coffee depends mostly on its colour and aroma. Both characteristics are developed during the roasting stage and this should be carefully monitored and controlled. Experience and skill are needed to produce a good quality product.

The traditional collection, drying and roasting processes are crude and unhygienic, producing a variable product with inferior flavour. They can be

Process	Notes
Coffee fruit	Pick when fully ripened.
Sort	Remove damaged or mouldy fruit.
Rot pulp	Pile into heaps or place in woven baskets to allow the pulp to rot and drain away over several days.
Separate pulp	Remove the beans.
Wash	Rinse in clean water.
Sort	Select healthy, undamaged beans.
Dry	Sun-dry for five to six days.
Dehusk	By rubbing the beans by hand.
Dry	Sun-dry for five to six days.
Store	In a cool, dry place in sacks until used.
Roast	At about 250°C/480°F for 10–15 minutes.
Cool	To room temperature.
Sort	Remove burned beans, recycle under-roasted beans.
Mill	To a fine powder in a plate mill.
Pack	In airtight, moisture-proof containers.
Store	In a cool, dry place.

improved by proper washing, roasting and grinding with improved quality control.

Packaging and storage

Roasted beans can be stored in sacks for many months provided that the store is cool, well-ventilated and dry. Milled beans should be packaged quickly as the volatile aromas will be quickly lost. The powder should be packed in airtight and moisture-proof containers such as jars, cans or composite plastic bags. Polythene is not a suitable material for this product because of its low barrier to moisture and air, leading to a loss of aroma and moisture pick-up after a few days.

Equipment
Roaster
Plate mill
Heat sealer
Scales

Coffee beans should be fully ripened and red for processing [IT/KD]

Alcoholic beverages and vinegar

Palm wine

Product description

Palm wine is the fermented sap of certain varieties of palm trees, obtained by tapping the top of the trunk or, in some countries, by felling the palm tree and boring a hole into the trunk. It is a cloudy, whitish beverage with a sweet, alcoholic taste and a shelf-file of one day.

Principles of preservation and processing

The product is not preserved for more than one day. After tapping, the palm wine is sweet and during the day a natural fermentation takes place, converting sugars in the sap to alcohol.

Process	Notes
Cut ↓	Cut 10–15cm from the top of the trunk.
Collect	A gourd is fixed below the cut. The sap is collected each day and sold within 5–12 hours.

Raw material

The raw material should be collected from a growing palm. The sap is not heated and the wine is an excellent substrate for microbial growth. It is therefore essential that proper hygienic collection procedures are followed to prevent contaminating bacteria from competing with the yeast and producing acid instead of alcohol.

Process control

The main control points are extraction of a high yield of palm sap without excessive contamination by spoilage micro-organisms, and proper storage to allow the natural fermentation to take place. The main quality factors are colour, flavour and clarity of the wine. These are determined mostly by the conditions used in the collection of the sap and the extent of fermentation. Often the collecting gourd is not washed between collections and residual yeasts in the gourd quickly begin the fermentation. The resulting alcohol inhibits spoilage bacteria.

Packaging and storage

Packaging is usually required only to contain the product for its short shelf-file and to prevent contamination by dust and insects. The palm wine is poured into cleaned glass or plastic bottles, gourds etc. The product should be stored in a cool place, away from direct sunlight.

> **Equipment**
> Knives
> Collecting gourd or other vessel

Note Alcohol production requires a special licence in many countries. Alcohol production is sometimes criticized by health and social welfare authorities owing to the adverse effects of over-consumption.

Lubisi (banana beer)

Product description
Lubisi is made from bananas of the Jamaican variety, mixed with sorghum flour and fermented to an orange, alcoholic beverage. It is sweet and slightly hazy with a shelf-life of several days under correct storage conditions.

Principles of preservation and processing
Preservation is achieved by the relatively high levels of alcohol which inhibit the growth of many spoilage micro-organisms. The process involves preparation of the banana juice, mixing with sorghum flour and fermentation by yeasts to produce the alcohol. There is no boiling of the wort in traditional processing and this contributes to the relatively short shelf-life. Improved processing could introduce a boiling stage for the wort and pasteurization of the product to achieve improved quality and a longer shelf-life.

Process	Notes
Raw material	Ripe banana.
Peel	Peel by hand; if peels are not easily removed then the banana is not ripe enough.
Extract residue	Use grass to knead or squeeze the banana such that only clear juice is obtained. Residue will remain in the grasses.
Mix with water	The ratio water:banana juice should be 1:3. This makes the total soluble solids low enough for the yeast to act.
Mix with sorghum	Sorghum flour:banana juice ratio should be 1:12. Stir the mixture well. Sorghum is used to improve the flavour and colour of the beer.
Ferment	In plastic container, covered by polythene bags or flat wood pushed down by heavy stone. Leave to ferment for 18 to 24 hours. An improved process uses a fermentation vessel with a fermentation lock.
Filter residue	Filter the liquid by putting in a cotton cloth bag and squeezing by hand or in a press.
Pack	Package in one-litre plastic bottles with cork stoppers or similar.
Store	In a cool place, away from sunlight.

Hygiene
The raw materials are not sterilized by boiling and the wort is therefore an excellent substrate for microbial growth. It is essential that proper hygienic procedures are followed and that all equipment is thoroughly sterilized to prevent contaminating bacteria from competing with the yeast and producing acid instead of alcohol. This can be done by cleaning with boiling water or with chlorine solution. Care is necessary to wash the equipment free of residual chlorine as this would interfere with the actions of the yeast. Strict personal hygiene is also essential.

Raw material
Bananas should be harvested when fully ripe, to maximize the sugar content and flavour. Overripe bananas should not be used as they may impart off-flavours to the final product.

Process control
The main control points are extraction of a high yield of banana juice without excessive browning or contamination by spoilage micro-organisms, and proper filtration to produce a clear product.

The main quality factors are colour, flavour, and clarity of the beer. The colour and flavour are determined mostly by the preparation of the banana/sorghum mixture. The clarity of the final product is determined by the success of filtration.

Packaging and storage
Packaging is usually required to contain the product only for its relatively short shelf-life and to prevent contamination by dust and insects. Cleaned glass or plastic bottles or gourds are sufficient. The product should be stored in a cool place, away from direct sunlight.

```
Equipment
Knives
Filter bags
Fermentation vessel
```

Product note Similar beers are made in most countries using saps, juices and extracts from cereal grains. This example is typical of the stages used in many other processes.

Pineapple peel vinegar

Product description
This product enables the utilization of pineapple peels which are usually discarded during the processing or consumption of the fruit. The product

Process	Notes
Fruit ↓	100 washed ripe pineapples, well washed in clean water.
Peel ↓	Take care not to damage hands.
Cut ↓	Cut into thin strips and put into clay or pewter pots. Aluminium or iron containers are not recommended.
Mix with sugar syrup ↓	Sugar (panela) is dissolved in potable water in a ratio of 45kg of panela to 680 litres of water and added to the peels from one standard ripe fruit.
Add and ferment inoculum ↓	Each pot is then inoculated and covered with a clean cotton cloth, held around the pot with an adhesive tape, to prevent contamination by insects or dust. Ferment at room temperature (about 20–22°C/70°F) for about eight days, checking the acidity daily. The water level should be maintained during this period. The product should be increasingly acid and by the eighth day it should have the required concentration of 4 per cent acetic acid in vinegar. If higher acidity is desired the product is left to ferment for another one or two days.
Filter residue ↓	Strain through a cheese cloth. The residual bacteria removed may be reused as an inoculum two or three times.
Fill ↓	The vinegar is bottled using the cleaned and steam-sterilized bottles and lids, closing them loosely.
Pasteurize ↓	The filled bottles, if desired, may be immersed in a waterbath and heated to boiling for about 10 minutes to pasteurize the product and improve its stability.
Cool ↓	Caps should be tightened during cooling.
Store	In a cool, dark place.

has a distinct, very light, pineapple flavour and has the same uses as any commercial vinegar.

Raw material
The peels should be from very well-washed ripe pineapples (damaged, rotten or infected fruits should not be used as a source of peels). Use only the peels, not the leaves or stems. The water used should be potable water, boiled if necessary. All the equipment should be well-cleaned, as well as the bottles, which should also be steam-sterilized before use.

Process control
The development of acidity should be checked by tasting the product during fermentation. The residue may be reused about two times, until its texture breaks apart. The filtration should yield a transparent product.

Packaging and storage
Suitable packaging materials include glass bottles with tight-fitting caps to prevent evaporation of the acetic acid in the vinegar. The product should be stored in a cool place.

> **Equipment**
> Pots
> Cotton cloth
> Cheese cloth
> Boiling waterbath (optional)

Note The traditional process may be improved by a two-stage fermentation in which alcohol is first formed by yeast (*Saccharomyces cerevisiae*) and the 'must' is then inoculated with acetic acid bacteria (*Acetobacter pasteurianus*). In outline, the process involves liquidizing the peels and diluting with water (water:pulp is 4:1), adjusting the pH to 4.0 using sodium bicarbonate and adding yeast nutrient (ammonium phosphate) at 0.14g per litre. A starter culture is added at 2.7g per litre and the fermentation allowed to take place at 25°C (77°F) for two days. The 'must' is then filtered and inoculated with acetic acid bacteria and allowed to ferment for 11 days with aeration of the must. Other parts of the process are similar. Additional equipment includes a pH meter, refractometer, liquidizer, fermentation locks and equipment for preparing the starter cultures.

Pineapples which are to be dried or used to make juice can also provide peels from which to make vinegar [IT/SB]

Pickles and chutneys

Lime pickle

Product description

This product is made from salted pieces of lime packed in a salty, spicy liquor, like a semi-solid gravy. It is brownish red and the lime peels are yellow or pale green with a sour and salty taste. It is eaten as a condiment with curries or other main meals. If processed well, the product can be kept for several months.

The process and the principle of preservation

Limes (*Citrus aurantifolia*) are cut to expose the interior and allow salt to be absorbed more quickly. They are dipped in salt solution and this causes water to be drawn out of the pieces (osmosis). Some sugar is also drawn out and this allows certain types of salt-tolerant micro-organisms to grow and ferment the product. The micro-organisms produce acid, helping to develop the flavour and soften the product. The limes are dried in the sun and this also concentrates the juice on the surface.

Preservation is therefore achieved by a combination of salt, increased acidity and lower moisture content. Packaging prevents contamination by dirt and moulds. In alternative methods the limes may not be fermented or dried, but packaged with the liquor.

Raw material

Ingredients

5kg/11lb limes
1kg/2.2lb salt
5g/1 teaspoon turmeric powder
150g/5½oz chilli powder
100g/3½oz fenugreek seeds
100g/3½oz mustard seeds

Good quality, fully mature fruit is used without bruising or damage. All spices should be good quality and free of mould or adulteration.

Process control

In one process, the drying stage in which a degree of fermentation takes place has the main influence on the quality of the final product. This should be

Process	Notes
Sort	Select ripe (but not overripe), healthy lime fruits with dark yellow skins without infection or mould growth.
Wash	In clean water.
Heat	Dip in hot water (60–65°C/110–120°F) for about five minutes.
Cut	Cut into four pieces or alternatively cut into smaller, uniform-sized pieces.
Mix with salt	Dip in saturated salt solution for 20–30 minutes. Alternatively, pack the limes and salt in layers (1kg salt per 5kg limes), ensuring that the surface is covered with juice, and leave for 24 hours. If necessary, the fruits should be pressed down to hold them below the liquid.
Dry	Dry in the sun for 2–3 days. Sometimes salt crystals are sprinkled on the lime while drying. Drying is continued until the skin becomes brown and the pieces are soft and breakable.
Mix spices	Roast fenugreek seeds until they 'splutter' and grind all seeds together to a powder before adding to the fruit.
Pack	Fill into pots or glass jars and seal.
Store	Store in a cool place away from sunlight. With the fermented product, store for one month to allow fermentation to take place.
Pack	Repack in pre-sterilized glass jars or plastic bags, ensuring that no air bubbles are trapped in the pickle and that a layer of oil covers the surface.
Store	In a cool place, away from sunlight.

carefully monitored to ensure that a consistent product is produced, and this requires skill and experience. In the other process the fermentation takes place in containers during storage for one month. While this takes place, the containers should be stored in cool, dry conditions.

Packaging and storage

Lime pickle can be packed in small polythene bags and sealed or in clean jars and capped. It keeps well if stored in a cool place. Although the product is salty and acidic, and therefore not at serious risk from food poisoning, strict hygiene should be enforced because the product is not cooked before consumption and therefore unhygienic conditions will also promote mould growth or excessive fermentation during storage.

Equipment
Scales
Heat sealer or jar capper
Filler
Stainless steel mixing pan

Note The cut fruit is sometimes boiled in salt water, then dried after straining out the salt. Sometimes the final product is squeezed by hand to remove the juice, the pieces packed into bottles and the juice re-added. Similar products are made using fruits of *Averrhoea bilimbi* (Billing). There are possibilities for product development in this area and also for packaging less sweet fruits in vinegar and salt.

Different products, including mango pickle (see page 119), can be made using a similar process.

Tamarind pickle

Product description

This is a hot, spicy pickle with a salty, sour taste. It is a mixture of tamarind and spices with a layer of oil on the surface. It is eaten as an accompaniment to curries or other main meals. If processed well, the product can be kept for several months.

The process and the principle of preservation

Preservation is caused by a combination of added salt, increased acidity and spices. Packaging prevents contamination by dirt and moulds.

Process	Notes
Sort	Select fresh, mature but unripe tamarind fruits. Reject ripe fruits or those with infection, damage or mould growth.
Wash	Rinse in clean water.
Soak	Use clean water, for 12 hours.
Separate water	Strain the tamarind.
Mix sugar	For each 1kg tamarind, add 1kg sugar.
Heat	Boil while stirring continuously. When the mixture thickens, add the spices.
Fry	For each 1kg of tamarind use: 40g coriander, 50g cumin, 30g black cumin, 3–4 pieces of cloves, 3–4 pieces of cardamom, 3–4 pieces of cinnamon, 10–12 chillies, 30g salt, 250ml mustard oil, 15g caraway seeds, 30g pepper.
Grind	Grind the spice mix to a paste.
Mix spices	Add the spice paste to the tamarind and mix thoroughly.
Pack	Hot-fill (above 80°C/146°F) into pre-sterilized glass jars or cold fill into plastic bags.
Cool	To room temperature.
Store	In a cool place, away from sunlight.

Raw material

Use good quality, fully mature but unripe fruit without bruising or damage. All spices should be of good quality and free of mould or adulteration. Oil should be of good quality without rancidity.

Process control

Strict control over hygiene and sanitation is needed to prevent spoilage during storage. The main control points are:

○ Weighing all ingredients to the correct formulation.

○ Monitoring the boiling stage to ensure a consistent product from each batch.

Packaging and storage

The pickle can be packed in small polythene bags and sealed or in clean jars and capped. It keeps well if stored in a cool place. Care should be taken to prevent air bubbles becoming trapped in the pickle and to ensure that a layer of oil covers the product.

Equipment
Scales
Heat sealer or capper
Filler
Stainless steel mixing pan

Product variation Olive pickle is a hot, spicy pickle with a salty, sour taste. It is a mixture of dried olives and spices with a layer of oil on the surface. The process is similar to that described above, except that 30g turmeric is mixed with each 1kg of fruit which is then dried in the sun for 3–4 days. Then the following spices are added per 1kg fruit: 250ml mustard oil, 40g ground ginger, 50g coriander, 30g garlic powder, 250ml vinegar, 40g mustard seed, 50g mixed spice. The spices are ground with the vinegar and added to hot oil. This is then mixed with the olives and boiled while stirring continuously until it thickens. Sugar (400g) is added and the mixture is finally hot-filled into pre-sterilized glass jars.

Mango pickle

Product description

This is a hot, spicy, red pickle with a salty, sour taste. It is a mixture of salted pieces of mango and spices with a layer of oil on the surface. It is eaten as an accompaniment to curries or other main meals. If processed well the product can be kept for several months.

Process	Notes
Mango fruits	Fresh, mature but unripe fruits, particularly varieties that have a sharp, acidic taste.
Sort	Reject ripe fruits or those with infection damage or mould growth.
Wash	Wash in clean water.
Destone	Remove stones by hand.
Cut	Slice fruit into uniform-sized pieces.
Soak in salt	Hold in 2–3 per cent salt solution to prevent darkening of the surfaces.
Mix salt and spices	Per 20kg fruit pieces, add 3.5–4kg salt and 0.2kg turmeric.
Ferment	Ferment for four to five days in pre-sterilized jars, in the sun, ensuring that the surface is covered with juice. If necessary the fruits should be pressed down to hold them below the liquid. The mango pieces become pale yellow and all salt is converted into brine.
Mix spices	Per 20kg fruit: 0.4–0.8kg mustard pulse, roasted to a light brown colour, 0.4–0.8kg fenugreek similarly roasted, roasted asafoetida to taste, 0.4–1kg chilli powder and 2.0–2.5kg oil (any edible oil). *Note* other spices including mace, cumin, garlic, mint, aniseed, ginger, coriander, cloves, cardamom and pepper can be used depending on local tastes.
Pack	In pots or glass jars.
Store	In a cool place, away from sunlight.

The process and the principle of preservation

Preservation is caused by a combination of salt, increased acidity and spices. Packaging prevents contamination by dirt and moulds.

Raw material

Good quality, fully mature but unripe fruit is used without bruising or damage. All spices should be good quality and free of mould or adulteration. Oil should be of good quality without rancidity.

Process control

As the product is not heated, strict control over hygiene and sanitation is needed to prevent spoilage during storage. The main control points are:

○ Weighing of all ingredients to the correct formulation.

○ Ensuring that a brine is formed and completely covers the product.

Packaging and storage

Lime pickle can be packed in small polythene bags and sealed or in clean jars and capped. It keeps well if stored in a cool place. Care should be taken to prevent air bubbles becoming trapped in the pickle and ensuring that a layer of oil covers the product.

Equipment
Scales
Heat sealer or capper
Filler
Stainless steel mixing pan

Note A very wide range of pickles can be made by using the same basic recipe, but varying the spice mixture indicated above, or by combining different fruits.

Snackfoods

Fried breadfruit chips

Product description

These are chips of breadfruit (*Artocarpus nobilis*), packaged with chilli powder and salt sprinkled on them. They are golden yellow to golden brown, 1cm in length, 2–3cm wide and taste starchy, crisp, hot and salty. They are sold in packets of a few pieces (25–50g) which are stable for several months if packed in moisture-proof packs.

The process and the principle of preservation

Underripe but mature breadfruit is cut into chips and fried to a golden brown, sprinkled with salt and chilli powder and then packaged. Frying removes some water, gelatinizes the starch, destroys enzymes and micro-organisms, and yields a crisp product with a characteristic aroma and taste. The low moisture content inhibits microbial growth and packaging prevents recontamination.

Process	Notes
Breadfruit ↓	Picking fruit off the tree (rather than using those which have fallen) avoids contamination.
Sort ↓	Select nearly ripe fruit in which the flesh is stiff and starchy.
Wash ↓	Wash in clean water to remove dirt and surface micro-organisms.
Peel ↓	Remove skins.
Cut ↓	Cut into pieces, 1cm in length, 2–3cm wide.
Heat ↓	Deep fry in coconut oil at about 150°C/300°F until golden brown.
Mix ↓	Mix with salt and chilli powder to taste.
Pack ↓	In polypropylene bags.
Store	In a cool, dry place.

Raw material

Select nearly ripe fruit in which the flesh is stiff and starchy. Overripe fruit does not have a sufficiently firm texture to be used for this product.

Process control

The main control points are:

○ The size of the breadfruit pieces, which affects the frying time.

○ The temperature and quality of the oil used for frying should each be carefully monitored.

Packaging and storage

Moisture-proof and airtight packs are needed for a shelf-life of more than a few days. Polythene is not a sufficient barrier to moisture for this product, especially in humid climates. The product should be stored away from sunlight in a cool, dry place to avoid deterioration due to rancidity or mould growth.

Equipment
Wash tank
Deep fryer
Heat sealer
Scales

Note Semi-drying before frying gives a crisper but darker coloured product. The process can be improved by introducing blanching and sulphiting to maintain a better colour in the finished product. Similar products can be made from any low sugar, starchy fruit such as jackfruit (*Artocarpus heterophyllus*), plantain, or banana (see following).

Ipekere (fried plantain slices)

Product description

These are slices of green plantain (cooking banana), fried in palm oil with salt sprinkled on them. They are reddish yellow as a result of the palm oil, 0.2cm thick and taste starchy, crisp and salty. They are sold in packets of a few pieces (25–50g) which are stable for several months if packed in moisture-proof packs.

The process and the principle of preservation

Underripe but mature plantain is cut into thin slices, washed in salt water and fried to a crisp texture. Frying removes some water, gelatinizes the starch, destroys enzymes and micro-organisms, and yields a crisp product with a characteristic aroma and taste. The low moisture content inhibits microbial growth and packaging prevents recontamination.

Raw material

Select nearly ripe fruit in which the flesh is stiff and starchy. Overripe fruit does not have a sufficiently firm texture to be used for this product.

Process control

The main control points are the thickness of the slices which affects the frying time and also the temperature and quality of the oil used for frying. These should both be carefully monitored and controlled.

Packaging and storage

Moisture-proof and airtight packs (not polythene) are needed for a shelf-life of more than a few days. The product should be stored away from sunlight in a cool, dry place to avoid deterioration due to rancidity, softening or mould growth.

Process	Notes
Plantain fruit	Picking fruit off the tree avoids contamination from dirt and dust.
Sort	Select nearly ripe fruit in which the flesh is stiff and starchy.
Wash	Wash in clean water to remove dirt and surface micro-organisms.
Peel	Remove skins.
Cut	Cut by hand or using a manual slicer, to slices approx 0.2cm thick.
Mix with salt water	Dip the slices in a solution of 5 per cent salt for 10–20 minutes.
Heat in oil	Deep fry in palm oil at about 150°C/300°F for 25–30 minutes until crisp.
Drain oil	Allow to drain and cool on wire mesh.
Pack	In polypropylene bags.
Store	In a cool, dry place.

Equipment
Wash tank
Deep fryer
Heat sealer
Scales

Note Semi-drying before frying gives a crisper but darker coloured product. Similar products can be made from any low sugar, starchy fruit such as jackfruit (*Artocarpus heterophyllus*) or banana.

3. VEGETABLE AND ROOT CROP PRODUCTS

A very high proportion of vegetables and root crops are harvested, stored for a short time, then cooked and eaten straight away. There is, however, a surprising variety of processed foods made from vegetables and root crops and a selection is included in this chapter.

Vegetables and root crops are low acid foods that have the potential to cause food poisoning. Although the risk may be lower than that associated with meats and dairy products, vegetables and root crops should be carefully handled under hygienic conditions to minimize such risks.

Dried and salted vegetables and root crops

Gari (cassava flour)

Product description

Gari is a creamy-white, granular flour with a slightly fermented flavour and slightly sour taste. It is produced from cassava tubers and eaten as a main meal with soup or stew. It is also consumed as a drink with sugar and milk. When properly stored it has a shelf-life of six months or more.

Principles of preservation and processing

As in all cassava products, especially those made from bitter cassava, it is necessary to detoxify the cassava by removing or deactivating the components that yield cyanide. In this product, the cassava is fermented to remove cyanide and produce the desirable flavours. It is then roasted to destroy enzymes and micro-organisms, to drive off cyamide gas and to dry the product.

Preservation is achieved by heat during roasting and the low moisture content inhibits recontamination by bacteria. Packaging is needed, especially in areas of high humidity, to retain the low moisture content.

Hygiene

Fresh cassava is a moist, low-acid food that is susceptible to bacterial and fungal growth. Hygienic practices, especially in the early stages of processing, should therefore ensure that contamination is minimized. All waste materials from the process should be removed from the site as they are produced to avoid the risk of cross-contamination.

Raw material

Fresh cassava should be free from microbial or insect damage and without serious bruising or cuts. It should be processed within two days of harvest to prevent deterioration and loss of quality in the gari.

Process control

Washing should be carried out thoroughly to avoid contamination of the final product with peels, sand and so on. Fermentation must be properly controlled as too short a period will result in incomplete detoxification and a bland product.

Process	Notes
Sort	Select fresh, mature cassava tubers without rot.
Peel	Peel by hand and remove woody tips.
Wash	Wash in clean water to remove pieces of peel, sand etc.
Grate	Use a manual or motorized cassava grater.
Ferment	Pack into baskets made from cane, bark or palm branches and leave for 24–48 hours at room temperature.
Press liquor	The fermented paste is filled into hessian or polypropylene sacks and placed in a manual screw press or weighted down with rocks. If the latter is used, the fermentation and pressing take place at the same time.
Sieve fibres	Using a wooden sieve, separate fibrous materials to control the size of the particles.
Heat	Roast in a large, shallow cast-iron pan over a fire, with constant stirring, usually with a piece of broken calabash (gourd) or a wooden paddle for 20–30 minutes.
Cool	To room temperature.
Sieve	Sieve to obtain granules of uniform size. Larger particles of gari that are separated on the sieve may be sold as a cheaper grade.
Pack	In polythene bags.
Store	In a cool, dry place.

Too long a period and the product will have a strong sour taste. Both over- and under-fermentation also badly affect the texture of the final gari.

If too much liquid is pressed from the grated cassava, the gelatinization of starch during subsequent roasting is affected and the product is more white. If sufficient liquid is not removed, however, the formation of granules during roasting is affected and the dough is more likely to form into lumps. The ideal moisture content is 47–50 per cent, and this is assessed visually by experienced gari producers.

Sieving is important to obtain a high-quality product, free of fibrous contaminants and having similar-sized granules. The granules must be roasted to about 80°C/175°F to achieve partial gelatinization of the starch. If lower temperatures are used, the product simply dries and produces a dry white powder. Too high a temperature will cause charring of the product and make it stick to the roasting pan.

Packaging and storage

The product is hygroscopic (absorbs moisture from the air) and should be packed in airtight and moisture-proof bags, especially in areas of high humidity, to prevent mould growth.

Equipment
Cassava press
Grater
Wash tank
Sieves
Roasting pan
Heat sealer (optional)

Bitter gourd

Product description

Dried slices of bitter gourd (*Momordica charantia*) are brown to black in colour and have a hard texture. A green/white product can also be made if the gourd is blanched and/or sulphited before drying. It is eaten in a curry with coconut milk and spices, or lightly fried in coconut oil with onion and spices. The product keeps well for about three months if packaged in airtight bags.

Process	Notes
Raw material	Bitter gourd.
Sort	Discard mouldy or rotten vegetables.
Wash	Rinse in clean water.
Slice	Slice into rings about 0.25cm thick.
Dry, blanch, sulphite, salt	Gourd slices may be: ○ dried directly (to give a brown/black product); ○ blanched in boiling water for one minute and dried; ○ blanched in a 1 per cent solution of sodium sulphite for one minute ○ dipped in a 10–15 per cent salt solution for two hours and dried. The last three methods prevent darkening of the product.
Dry	Directly dried under the sun on woven mats for about three days in dry, hot weather or up to eight days in cooler weather.
Pack	In moisture-proof bags.
Store	In a cool dry place.

Principles of preservation and processing

Preservation is caused by the low moisture content of the product. Blanching and/or sulphiting may be used to prevent enzyme activity during drying and storage, thereby preventing darkening of the product.

Raw material

Nearly ripe gourds are harvested. They should be free from mould or rotting and have no serious surface damage.

Process control

During drying there will be a loss of green colour which continues during storage unless blanching, sulphiting or salting is used. The method chosen reflects the demand for different types of product. Drying should be monitored to ensure that the product is fully dried and will not become mouldy in storage. Uniformly thick slices ensure even drying.

Packaging and storage

The product is stable under most conditions and little protection is needed from packaging. However sealing in moisture-proof bags will enhance the shelf-life.

Equipment
Wash tank
Blanching pot or salting pan
Trays or woven mats for drying
Solar or mechanical dryer (optional)
Heat sealer (optional)

Product variation   A large number of vegetables, including aubergine (eggplant) and leafy vegetables, can be processed in this way.

Aubergines (eggplants) can be dried or salted to extend their shelf-life [Panos/Fram Petit]

Crystallized vegetables and snackfoods

Carrot halva

Product description

This is a deep golden orange, sweet product which has a soft texture and sweet carrot flavour. It is cut into rectangles or diamond shapes 3–4cm thick and has a shelf-life of a few days.

Principles of preservation and processing

Carrots are boiled, formed to a paste with ghee, sugar and flavouring and cut to shape. Heat destroys enzymes and micro-organisms and preserves the food for a few days.

Process	Notes
Sort	Select fresh carrots, free of rot or mould.
Peel	Remove the skin.
Wash	Wash in clean water.
Grate	Grate to a fine pulp.
Mix milk	Add milk.
Heat	Boil gently for 25 minutes or until all liquid has evaporated.
Mix ingredients	Add ghee or butter, sugar and ground cardamom.
Cool	To room temperature.
Mould	Spread on a greased tray in a layer 3–4cm thick.
Cut	Into rectangles or diamond shapes.
Store	In a cool place.

Raw material

Ingredients
250g/9oz carrots
100ml/3½fl.oz milk
50g/1¾oz ghee/butter
120g/4¼oz sugar
5g/1 teaspoon ground cardamon

Good quality fresh carrots should be used and water should be of drinking quality.

Process control

The main control points are:

○ Finely grating the carrot to enable easy cooking and give the required texture.

○ Boiling in milk which gives flavour to the product and softens it.

○ Adequate heat treatment to ensure micro-organisms and enzymes are destroyed.

○ Correct mixture of other ingredients to give the required texture and flavour.

Packaging and storage

The product has a short shelf-life and should be handled correctly to prevent recontamination. It should be stored in a cool place, protected from insects and dust.

Equipment
Scales
Boiling pan

Ojojo (fried yam cake)

Product description

A golden brown, fried savoury snackfood made from grated yam, chilli pepper, onion, tomato and okra, fried in palm oil. It has a shelf-life of one to two days.

Principles of preservation and processing

The principle of preservation is the destruction of enzymes and micro-organisms during frying. The dry exterior provides some resistance to recontamination but the short shelf-life does not require inhibition of spoilage micro-organisms during storage.

Process	Notes
Yam ↓	Select healthy, mature tubers without infection.
Peel	Remove skins by hand.
Wash	Wash in clean water.
Grate	Use a fine grater.
Mix ingredients	Thoroughly mix in red chilli powder, freshly chopped onion and tomatoes, and salt to taste. The consistency should be thick, but if it does not bind well, pulped okra can be added as a binder.
Mould	Take spoonfuls of the mixture and shape into patties 3mm thick. Use floured hands to avoid sticking.
Fry	Deep fry in palm oil at 150°C/300°F until both sides are golden brown.
Drain	Remove excess oil.
Cool	To room temperature.
Store	Store in glass boxes in a cool place, in the shade to slow the onset of rancidity.

Hygiene

Heat during frying destroys most contaminating bacteria and the short shelf-life restricts recontamination during storage. Good hygienic practices should be ensured during preparation of the mix to prevent gross contamination and possible survival of large numbers of bacteria after frying. Careful handling and storage are needed after processing to reduce the risk of food poisoning.

Raw material

Ingredients
Yam
Chilli powder
Tomatoes, freshly chopped
Onions, freshly chopped
Okra, pulped (optional)
Palm oil (for frying)

The main quality factors are the colour and particle size of the grated yam and freedom from soils, mould and insect damage. Oil used for frying should be clear, of good quality and free from rancidity.

Process control

The main control points are:

○ Accurate weighing and thorough mixing of ingredients, as even small variations can cause large differences in the final product.

○ The use of okra to bind the mixture during forming.

○ Time and temperature of frying, which controls the colour, texture, flavour and moistness of the product.

The main quality factors are the colour, size and shape, aroma, texture and flavour of the product, and freedom from contamination and soils. Each is determined by the amounts and types of ingredients, control over mixing and frying stages. In particular the type and quality of the frying oil is a major influence on the product quality and only good quality palm oil should be used.

Packaging and storage

The product is eaten within a few hours and packaging is rarely necessary except to keep the product clean. The product should be stored in a cool, dry place, away from sunlight which accelerates rancidity of the oil in the product.

Equipment
Mixer (optional)
Scales
Grater

Crystallized vegetables and snackfoods

Cassava fritters/tortitas

Product description

Cassava fritters (from southern Africa) are thin, round, fried products which are approximately 8cm in diameter and 0.3cm thick. Tortitas, from Latin America, are similar but thicker. They are both made from fresh grated or pulped cassava bound together with egg, breadcrumbs and/or cassava flour. The texture is harder than that of baked products and whereas fritters have a shelf-life of a day or so, tortitas can keep for up to a week. They are used as an appetizer, a snackfood or in packed meals.

Process	Notes
Cassava ↓	Select fresh, mature tubers without mould or rot.
Peel skin	Peel by hand.
Wash	Wash in clean water.
Grate, cut	Grate cassava and onions together using a fine grater for fritters. Cut into 5cm pieces for tortitas.
Mix ingredients	4 cups grated cassava, ½ cup grated onions, ½ teaspoon salt, 3 eggs (beaten), 1 cup wheat/cassava flour and other spices. For tortitas: add salt to taste. Consistency should be thick, like a scone mixture.
Heat ↓	For tortitas only: boil for 20–30 minutes until soft.
Mash	Mash to a pulp.
Shape	Take spoonfuls of the mixture and shape into patties 3mm thick. Use floured hands to avoid sticking, or use a moulding machine. In tortitas, the breadcrumbs (1kg per 5kg cassava) and egg (5 eggs per 5kg/11lb cassava) are added before the mixture is shaped.
Coat	Dip patties into beaten egg.
Fry	Deep fry in oil at 180°C/350°F until both sides are golden brown.
Drain	Remove excess oil from fritters.
Cool	Cool to room temperature.
Pack	Pack into waxed paper or sealed plastic bags.
Store	Store in a cool place, in the shade to combat rancidity.

Principles of preservation and processing

As with all cassava products, especially those made from bitter cassava, it is necessary to detoxify the cassava by removing or deactivating the components that yield cyanide. The principle of preservation is the heat destruction of enzymes and micro-organisms during frying. The short shelf-life does not require the inhibition of spoilage micro-organisms during storage.

Hygiene

Heat during frying destroys most contaminating bacteria and the short shelf-life restricts recontamination during storage. Good hygienic practices should be ensured during preparation of the dough to prevent gross contamination and possible survival of large numbers of bacteria after frying.

Raw material

Ingredients

Cassava
Onions
Eggs
Wheat/cassava flour
Spices to taste
Salt to taste (tortitas)
Breadcrumbs (tortitas)
Vegetable oil (for frying)

The main quality factors are the colour and particle size of the grated cassava and its freedom from soils, mould and insect damage. Oil used for frying should be clear, of good quality and free from rancidity.

Process control

The main control points are:

○ Accurate weighing and thorough mixing of ingredients, as even small variations can cause large differences in the final product.

○ The use of flour to prevent the batter sticking during forming.

○ Coating with egg to prevent the product disintegrating during frying.

○ Time and temperature of frying, which control the colour, texture, flavour and moistness of the product.

The main quality factors are the colour, size/shape, aroma, texture and flavour of the product, and freedom from contamination and soils. Each is determined by the amounts and types of ingredients, control over mixing and frying stages. In particular, the type and quality of the frying oil is a major influence on the product quality.

Packaging and storage

The product is eaten within a few hours and packaging is rarely necessary except to keep the product clean. The product should be stored in a cool, dry place, away from sunlight which would accelerate rancidity of the oil in the product.

Equipment
Mixer (optional)
Scales
Grater
Fryer

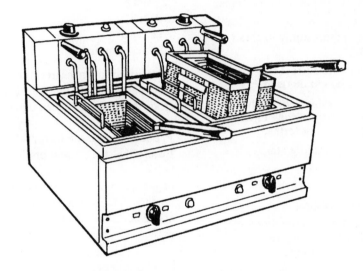

Oil for deep fat frying should be changed regularly

Bottled vegetables

Palmitos (bottled palm hearts)

Product description

Palmitos are cooked and cured palm hearts in vinegar, packed in glass jars. They are consumed cold either as a snack or as part of a green salad when they can be seasoned with a dressing.

Process	Notes
Palm hearts	Hearts are cut from the trees.
Clean	Wash thoroughly in clean water.
Cut	Cut to the correct size for the glass jars to be used.
Heat	Boil in water until the hearts soften, periodically removing the foam that forms.
Separate	Drain cooking water.
Mix ingredients	Add vinegar, salt and sugar.
Heat	Heat to boiling.
Fill	Hot-fill the hearts and liquid (80°C/170°F) into steam-sterilized, hot glass jars.
Pack	Fit an hermetically sealed lid and cool to room temperature.
Store	In a cool, dry place.

Principles of processing and preservation

The process is a straightforward bottling process with the palm hearts preserved by a combination of vinegar and pasteurization. The packaging prevents recontamination.

Raw material

Ingredients

72 palm hearts
170g salt
170g sugar
1.5 litres vinegar

Select sweet palm hearts (for example, the Cohune palm) and ensure that they are thoroughly cleaned, removing all their outers.

Process and packaging

Ensure that the packed product has a pH value below 4 and ensure that the glass jars are thoroughly cleaned and steam sterilized for at least 10 minutes. Filling temperatures should be at or above 80°C/175°F to ensure that a vacuum forms in the cooled jar.

Equipment
Boiling pans
Mixing vessel
Filler
Jar steamer

Vegetable pickles

Atchar

Product description
Atchar is a hot, mixed vegetable pickle consisting of slices of carrots, green peppers, onions and cabbage, mixed with vinegar, salt, oil and spices (the main one being chillis). It is packed in jars or polythene bags and is eaten with main meals.

The process and the principle of preservation
The process involves preparing the materials and mixing with the correct amount of salt and vinegar which act as preservatives. It is important that the ratio of salt to vinegar is correct, to prevent fermentation or mould growth.

Raw material

Ingredients for 3kg pickle

750g/1½lb carrots
600g/1¼ cabbage
100g/4oz green pepper (capsicum)
450g/1lb onions
120g/4½oz cayenne pepper
15g/½oz ginger powder
40g/1½oz salt
30g/1oz curry powder
750ml/25fl oz sunflower oil
300ml/9½fl oz vinegar

Good quality vegetables should be used.

Process control
The size and amounts of ingredients have the main influence on the quality of the final product. These should be carefully weighed out and thoroughly mixed to ensure that a consistent product is produced, and this requires some experience. Uniform heating is needed for each batch.

Packaging and storage
The pickle can be packed in small polythene bags and sealed or in clean jars and capped. It keeps well for six to twelve months if stored in a cool place.

Process	Notes
Raw vegetables	Carrots, cabbage, green peppers, onions.
Wash	Wash in clean water.
Sort	Remove mouldy or damaged vegetables.
Peel	Peel the onions and carrots.
Cut	Chop onions, cabbage and peppers to small pieces or slices about 5cm (2in) long.
Grate	Grate carrots to fine shreds.
Mix ingredients	Mix cayenne pepper, ginger powder, salt, and curry powder.
Heat spices	Heat dry spices in a little sunflower oil (about 50ml/1¾fl oz).
Heat onions	Use spicy oil to fry onions at 150°C/300°F until soft (about 5 minutes).
Mix oil, vinegar	Add 700ml/22fl oz oil and the vinegar.
Mix cabbage, heat	Cook for 5 minutes.
Mix carrots, pepper, heat	Cook for 5 minutes.
Pack	Hot-fill into pre-sterilized glass jars or polypropylene bags.
Seal	Seal on caps, or heat-seal bags.
Store	In a cool place.

```
Equipment
Mixing vessel
Boiling pan
Grater
Heat sealer or jar capper
Scales
```

Note Nearly any combination of vegetables can be used to make this product, depending on local tastes (see also fruit pickles (Chapter 2) for alternative, similar products using fruits).

4. HONEY, SYRUPS AND SUGAR CONFECTIONERY

Honey and syrups made from sugar cane or tree saps are traditional products that are found throughout the world. Similarly, in all regions there are traditional, unrefined sugars that are widely used as sweeteners and cooking ingredients. These are described in this chapter together with an example of a confectionery product made from sugar. There are also examples of confectionery products in the chapters describing cereal products, fruit products, vegetable products, nut products and animal products.

Preservation is achieved by a combination of heat, which destroys enzymes and micro-organisms, and a low moisture content in the final product, which inhibits recontamination. Many products are hygroscopic (absorb moisture from the air) and these may require packaging, especially in humid areas.

A number of medical and dental authorities sometimes criticize confectionery products because of damage to health, particularly teeth, caused by the high sugar content and a lack of other more nutritious ingredients. Although space does not permit a detailed discussion of the complex arguments surrounding these products, another view is that they are often in great demand, particularly for special occasions, and it is preferable that the demand is met by small, local entrepreneurs rather than large foreign manufacturers. When eaten in moderation as part of a mixed diet, confectionery products increase the variety and choice of foods available, and the illnesses caused in part by over-consumption in Western countries should be avoidable.

Honey and syrups

Honey

Product description

This is either a clear, viscous syrup varying in colour from pale white/yellow to dark brown, or a crystalline paste with the same colour range. It has a sweet taste and is widely used as a medicine, as a replacement for sugar, as a sweet confectionery or in cooking. It is usually sold in glass jars or bottles and has a shelf-life of many months.

Principles of preservation and processing

Honey is extracted from the honeycombs of beehives. The moisture content is standardized and it is packaged in moisture-proof containers. It is not usually heated to inactivate enzymes or destroy micro-organisms as heat reduces the quality by changing the colour and flavour. Preservation is therefore a result of the low moisture content.

Raw material

Only sealed honeycombs should be used as unsealed combs are not mature and have a higher moisture and pollen content. Honey should be fresh and without contamination by insects and with no sign of fermentation. Undamaged honeycomb should be used to reduce the amount of wax and comb pieces in the honey.

Process control

Honey should be processed as quickly as possible to prevent contamination. Processing is a slow and sticky operation which requires patience and careful control of insects. All equipment should be carefully dried to prevent moisture contaminating the product. Careful uncapping reduces the amount of wax and comb debris in the honey. Control of insects and regular cleaning of equipment is needed to prevent contamination. Heating should be avoided if possible but, where required, it should be done very carefully using a hot water bath and not directly over a flame. The moisture content must be below 19 per cent (i.e. the sugar content must be more than 81 per cent), to prevent honey fermenting during storage.

Process	Notes
Honeycombs	Collect combs that are sealed and undamaged from the hives.
Uncap	Remove the wax cappings of the honeycomb with a heated capping knife (either electrically heated or allowed to stand in hot water when not in use). Start cutting from the base of the comb and collect the wax in a clean dish. Turn the comb and remove wax from the other side.
Separate wax combs	Either allow the honey to drain out into a clean, dry stainless steel or ceramic container or use a honey centrifuge to spin the combs and extract the honey. The wax is a valuable by-product. It is collected, melted using hot water and formed into blocks.
Filter	Filter through coarse and then fine stainless steel meshes or cloth bags to remove pieces of comb, wax and pollen. *Note* Filters should be carefully washed after each use to prevent contamination of the honey.
Evaporate	The moisture content should not exceed 19 per cent to prevent fermentation. This can be checked using a refractometer and if necessary water can be removed by either blowing air across the honey using a fan or by very gentle heating. *Note* Heat causes production of a chemical named HMF following the breakdown of some sugars in honey. HMF lowers the value of the honey and in some countries there is a maximum HMF limit. Heating should therefore be reduced to the minimum to maintain the honey quality.
Pack	Fill into glass or plastic containers and seal.

Packaging and storage

Honey is hygroscopic (absorbs moisture from the air) and should therefore be stored in airtight and moisture-proof jars or bottles. Careful filling is needed to prevent honey from contacting the outside of the container as this will attract insects. It should be stored in a cool, dark place.

Equipment

Jar or bottle sealer
Scales
Refractometer
Fan or waterbath
Uncapping knife
Honey centrifuge
Coarse and fine filters

Note Some honeys are more likely to granulate (or crystallize) than others, but nearly all will granulate if the temperature falls to below 24°C/75°F. This is a natural process and there is no nutritional difference between solid and liquid honeys. However, there are strong customer preferences for solid or liquid honeys in different regions.

The colour, aroma and taste of honey are the most important features. Usually dark coloured honey has a stronger flavour whereas pale honey has a more delicate flavour. Generally, light coloured honey has a higher value. Dark colour is due in part to the sources of nectar and pollen collected by the bees, in part to the amount of heating used in the process and in part due to the temperature of storage. Where possible, heat should be avoided during processing and the honey should be stored in a cool place to prevent darkening.

Some honeys have a very high pollen content making them appear cloudy, and this is considered to be low quality. Other contaminants such as wax, dust or insects make the honey of very low value.

The wax from a honeycomb is a valuable by-product and should be collected, melted and formed into blocks [IT/MJB]

Honey and syrups

Black syrup

Product description

Black syrup is a thick, viscous liquid treacle that is dark brown to black with a sweet taste. It is made by concentrating sugarcane juice and has a shelf-life of a year or more. It is eaten as a replacement for honey in many dishes. Similar products can also be made from palm sap (see Chapter 5, Coconut treacle) or other tree saps.

Principles of preservation and processing

Boiling the juice inactivates enzymes and destroys micro-organisms and also produces the required viscosity by evaporating water from the juice. The high solid content (around 75 per cent sugar) prevents recontamination by micro-organisms. The viscous liquid is hot-filled into pre-sterilized glass bottles.

Raw material

Sugarcane should be fresh and fully mature to give a good yield of juice.

Process control

Juice is filtered to removed any plant materials or insects. Boiling should be carried out slowly to evaporate the water without burning the product—especially during the later stages when the treacle is thick.

Packaging and storage

Black treacle can keep for up to one year under ambient conditions, provided it is protected from moisture. Airtight and moisture-proof glass bottles are used.

Process	Notes
Sugarcane	Cut canes and remove leaves.
Mill	Crush the canes in a roller mill.
Extract bagasse	Collect the juice.
Filter can pieces	Sieve through wire mesh to remove extraneuous materials.
Heat	Heat slowly over a low heat with regular stirring until the syrup thickens to a viscous liquid. In traditional methods this is judged visually, but in improved processes a refractometer can be used.
Fill	Hot-fill into pre-sterilized glass bottles.
Seal	Cap the bottles.
Cool	Cool to room temperature.
Store	Store in a cool dry place.

Equipment
Roller mill
Wire mill
Boiling pan
Bottle sealer
Refractometer (optional)

Product variations A large number of treacles and syrups can be made using this process, from a wide variety of sweet juices and saps. Common examples include palm saps (Chapter 5) and fruit juices (Chapter 2).

Honey, syrups and sugar

Unrefined sugar

Panela

Product description
A solid, black, crystalline sugar product made by concentrating sugar cane juice. The product is sweet with a crystalline texture and is sold in moulded shapes, particularly in rural areas. It is eaten as a sweet, used in traditional confectionery products or instead of refined cane sugar. It has a shelf-life of a year or more.

Principles of preservation and processing
Boiling the juice inactivates enzymes and destroys micro-organisms and also evaporates water to give the required texture and flavour. The high solids content (around 84 per cent sugar) prevents re-contamination by micro-organisms. After boiling, the treacle-like viscous liquid is poured into moulds and allowed to cool slowly and crystallize to a solid product.

Raw material
Sugar cane should be fresh and fully mature to obtain a good yield of juice.

Process control
Juice is filtered to remove any plant materials or insects. Boiling should be done slowly to evaporate the water without burning the product—especially during the later stages when a thick treacle is formed. Cooling should also be allowed to occur slowly to enable a crystalline product to form.

Process	Notes
Mill	Crush the sugar cane in a roller mill.
Extract	Collect the juice.
Filter juice	Filter through wire mesh to remove extraneous materials.
Heat	Heat slowly over a low heat with regular stirring until a sample of the treacle solidifies when placed in cool water.
Cool	Fill into moulds that hold a known weight of product. Cool slowly without agitation to allow crystallization.
Pack	Pack in polythene bags, or in humid areas use polypropylene.
Store	Store in a cool, dry place.

Packaging and storage
Panela can keep for up to one year under ambient conditions, provided it is protected from moisture. Airtight and moisture-proof plastic wrapping can be used.

Equipment
Roller mill
Wire mesh
Boiling pan
Heat sealer (optional)

Note Similar products are made in Asia from palm saps. Another product made from sugar cane juice is known as gur. It is boiled to a lesser extent and is a light or dark brown colour. It is usually sold as small crystals.

Coconut jaggery

Product description

A solid, crystalline sugar product made by concentrating the unfermented flower sap of the coconut palm (*Cocus neusifera*). The product is brown/black, sweet and with a crystalline texture. It is sold in cubes, small pieces or in moulded shapes. It is eaten as a sweet or used in traditional confectionery products or instead of refined cane sugar. If packaged in moisture-proof containers, it has a shelf-life of a year or more. Similar products can also be made from other species of palm, including thal (*Borassus flabalifer*) and kitul (*Caryota urens*).

Principles of preservation and processing

Boiling the sap inactivates enzymes and destroys micro-organisms and also provides the required texture and flavour. The high solids content (around 84 per cent sugar) prevents recontamination by micro-organisms. The unfermented sap has a sugar content of 18–22 degrees Brix and this is increased to 80–84 degrees Brix by evaporating the water over an open fire. This treacle-like viscous liquid is then poured into coconut shells and allowed to cool slowly and crystallize to a solid product.

Raw material

Flower sap should be fresh and not fermenting, as this would lower the yield of sugar.

Process control

Sap is filtered to remove any plant materials or insects. Boiling should be done slowly to evaporate the water without burning the product, especially during the later stages when a thick treacle is formed. Cooling should also be allowed to occur slowly to enable large crystals to form.

Process	Notes
Filter	Pass flower sap through clean muslin cloth to remove extraneous materials.
Heat	Concentrate slowly over a low heat with regular stirring, until a treacle is formed.
Cool	Fill into coconut shells, shallow trays or other containers. Cool slowly without agitation to allow large crystals to grow.
Mould	If required, the partially solidified mass can be shaped in moulds or cut into, for example, squares.
Pack	Package in polythene or wrap in dry plantain leaves.
Store	Store in a cool, dry place.

Packaging and storage

Coconut jaggery can keep for up to one year under ambient conditions, provided it is protected from moisture. Airtight and moisture-proof plastic or glass containers, polythene or other types of plastic wrapping can be used.

Equipment
Collecting pots
Filter cloth
Boiling pan
Heat sealer
Refractometer (optional)
Scales

Sugar confectionery

Milk burfi

Product description

Milk burfi is a confectionery made by concentrating a mixture of sugar, milk and water, sometimes with added vanilla flavour. It is off-white to brown with a smooth soft chocolate-like texture. It is eaten with tea or savouries and also as a special dish during festivals.

The process and the principle of preservation

Ingredients are boiled until the mixture becomes viscous. It is then poured onto a tray as a 1cm thick sheet and cooled. Boiling the mixture destroys micro-organisms and concentrates the sugar solution. Heat is also used to partially invert sugar and therefore control the consistency of the product.

Preservation is due to the heat and low moisture content of the product. Packaging protects against moisture pickup from the air and prevents further contamination.

Raw material

Ingredients

1kg/2lb sugar
1 litre/32fl oz potable water
1kg/2lb milk powder
600g/19oz hydrogenated fat
Vanilla flavouring

Good quality materials should be used. The milk powder and fat should have no evidence of rancidity.

Process control

The sugar solution should be filtered to remove impurities. Controlled heating of the mixture is essential to give a mass of the correct consistency. Over-cooking results in a hard and powdery texture in the final product.

Process	Notes
Mix sugar with water	Dissolve sugar in water.
Heat	Heat to ensure sugar is fully dissolved.
Mix milk powder and fat	Melt the fat in a clean pan and let it cool; add milk powder and blend thoroughly. Add this to the syrup with constant stirring.
Heat	Heat to boiling with constant stirring for 5 minutes.
Mix vanilla flavouring	If required, a few drops of vanilla are sufficient.
Pour	Pour onto oiled metal trays in a layer 1cm thick.
Cool	Cool to room temperature.
Cut	The sheet is marked and cut while cooling. Diamond or square-shaped pieces are then separated.
Pack	In moisture-proof plastic bags or glass jars.
Store	In a cool, dry place.

Packaging and storage

Milk burfi is hygroscopic (it will absorb moisture from the air) and it is therefore packaged in moisture-proof bags or glass jars. Polythene is a poor moisture barrier and the product will keep for only a few days in this material, especially in humid areas. Packs should be stored in a cool, dry place, away from sunlight.

Equipment
Boiling pan
Metal trays
Knife for marking and cutting
Heat sealer
Scales

---

5. NUT AND OILSEED PRODUCTS

Nuts and oilseeds are characterized by the stable nature of the raw materials which, if properly dried and stored, can be kept for many months before processing. This enables production to be spread throughout the year after the raw materials have been harvested. The main problem with raw material occurs if the nuts are allowed to become moist (through incorrect drying or poor storage conditions). There is then a risk of mould growth which may result in a complete loss of the materials or the development of off-flavours which are transferred to the products, making them unacceptable. A particular risk is the growth of moulds that produce a poison named 'aflatoxin', and great care is needed to ensure that the nuts and seeds remain dry and free from mould. Milling to make flours has no preservative effect and may actually promote deterioration, unless care is taken to store the flours properly in a cool dry place.

Whole nuts and seeds

Cashew nuts

Product description

These are kernels of dry seeds of *Annacardium accidentale*, curved to the shape of the letter C, and with or without the testa. The unprocessed product tastes starchy with the characteristic flavour of cashew. It is dried and sometimes smoked to give a shelf-life of six to seven months when kept dry.

The process and the method of preservation

The processes of drying remove water from the kernel and thereby inhibit microbial growth. The smoking process is quicker as the temperature is higher and this causes destruction of some enzymes and contaminants on the shell. The smoke also contributes favourably to the flavour. Packaging prevents further contamination.

Process	Notes
Cashew nuts	Select those free of mould, full-sized.
↓	
Dry/ smoke	Dry for three to four days, or smoke at 50–70°C/120–160°F for 10–12 hours.
↓	
Split	Split by hand or using a manual cashew splitter. *Note* Cashew nut oil is hazardous and care should be taken to prevent the oil contacting skin as it will cause burns.
↓	
Remove testa	Remove by hand.
↓	
Sort	Sort into whole and broken nuts.
↓	
Dry	Dry for two to three days in the sun.
↓	
Pack	Pack into gunny bags or polythene packs.
↓	
Store	In a cool, dry place away from sunlight.

Raw material

Cashew seeds are picked when fully ripe (after falling to the ground).

Process control

Cashews are dried in the sun for several days until it is possible to feel the movement of the kernel inside the shell. A higher price is achieved for intact nuts and so a main control point is splitting the nut without breaking the kernel. This requires skill and practice if done manually, and there is also a risk of injury from the corrosive cashew nut oil that is released. Sorting the nuts into a uniform size also increases their value.

Drying and smoking should be carefully controlled and the product monitored closely to ensure that it does not scorch or burn. An under-dried product is highly susceptible to mould growth and will then lose its entire economic value.

Packaging and storage

Cashew nuts are packed in polythene or sold loose from large boxes or bags. The product keeps well for several months if packed in airtight and moisture-proof bags, provided that the processed nuts are low in moisture (lower than 12 per cent). They should be stored in a cool, dry place.

> **Equipment**
> Splitting hammer or cashew nut splitter
> Heat sealer
> Scales

Note Alternative processes include roasting the nuts instead of drying, coating in salt or chilli powder. Examples of some further alternative processes are described below.

Sugared cashew nuts

These are the kernels of cashew nuts with the taste and shape of cashew and a cyrstalline coating of sugar. They are sold in packets of 2–25g, and keep well for several months.

Heating in sugar syrup coats the kernel with sugar, causes some gelatinization of starch in the nut and inactivates enzymes and micro-organisms. The final product has a low moisture content and is stable in storage. The nuts are processed as above with the exception that they are placed in a concentrated sugar syrup (50 per cent sugar) and heated until the kernels develop an off-white colour (six to eight minutes).

Roasted cashew nuts

The roasted kernels of cashew nuts are golden brown and crisp, with a characteristic roasted flavour. The product is stable for several months if stored in moisture-proof containers.

Roasting subjects the kernel to heat which de-activates enzymes and micro-organisms. The process also gelatinizes the starch and causes development of flavour and colour. If chilli and salt are used to coat the kernels, these improve the keeping quality.

The main difference in the process is that nuts are roasted in a pre-heated steel pot to about 225°C (440°F) for 5–10 minutes until the product attains a characteristic golden brown colour. Heating should be done uniformly, with frequent mixing to ensure that the nuts have uniform colour and flavour development without burning.

Similar processes can be used for most types of nuts.

Processed cashew nuts can fetch a high price, but under-drying or breaking the kernels will reduce this value considerably [IT/ZUL]

Gingelly (sesame seeds)

Product description

The dry seeds of *Sesamum indicum* are light brown, oval and with the characteristic flavour of sesame. They are sold in packets of 100g–1kg, with a shelf-life of six or seven months when kept dry.

The process and the method of preservation

The process of drying removes water from the seeds and therefore inhibits microbial growth and enzyme activity. Packaging prevents moisture pickup and further contamination.

Process	Notes
Sesame seeds	Seeds should be whole and free of mould.
↓	
Clean	Wash in clean water and destone. Winnow to remove chaff.
↓	
Sort	Sort to remove discoloured or mouldy seeds.
↓	
Dry	Dry in the sun for 2–3 days, to a moisture content of about 5 per cent.
↓	
Pack	Pack in bulk, in gunny bags or in polythene bags for retail sales.
↓	
Store	In a cool, dry atmosphere.

Raw material

Sesame seeds should be carefully harvested, cleaned and sorted to ensure no discoloured or mouldy seed is mixed with the bulk.

Process control

An under-dried product is highly susceptible to mould growth and will then lose its entire economic value. The seed should be monitored during drying and turned regularly.

Packaging and storage

Seeds are packed in polythene or sold loose from gunny bags. The product keeps well for several months if packed in airtight and moisture-proof bags. They should be stored in a cool, dry place.

Equipment
Heat sealer
Scales

Product variation   The same general process can be used for most seeds and nuts.

Nut and oilseed products

Fried macadamia nuts

Product description

These are the fried kernels of macadamia nuts which are used as a snackfood and in bakery and ice-cream products. They are light brown to tan coloured with a crunchy texture and a characteristic mild flavour. They have a shelf-life of six to seven months when packaged in airtight, light-proof containers and kept in cool conditions.

The process and the method of preservation

The processes of frying removes water from the kernel and therefore inhibits microbial growth. The heat destroys enzymes and micro-organisms. However, the nuts are very prone to rancidity and sophisticated packaging is needed to provide an adequate shelf-life.

Raw material

Nuts should be picked when fully ripe.

Process control

A higher price is achieved for intact nuts and those with a light colour. The main control points are cracking the nut without breaking the kernel, drying to the correct moisture content and frying to the desired colour. Sorting the nuts into a uniform size also increases their value. Frying should be carefully controlled and the product monitored closely to ensure that it does not scorch or burn.

Packaging and storage

Nuts are packed in sealed bags, tins or jars. They are a high-value product and packaging can therefore be more expensive than for some other products. They keep well for several months if packed in airtight and moisture-proof containers, and they should be stored in a cool, dry place to prevent development of rancidity.

Process	Notes
Macadamia nuts	Nuts should be free of mould, full-sized.
Dehusk	Use a husking machine.
Dry	Dry for two or three days in bin dryers at 38°C/100°F until the moisture content falls to 8 per cent and then at 52°C/125°F until the level falls to 1.5 per cent.
Crack	Crack by hand or using a manual pressure cracker to avoid breaking the kernels.
Sort	Sort into whole and broken nuts, and sort by size and colour.
Fry in oil	Fry at 112°C/233°F for 12–15 minutes in coconut oil to a light brown colour.
Cool/drain	Cool to room temperature, then remove excess oil in a centrifuge or with absorbent paper.
Dry	Blow air over the nuts with a fan.
Coat with salt	Coat with an edible adhesive and then with salt.
Pack	Pack into sealed tins, glass jars or a high-barrier plastic film such as laminated foil/polyester.
Store	In a cool, dry place, away from sunlight.

Equipment

Nut cracker (rubber tyre type or counter-rotating scrolls)
Heat sealer
Scales
Bin dryer
Deep fat fryer

Nut pastes

Peanut butter

Product description
This is a thick, light brown, oily paste with the flavour of peanuts (groundnuts). It is used as a spread in some countries and in others as an ingredient in soups and stews.

Principles of preservation and processing
Peanuts are preserved in their dry form and have a long shelf-life provided that they are well-dried and properly stored. Peanut butter is preserved because of the heat during processing, which destroys enzymes and contaminating micro-organisms, and because of its relatively low moisture content which inhibits recontamination. It has a shelf-life of many months under tropical conditions if it is not allowed to become rancid by exposure to strong light, air or heat.

Process	Notes
Shell ↓	Shell peanuts (groundnuts) by hand or in a shelling machine.
Sort ↓	Remove nuts that are mouldy or discoloured.
Heat ↓	Roast in an oven at 235°C for 40–60 minutes. This is best carried out in a rotary roaster to allow each nut to be uniformly roasted.
Cool	Cool to room temperature.
Clean ↓	Remove the brown seed coat by gentle rubbing/brushing. Remove the dust using a winnowing basket.
Sort	Remove discoloured nuts.
Grind ↓	Grind to a paste using a small stone mill, a disc mill, a low speed liquidizer or a pestle and mortar.
Mix salt	2 per cent by weight salt may be added if required.
Pack	Pack in airtight and moisture-proof glass or plastic jars.
Store	In a cool, dry place, away from sunlight.

Hygiene
The product is often not re-heated before consumption, and as it is a low-acid product, strict hygiene rules for safe food handling should be observed.

Raw material
Peanuts should be harvested when fully mature. If the nuts are left in the ground for too long after reaching maturity they lose flavour and colour. Lifting before maturity produces shrivelled nuts that are difficult to process. The nuts should be dried in the field while in the shell, and then, while still on the stalk, turned upside down. Drying peanuts on iron sheets or a roof is not recommended because the nuts become baked in the sun and lose their flavour.

Process control

○ It is very important to dry the nuts thoroughly to prevent mould growth beneath the shell, and to shell them before storing. Some moulds produce aflatoxin, a poison which is highly dangerous. Care should be taken if shelling is done by hand not to moisten the nuts. Grit, shells, stones and leaves, and shrivelled or mouldy nuts should all be removed.

○ The nuts should be completely and uniformly roasted before grinding to produce a good quality peanut butter. Under-roasting produces a poor flavour, whereas over-roasting leads to a darkened product and burned flavour.

○ The degree of grinding and the size of the particles in the product depends on consumer preferences. In many countries a smooth paste has a higher market value than one that contains visible pieces of nut.

Packaging and storage
Peanut butter does not easily become contaminated by micro-organisms because of its low moisture content, but it can become rancid if it is not protected from air, light, or heat. It should not come into contact with metals, especially iron, copper or brass as these promote rancidity. It should be packaged in an airtight, light-proof container and stored in a cool, dry place.

Equipment
Shelling machine
Grinding mill, liquidizer or pestle and
mortar
Scales
Heat sealer/jar sealer

A shelling machine is not essential, but can save a great deal of manual work [IT/BLA]

Nut confectionery

Kashata (peanut brittle)

Product description
This confectionery is golden brown, very hard and crunchy, and contains peanut (groundnut) pieces. It is sweet, with the characteristic flavour of peanuts.

Process	Notes
Nuts in shell	These should be dry and free of mould.
Shell	Use a manual or motorized shelling machine.
Store	Store in gunny sacks in a well-ventilated room; keep sacks on pallets off the ground. Protect from rodents and insects.
Sort	Discard mouldy and shrivelled nuts.
Clean	Remove dust using a winnowing basket and pick out stones, stalks etc. by hand.
Roast	Dry-roast the nuts on a metal sheet or in a pan for 20–40 minutes at approximately 200°C/390°F.
Cool	Cool to room temperature.
Dehusk	Dehusk the nuts by rubbing them in a winnowing basket or tray.
Winnow	Use a winnowing basket.
Break	Break/crush nuts into smaller pieces using a manual or powered mill.
Sieve	Sieve through a 2–4cm sieve.
Add sugar	Add sugar, glucose and butter.
Melt	Gently stir to melt sugar without burning.
Mix	Stir the nut pieces into the melted sugar until well mixed.
Cool	Pour the mixture onto a flat tray to a depth of 1–2cm and leave to cool. Mark out 2cm squares or other shapes with a sharp knife while the mixture is still warm.
Break	When fully cooled, break the pieces along the markings.
Pack	Pack in polypropylene bags and seal.
Store	Store in cool, dry place.

Principles of preservation and processing
Preservation is achieved by heat, which destroys enzymes and contaminating micro-organisms, and by the low moisture content of the final product which inhibits recontamination. The product is hygroscopic and requires a moisture-proof package for an expected shelf-life of several weeks.

Hygiene
The raw material and product remain dry throughout the process and problems of contamination are therefore less than for wet foods. However, normal hygiene rules for safe food handling should be observed.

Raw material

Ingredients
440g/1lb sugar
200g/7oz fresh peanuts
75g/2½oz glucose syrup
50g/1¾oz butter

Peanuts should be harvested when fully mature. If the nuts are left in the ground for too long after reaching maturity they lose flavour and colour. Lifting before maturity produces shrivelled nuts that are difficult to process. The nuts should be dried in the field while in the shell, and then, while still on the stalk, turned upside down. Drying nuts on iron sheets or a roof is not recommended because the nuts will become baked by the sun and lose their flavour.

Process control
It is very important to shell nuts before storing and to dry them thoroughly to prevent mould growth beneath the shell. Some moulds produce 'aflatoxins', a poison which is highly dangerous. Shells, stones and leaves, shrivelled or mouldy nuts should be removed. The quality of the nuts in the final product is mostly determined by the time and temperature of heating (roasting) and the size and moisture content of the nuts. The colour and texture of the final product is determined by the degree of heating of the sugar and the ratio of nuts:sugar.

Product control

The main quality factors in the product are colour, texture (hardness) and flavour. The colour depends on the amount of heating of the sugar; the hardness depends both on the amount of heating and the size and amount of nut pieces added to the mixture.

Packaging and storage

The crispness of the product is maintained by packaging in sealed, strong moisture-proof plastic bags and storing in a cool, dry place. Polythene is an inadequate barrier to moisture and polypropylene or sealed glass jars should be used.

Peanut ladoo

This product is similar to kashata, described above. Peanut ladoo is a popular sweet in South Asia. It has a distinct nutty flavour and is sweetened with jaggery (raw lump sugar). The product is usually shaped into small balls (the size of a lime) and has a crunchy texture and dark brown colour.

After initial processing, the nuts are ground to a coarse flour rather than broken into pieces, and then 20g butter and 400g grated jaggery are mixed in and heated gently. Then 1g cardamom powder and 400g peanuts are mixed in. The product is formed into balls and lightly dusted with flour.

In West Africa the product is named 'groundnut biscuit' and is a dark-brown, gritty, roundish flat cake, made from roasted peanuts and caramelized sugar. The product has a sweet, nutty flavour and is eaten as a snack. It is a dry, hardened product which is very stable under tropical conditions. The nuts are roasted as above and a caramel is prepared by heating granulated sugar in a pan until it starts to turn brown. They are mixed and heated for 30 minutes until the mixture thickens, and then scooped onto a flat tray and spread with a wooden roller to form a flat sheet. The sheet may be cut into round, flat discs using a disc mould or cut with a knife.

Equipment
Shelling machine
Grinding mill
Scales
Heat sealer
Sieve
Roasting trays/pans

Coconut treacle

Product description

A thick, viscous liquid treacle, dark brown to black with a sweet, smoky flavour, made by concentrating the unfermented flower sap of the coconut palm (*Cocus neusifera*). It is sold in glass bottles or specially prepared bottles made from areca nut leaves and has a shelf-life of a year or more. It is eaten as an accompaniment to curd or used in traditional confectionery products. Similar products can also be made from other species of palm including thal (*Borassus flabalifer*) and kitul (*Caryota urens*).

Process	Notes
Filter	Filter flower sap through clean muslin cloth to remove extraneous materials.
Heat	Concentrate slowly over a low heat with regular stirring until a treacle is formed.
Fill	Hot-fill into pre-sterilized glass bottles or newly-dried areca nut leaf bottles.
Cool	To room temperature.
Store	In a cool, dry place.

Principles of preservation and processing

Boiling the sap inactivates enzymes and destroys micro-organisms and also provides the required viscosity and flavour. The high solids content (around 70 per cent sugar) prevents recontamination by micro-organisms. The unfermented sap has a sugar content of 18–22 degrees Brix and this is increased to 68–72 Brix by evaporating the water over an open fire.

Raw material

Flower sap should be fresh and not fermenting, as this would lower the yield of treacle.

Process control

Sap is filtered to remove any plant materials or insects. Boiling should be done slowly to evaporate the water without burning the product—especially during the later stages when the thick treacle is formed.

Packaging and storage

Coconut treacle can keep for up to one year under ambient conditions, provided it is protected from moisture. Airtight and moisture-proof glass containers or areca nut bottles are used.

Equipment
Filter cloth
Bottle sealer
Refractometer (optional)

Thala bola (sesame balls)

Product description

These are spherical balls, about 1.5cm or smaller, made from a mixture of sugar, glucose syrup and roasted sesame seeds. They are dark brown to black with the sesame seeds visible. They are stable for several months and are sold singly or in packs of a few balls.

The process and the principle of preservation

Washing the seeds removes dust and also some micro-organisms. Drying removes water from the seeds, thus stabilizing them. Roasting removes water, inactivates enzymes and micro-organisms and develops colour and the roasted flavour. Heating sugar partially converts it to sucrose syrup, which prevents crystallization, destroys micro-organisms, and also concentrates the sugar syrup to reduce the moisture content and extend the shelf-life. Packaging prevents further contamination.

Raw material

Ingredients
1kg/2.2lb sesame seeds
500g/1.1lb sugar
200ml/6½fl oz water
200g/7oz glucose syrup

Sesame seeds should be mature, of good quality and free from mould.

Process control

Discoloured seeds should be removed, sugar syrup should be filtered to remove foreign matter. The temperature used to invert the sugar and the time of inversion should be carefully controlled. Too little heat results in crystallization of the product and too much causes an excessively soft, sticky product.

Packaging and storage

Sesame balls can be packed in polythene bags. The packs can be stored in boxes and excessive weight on the packs should be avoided as the product can be easily damaged by crushing. The product should be stored in a cool, dry place.

Process	Notes
Sesame seeds	Should be whole, mature, not mouldy.
Clean	Wash in clean water.
Dry	Sun-dry for two to three days.
Roast	Roast for a few minutes at about 180°C/355°F to a slightly brownish colour.
Dissolve sugar	Dissolve the sugar in the water and bring to the boil.
Mix glucose syrup	Add glucose syrup and heat the mixture quickly to 118°C/245°F for five minutes; then cool.
Mix	Place sesame seeds in another pan, add the liquid sugar mix, and mix well.
Shape	Mould into balls.
Cool	
Pack	Pack in polythene (optional).
Store	Store in a cool, dry place.

> **Equipment**
> Thermometer
> Boiling pan
> Heat sealer
> Scales

Product variations An alternative product involves making a sheet about 1cm thick, and then cutting into pieces of the desired shape and size. Other seeds (e.g. poppy seeds), roasted or otherwise, could be used with the above sugar syrup mix and made into a similar product.

Beverages

Coconut toddy

Product description

An alcoholic drink made by fermentation of flower sap from the coconut palm (*Cocus neusifera*). It is white and sweet with a characteristic flavour and contains 4–6 per cent alcohol. It has a shelf life of about one day unless refrigerated.

Method of processing and principles of preservation

A natural fermentation takes place due to yeasts contaminating the sap and those added from a previous batch of toddy. The sugar in the sap is partly fermented to alcohol and this offers a degree of preservation. However, refrigeration is needed to extend the shelf-life.

Process	Notes
Raw material	Flower sap.
Collect	Slice off the tip of the unopened flower; the sap that oozes out can be collected in small pots tied underneath. A small amount of toddy from the day before should be left in the pot to start the fermentation.
Ferment	After emptying the pots into a larger vessel, allow the fermentation to continue for a further six to eight hours and the product is then ready for sale to customers or to distilleries.
Store	The product is usually sold immediately, but can be stored under refrigeration for a day or two.

Hygiene

It is necessary to avoid cleaning the pots and therefore retain an inoculum for future fermentations. However, storage vessels must be kept clean and the product must be hygienically handled.

Raw material

Flowers are selected to be free from infection or mould. They are used until they cease to provide sap or become infected.

Process control

The only control factor is the time that fermentation is allowed to continue. The longer the time the higher the alcohol content and lower the level of sweetness in the product.

Packaging and storage

The product is not packaged, but is stored away from heat until used.

Equipment
Collecting pots
Storage barrels/drums

Note Toddy can be distilled to a brandy-like spirit (named 'Arrack' in Sri Lanka). It should be noted that special licences are required for alcohol production in many countries.

Nut and oilseed products

The oil palm is one of many different sources of vegetable oil [IT/VH]

Oils

Production of nut and seed oils is a major source of income and employment in many countries. Different regions have one or more main oils that are used for cooking (for example, coconut and mustard seed oils in South Asia), peanut (groundnut) and sunflower oils in Eastern and Southern Africa and palm oil in West Africa). Oils are also used as a raw material for small-scale soap manufacture.

Raw materials

Oilseeds and nuts should be fully dried before storage. Inadequate drying and/or poor storage conditions allow mould or bacteria growth. This causes spoilage which reduces the oil yield and may affect the oil flavour and colour. More importantly, a mould can grow on nuts or seeds that are not fully dried, which produces poisons called 'aflatoxins'. This is highly dangerous and all precautions should be taken to dry nuts/seeds properly and keep them dry before use. This is a particular problem with peanuts (groundnuts) and these should be shelled before storage to prevent mould growth beneath the husk.

Preservation of oils and fats

The most important cause of spoilage is a change in flavour of the oil due to rancidity. If correct storage conditions are not used, the shelf-life of the oil is reduced from many months to as little as a few days or weeks. The main factors that cause rancidity during storage are:

○ Oxidative rancidity takes place in air and is accelerated by light, by contact with copper and iron from equipment, and by high temperatures. Oil should be stored away from heat or sunlight, in a light-proof and airtight container which is filled to the top, and does not have iron or copper on the inner surface.

○ Hydrolytic rancidity is caused by enzymes present in the raw materials or produced by contaminating bacteria. Bacteria grow on the oil if moisture, plant material or dust are present. The enzymes increase the levels of fatty acids and cause rancidity. They can be prevented by filtering the oil after extraction, heating oil to remove moisture and destroy enzymes and bacteria, and preventing moisture pickup during storage by using moisture-proof containers.

In practice, suitable storage containers include sealed glass bottles, preferably made from coloured glass or kept in a dark box, metal oil cans, where the metal is tin coated (to prevent oil from reaching the iron of the can), or glazed ceramic pots, sealed with a cork and wax stopper. Only certain types of plastic bottles are suitable for storing oils. Soft pliable plastics contain poisonous

Properties of selected oils and fats

Type of oil	Melting point (°C)	Colour/flavour	Uses
Sunflower	16–20	light yellow	cooking, soap
Cocoa	45–50	white, yellow	confectionery, chocolate
Safflower	15–18	pale yellow	cooking
Soybean	20–21	light brown	cooking
Sesame	20–25	light brown	cooking
Maize	14–20	golden yellow	cooking
Mustard	6–8	yellow	cooking
Olive	17–26	light brown	cooking, skin cream
Coconut	20–24	white/yellow	cooking, skin cream, shampoo, soap
Palm kernel	20–28	yellow/white	cooking, skin cream, shampoo, soap
Palm	40–47	yellow to deep red	cooking, soap
Peanut (groundnut)	26–32	white/light brown	cooking, soap
Cottonseed	30–37	dark/light brown	cooking, soap

Nut and oilseed products

plasticizers which will be absorbed by the oil. For example, polythene should not be used for the storage of oils.

Great care should be taken to properly clean oil containers if they are to be reused. A film of old, rancid oil on the inside of an empty container will quickly make fresh oil go rancid. The containers should be properly dried after cleaning to remove all traces of moisture.

Oilcake should be dried to prevent mould growth and stored in a cool, dark place to prevent rancidity of the oil remaining in the cake. It should be protected from insect and rodent attack using the same methods as those used for the raw materials.

Clarification

Fresh oil contains a suspension of fine pulp and fibre from the plant material with small quantities of water, resins, colours and bacteria which make it darker and opaque. These are removed by clarifying the oil, by allowing it to stand undisturbed for a few days and removing the upper layer, or by using a clarifier. If the oil is still not sufficiently clear for the consumer's requirements, it can be filtered through a plastic funnel fitted with a fine filter cloth. Finally, the oil is heated to above 100°C/212°F for a short time to boil off traces of water and destroy bacteria.

When these impurities are removed, the shelflife of oils can be extended from a few days to several months, provided proper storage conditions are used. Further clarification and extension of shelf-life by boiling the oil with 1 per cent salt is possible, but rarely used due to the extra time and cost which may not be reflected in a higher price for the product.

Refining

Large-scale, commercially produced oil is further refined by degumming, neutralizing and bleaching. This is rarely necessary for small-scale producers who are supplying domestic customers, but one or more of these stages may be necessary for export markets. The correct control of these stages (particularly neutralization) requires more complex chemical determinations and analytical equipment than is likely to be available for small-scale producers.

Peanut (groundnut) oil

Product description

This is a clear, light yellow-brown oil with a mild characteristic odour of peanuts. It is used extensively for cooking and gives flavour to many traditional dishes in West Africa.

Method of processing and principle of preservation

Kernels are dried, roasted and crushed to release the oil. Heating destroys enzymes and micro-

Process	Notes
Sort	Select mature nuts with the shells removed. Remove any discoloured or mouldy nuts.
Clean	Winnow and sieve to remove sand, straw, metal, stones, etc., either manually or with a machine.
Dry	Dry in the sun for five to eight days.
Heat	Roast for 20–30 minutes at approximately 150–200°C/300–400°F with an electrically or wood-fired roaster. The shell is often used as a fuel.
Winnow	Winnow to remove brown seed-coat.
Grind	Grind to a paste using a plate mill, a hammer mill or a pestle and mortar.
Mix water	Add four parts of water to one part paste to obtain a slurry.
Heat	Boil the slurry for 8–10 hours.
Separate paste	Skim off the floating oil with a ladle. Small amounts of water can be added to the slurry as it thickens. This part of the process may be repeated several times over a period of 8–10 hours to obtain the maximum yield of oil.
Heat	Boil the oil for one to four hours in drums to remove excess moisture.
Cool	Cool to room temperature.
Pack	Pack in airtight, light-proof containers such as oil cans or pottery vessels.
Store	Store in a cool, dry place, away from direct sunlight.

Process modification

After roasting and winnowing:

Grind	Grind to a flour using a plate mill, a hammer mill or a pestle and mortar.
Mix water	Add 8–10 per cent water (as percentage of flour weight) to condition the flour.
Heat	Heat to 80–90°C/175–195°F for 20–30 minutes with constant stirring, until the flour forms a loose ball when squeezed in the hand.
Press cake	Use a screw press. The oil from the press is passed through a screen to trap larger solid particles.
Filter residue	Filter the oil using a canvas filter cloth.
Pack	Pack in 200-litre metal or plastic drums and deliver to the retail shops for sale.
Store	Store in a cool, dry place, away from sunlight.

organisms and the oil is preserved by its low moisture content. The product is liable to rancidity and should be stored as described. The improved traditional process is also applied to many other nut and seed oils.

Raw material

The nuts must be stored in a dry place to prevent mould growth and possible aflatoxin contamination.

Process control

The yield of oil is determined mainly by the temperature and moisture content of the heated flour or paste. This is judged by experience. Secondary boiling of the oil is needed to remove all traces of water.

Packaging and storage

Reused oil drums must be thoroughly washed with hot water and, if possible, with caustic soda after each use to prevent rancid oil from contaminating fresh oil. All containers should be airtight and light-proof. Oil should be stored in a cool place to minimize the development of rancidity.

Nut and oilseed products

By-product use The cake remaining after oil extraction is a valuable raw material for use in snackfoods, in stews or soups or as animal feed.

Process variations There have been many developments of the traditional process and most oil is now made using one of the many different designs of oil press. If an expeller or ram press is used, the nuts may be pressed directly without grinding to a flour (see Further reading).

Shea butter

Product description

This is a soft, yellowish-white fat, which is solid at tropical temperatures. It is made from the kernels of the shea nut tree (*Butyrospermum parkii*) and has a strong characteristic odour. It is used for cooking and as a flavouring in traditional dishes.

Process	Notes
Shea nuts	Remove from ripe but not mouldy or rotten fruits.
Wash	Wash in clean water to remove pulp.
Dry	Dry in the sun if they are not to be used immediately.
Heat	Boil in water for one to three hours.
Dehusk	Crack shells by hand or in a cracker and remove shells.
Pound	Pound to small pieces with a pestle and mortar.
Heat	Roast at 85–100°C/185–212°F for two to three hours until nearly all moisture has been removed. The shell is often used as the fuel.
Grind	Grind to a paste using a pestle and mortar or a plate mill.
Separate pulp	The fat is squeezed out by hand or in a press.
Heat	Boil in drums to remove any remaining water.
Cool	Cool to room temperature.
Store	In airtight, light-proof containers in a cool place, away from direct sunlight.

The process and principles of preservation

Kernels are removed from the fruit, cooked, crushed and pressed to release the fat. Heating destroys micro-organisms and enzymes and the low moisture content of the separated fat prevents recontamination. The product is susceptible to rancidity and should be stored as described at the beginning of this section.

Raw material

Fruits should be fully ripened, as ripe kernels will contain more fat. They should not be mouldy or rotten as this will give off-flavours to the fat.

Process control

The kernels should be thoroughly crushed to small pieces to get a good yield of fat. Roasting should take place for a sufficient time to release the fat and remove water. If water is present it will promote rancidity in the fat. However, in the traditional product a certain amount of rancidity is acceptable as it gives flavour to the foods in which the oil is used.

Packaging and storage

The product is often not packaged and a block of fat is wrapped in clean paper. However, for longer storage it should be sealed in airtight containers. It should be kept cool and away from sunlight to give a shelf-life of up to twelve months.

> **Equipment**
> Pestle and mortar or powered cracker
> Boiling pan

Nut and oilseed products

Breadfruit oil

Product description
There are two varieties of breadfruit (*Treculia africana*) of interest: one is large (about 45cm/18in diameter) and the other is about the size of a tennis ball with very small seeds. Both are suitable for making this product. It is a clear brown oil used for cooking and as a flavouring in traditional dishes.

The process and principles of preservation
Seeds are removed, dried, crushed and then boiled to release the oil. Heating destroys microorganisms and enzymes and the low moisture content of the separated oil prevents re-contamination. The product is susceptible to rancidity and should be stored as described at the beginning of this section.

Process	Notes
Breadfruit	Ripe but not mouldy or rotten.
Cut	Cut open to release seeds.
Separate fruit	Remove seeds.
Wash	Wash in clean water to remove pulp.
Dry	Dry in the sun if they are not to be used immediately.
Crush	Grind seeds in a pestle and mortar or in a plate mill to a fine powder.
Mix water	Mix to a thick paste.
Heat	Boil for one to two hours to release oil.
Separate cake	Skim off the oil.
Cool	To room temperature.
Store	In airtight, light-proof containers.

Raw material
Breadfruit should be fully ripened but not mouldy or rotten as this will give off-flavours to the oil.

Process control
The seeds should be thoroughly crushed to a fine flour to get a good yield of oil. Boiling should take place for a sufficient time to release the oil from the flour and skimming should be carefully done to collect as much oil as possible without significant amounts of water. If water is present it will promote rancidity in the oil and a second boiling may be needed to remove it. In the traditional product a certain amount of rancidity is acceptable as it gives flavour to the foods in which the oil is used.

Packaging and storage
The product is packaged in airtight containers such as sealed calabashes, plastic or glass containers. It should be kept cool and away from sunlight.

Equipment
Pestle and mortar or powered mill
Boiling pan
Skimming ladle

Note In South Asia, sesame oil is produced by a similar process.

Sesame oil (thala thel)
This is a clear, brownish oil, with a characteristic odour, used in many Asian countries.

Oil is prepared by expelling from dried seeds (commercially) or by using hot water and pressing from crushed sesame seed pulp (in the home). At the industrial scale the seeds are cleaned, washed and destoned. They are then dried, transferred into a mechanical expeller, and the oil is expelled.

In the cottage-scale process, the cleaned, destoned and dried seeds are pounded with the addition of a little boiling water. The flour is then placed in a cloth and pressed by hand. The process is repeated several times until nearly all of the oil is extracted. The oil is then decanted and packed.

6. MEAT, FISH AND DAIRY PRODUCTS

The animal products contained in this chapter are each characterized by the highly perishable nature of the raw materials and the high risk of food poisoning. Meat, fish and dairy products are all low acid foods that can support the growth of a wide range of bacteria. These can rapidly spoil the foods if processing is not done quickly and properly. Some bacteria can grow and cause severe food poisoning and it is essential that correct hygiene and food handling are carried out with these products. In general, processing these products should not be carried out by inexperienced people, and training to deal with the risks associated with these products should be given.

Dried meat and fish

Kilishi (spiced meat)

Product description
Kilishi is a spiced, sun-dried beef snack. It will keep for up to six months at ambient temperatures if properly processed.

Principles of preservation and processing
The meat is cut into thin slices, spiced and sun-dried. Preservation is mainly due to the low moisture content but the spices also have an anti-microbial effect.

Process	Notes
Meat ↓	Meat from any part of healthy cattle can be used.
Separate fat	Cut off the fat using a sharp knife.
Cut ↓	Cut the meat into thin slices, 1–2cm thick.
Wash	Wash in clean water.
Mix ↓	Add yaji (mixed spice) to the strips.
Pound ↓	Pound the meat-spice mixture with a pestle into thin sheets.
Dry ↓	Dry in the sun on drying racks for two to three days (to about 5 per cent moisture).
Pack	Kilishi is stored in jute bags. It is sold from bowls, wrapped in paper (newspaper should be avoided as the print is poisonous).

Hygiene
Meat is a low acid food that is able to cause food poisoning. Care should be taken to ensure hygienic procedures are followed.

Raw material
Only meat from healthy animals should be used. The meat should be prepared quickly to prevent bacterial growth. As the product is not cooked it should be processed hygienically to prevent the risk of food poisoning.

Process control
The main quality control points are:

○ The thickness of the slices, which determines both the drying time and the texture of the final product. Pounding is an important stage because the meat is eaten by tearing pieces off the strip, and it must therefore be thin and soft.

○ The spice mixture should be evenly distributed through all parts of the meat during the pounding stage.

Packaging and storage
The meat is not packaged, but is sold from bowls. It is cut into different-sized pieces depending on the price paid.

> **Equipment**
> Drying racks
> Pestle and mortar

Sun-dried meat will keep for up to six months [IT/KM]

Dried fish and shellfish

Product description
These dried products are made by laying wet fish or seafoods (e.g. shrimps) on raised platforms to be dried by the sun. Drying times depend on the type of raw materials, desired quality of end product, traditional practice within the locality, and climatic conditions. Sun-dried fish products are very popular in the north of Cameroon where the climate enables this method of processing. These products are essential ingredients of many traditional soups and are important sources of protein and minerals. They are also used as condiments for different types of soups and as essential flavourings. They are used as a delicacy to prepare foods for special occasions.

Principles of preservation and processing
Preservation is achieved by the low moisture content of the products. The optional treatment with salt improves the rate of drying, reduces the initial level of micro-organisms and extends the shelf-life by inhibiting the activity of enzymes and micro-organisms. It also improves the flavour of the products and gives them some protection against insects and mites.

Process	Notes
Fresh fish/ shellfish	Large fish should be gutted and cut into chunks; medium, gutted; small, used whole.
Wash	Wash to remove dirt, blood and reduce numbers of micro-organisms.
Mix salt	Various options: treatment by rubbing with dry salt, kenching or brining in 5 per cent salt solution.
Dry	Lay fish on raised platforms under the sun for 2–10 days.
Pack	Pack in paper, jute or hessian bags or in polythene bags, inside boxes for transport.
Store	In a cool, dry place.

Hygiene
Dressing operations (for example, gutting the fish) are important to reduce the numbers of micro-organisms and to facilitate drying. They also improve the appearance of the product. Fish is highly susceptible to spoilage and food poisoning bacteria and every care should be taken to use the highest standards of personal hygiene and process sanitation.

Raw material
It is important to use good quality shellfish and fish. Fish that are heavily loaded with spoilage and pathogenic bacteria are unacceptable for processing. Processing will do little to improve the quality of such fish. Washing removes dirt, blood and microflora present.

Process control
The main control points are:

○ Treatment with brine should be similar each time.

○ Drying conditions should be standardized.

Packaging and storage
Packaging should prevent rehydration, which would lead to microbial spoilage and changes in texture and flavour. Dried fish and shellfish are brittle and easy to break, so packaging should also offer protection against air, light and insects and should prevent the product breaking. Materials generally used are paper, jute or hessian bags sometimes lined with polythene, cartons or polythene-lined cane baskets.

> **Equipment**
> Drying rack
> Heat sealer (optional)

Product variation Salted and dried prawns (*Peaneaeus spp.*) have a dry texture and are either yellow or off-white in colour. They are cooked into curries or fried. Prawns are cleaned, boiled for a few minutes (until the colour of the cuticle becomes orange), strained of water and then salted by placing in salt solution (10–15 per cent salt) for two to three hours and sun-dried for several days to a moisture content of 15 per cent).

As the fresh prawns are a low-acid, moist food they are highly susceptible to microbial growth. It is therefore essential that all equipment and surfaces are thoroughly cleaned before processing. Strict personal hygiene and hygienic food handling practices should be enforced to prevent food poisoning bacteria from contaminating the product.

Note The carapace and cuticle of prawns, removed during processing, are sometimes dried and ground for use as a flavouring in curries.

Kapenta

Product description

Kapenta are small (2.5cm by 6cm) dried silver fish which are sold intact. They have a typically fishy flavour and salty taste and a hard, leathery texture. They are used domestically with a main meal and as a component of animal feed formulations. The expected shelf-life is several months under correct storage conditions.

Principles of preservation and processing

The principle of preservation is to inhibit enzyme and microbial action by addition of acetic acid to the surface of the fish, and removal of moisture by drying.

Process	Notes
Sort ↓	Use fresh, healthy fish without evidence of spoilage.
Store	Use damp sacking over fish to keep evaporation low and prevent them drying out. Keep the fish in the shade, out of direct sunlight. Ice can also be used. This helps to keep the fish wet and reduces the rate of microbiological and chemical deterioration.
Clean ↓	Remove weeds and snails by hand. Use clean water for washing away mud.
Acidify ↓	Dip the fish in vinegar diluted with water (50 per cent water : 50 per cent vinegar).
Dry ↓	Dry in the sun, turning at intervals for 3–4 days until hard and rubbery.
Pack	Pack in plastic or jute sacks.
Store	Store in a well-ventilated, cool, clean room.

Hygiene

As the fresh fish is a low-acid, moist food it is highly susceptible to microbial growth. This is an important factor with this product as it is not gutted, and gut bacteria therefore remain in the product. It is therefore essential that all equipment and surfaces are thoroughly cleaned before processing. Strict personal hygiene and hygienic food handling practices should be enforced to prevent food poisoning bacteria from contaminating the product.

Raw material

The fish should be freshly caught, free from disease and handled carefully to prevent contamination. They should appear shiny and metallic, with a wet sheen. The eyes should be clear and projecting and the gills should be pink.

Process control

The main control points are:

○ The fish should be thoroughly dried to a low moisture content. They should be protected from insects and animals during drying. The drying rate affects the product quality and moisture content and depends mostly on the climate and size of the fish.

○ The amount of acetic acid used must be carefully controlled, to prevent surface bacterial growth during the initial stages of drying.

Product control

The main quality factors are colour, taste and texture of the product. Colour and texture are determined by the drying conditions and taste is mostly determined by the freshness of the fish.

Packaging and storage

Kapenta needs packaging to prevent contamination by dust and insects and, if transported to a more humid region, to prevent moisture uptake and mould growth. If sold in the area of production, a simple container of paper or cloth is sufficient to keep the product clean. Sealed polythene bags are suitable for transport and distribution to other areas. The fish should be stored in a cool, dry place, away from sunlight to minimize rancidity and moisture uptake.

> Equipment
> Drying racks

Drying, salting or smoking will increase the shelf-life of fish as well as varying the flavour [IT/ Neil Cooper]

Salted/smoked meat and fish

Biltong

Product description

Biltong consists of strips of dried, salted meat which are dark brown with a salty taste and a flexible, rubbery texture. It is used in southern Africa as a snack or to accompany sadza (thick porridge). The expected shelf-life is several months under correct storage conditions.

Principles of preservation and processing

The principle of preservation is to inhibit enzyme and microbial action by the addition of salt to the surface of the meat and removal of moisture by drying. Where used, potassium nitrate/sorbate also has a preservative effect.

Process	Notes
Fresh meat	Good quality meat should be used. It must be kept cool and should be protected from flies. It should be handled in a hygienic way to protect it from dust and dirt.
Separate fat	Remove as much fat as possible by hand.
Slice	Slice meat into uniform-sized strips 2cm wide, 1cm thick and 20–25cm long (approx. 1in × ½ × 8–10in.).
Mix salt, spices	Rub salt into the meat slices (500g salt per 10kg sliced meat/1lb:22lb). Spices and flavourings can be mixed into the salt if required (typical spice mixture given below).
Dry	Hang each slice of meat on a hook and put the hooks on a hanging wire. Sun-dry the meat for 7–10 days depending on the climate (e.g. 25–30°C/77–86°F, <80 per cent humidity, with a gentle breeze). Enclose the meat in netting/gauze to protect it from flies while it dries.
Pack	Pack in polythene bags (e.g. 50g net weight) and heat-seal.
Store	Store in cool, dry conditions, away from sunlight.

Hygiene

It is essential that all tools and equipment are thoroughly cleaned and sterilized in boiling water for ten minutes before and after processing. Strict personal hygiene and hygienic food handling practices should be ensured to prevent food poisoning bacteria from contaminating the product. The meat should be protected from insects and animals during drying.

Raw material

Ingredients

Typical spice formulation (for 100kg meat—e.g. one week's production):

Salt	3.74kg
Sugar	1.87kg
Potassium nitrate	0.02kg
Potassium sorbate	0.2kg
Mixed spice	0.21kg
Black pepper	0.10kg
Onion powder	0.03kg
Garlic powder	0.03kg
Ground ginger	0.03kg
Mustard powder	0.03kg

The meat should be freshly slaughtered, free from disease and handled carefully to prevent contamination. Meat that can be easily cut into strips is best, but cheaper parts of the animal can also be used. Shin meat does not produce good biltong. The meat should be boned and trimmed of excess fat and any tendons. Spices should be from a reputable supplier as these are often a source of food poisoning bacteria. As biltong is not cooked this presents a potentially serious health hazard.

Process control

The main control points are:

○ The size of the strips, which should be uniform to give similar drying times.

○ The drying rate, which affects the product quality and moisture content. This depends mostly on the temperature and air speed of the drying air and size of the strips.

○ The amount of salt (and sometimes spices) rubbed into the meat, which prevents surface bacterial growth during drying.

Product control

The main quality factors are colour, taste and texture of the product. Colour and texture are determined by the drying conditions and taste is mostly determined by the amount of salt and spices used.

Packaging and storage

Biltong needs packaging to prevent contamination by dust and insects and, if transported to a more humid region, to prevent moisture uptake. If sold in the area of production, a simple container of paper or cloth is sufficient to keep the product clean. Sealed polythene bags are suitable for distribution to other areas. Biltong should be stored in a cool, dry place, away from sunlight to minimize rancidity and moisture uptake.

Equipment
Drying racks and mesh covers
Heat sealer

Smoked bream

Product description

Smoked bream is a dry, brown, leathery product that has a salty taste and a characteristic flavour. It has a shelf-life of several months when stored correctly. It is a valuable product which has a high domestic demand.

Process	Notes
Raw material	Fresh fish.
Clean	Clean the fish by removing sand, waste material and gills with clean water. Avoid contaminating flesh with internal organs. *Note* The removal of scales is optional; clean and wash with potable water.
Cut	Cut the fish from tail to head through the stomach using a sharp knife. The fish has to lie flat, supported by the spinal cord.
Mix salt	Place fish in salt water solution in several layers in a container. Let it stand for two hours.
Smoke	Place the salted fish on the smoking racks in an orderly pattern, and not one on top of the other, with the back of the fish downwards. Allow the fish to lie on the rack away from flames. Sprinkle fuel charcoal periodically on the wood chips. The fish must be kept for two to three days on the rack, turning every six hours. Break the fish to test the dryness. It should break crisply when fully dried. An enclosed smoke house is preferable because it keeps the smoke inside. The fire should have a composition of two-thirds dry firewood and one-third fresh wood to increase the smoke. The rack must be 2 metres above the fire.
Pack	Pack in jute/plastic bags or sacks.
Store	In a well-ventilated room at a cool temperature.

Principles of preservation and processing

Heat from the smoke destroys enzymes and micro-organisms in the fish. Smoke deposits hydrocarbons on the surface of the fish which, together with the salt that is rubbed into the surface, inhibit microbial growth.

Moisture is removed during smoking/drying, and the low moisture content of the final product inhibits re-contamination.

The process involves rubbing salt into the prepared fish and smoking the fish until sufficient moisture has been removed.

Hygiene

Fish is a low acid product that is extremely susceptible to bacterial spoilage and the transfer of food poisoning micro-organisms when it is moist. It is therefore essential that all equipment and surfaces are thoroughly cleaned before processing. Strict personal hygiene and hygienic food handling practices should be enforced to prevent food poisoning bacteria from contaminating the product. The fish should be thoroughly dried to a low moisture content and should be protected from insects and animals during drying.

Raw material

Fresh fish should have a shiny, metallic appearance, a firm texture and a fresh, seaweedy odour. Gills should be bright red and the eyes should be clear and protruding.

Process control

The main control points are:

○ Adequate cleaning and preparation of the fish to prevent contamination of the final product.

○ Correct smoking temperature and time; overheating causes excessive browning and underheating/inadequate time may result in incomplete drying and mould growth during storage.

Product control

The main quality characteristics are colour, texture and flavour in the final product. These are each determined by the type of wood used to smoke the fish and the time and temperature of smoking.

Packaging and storage

Packaging is needed to prevent contamination by dust and insects, and if transported to a more humid region, to prevent moisture uptake. If sold in the area of production, a simple container of paper or cloth is sufficient to keep the product clean. Sealed polythene bags are suitable for transport and distribution to other areas. The fish should be stored in a cool, dry place away from sunlight to minimize rancidity and moisture uptake.

Equipment
Smoke house

Product variation Smoked fish and shellfish in West Africa are glossy dark to golden brown in colour, with a tough texture, easy to break, and have a shelf-life of one to three weeks for un-brined samples and two to eight weeks for brined samples. Smoked fish and shellfish are essential ingredients in many traditional diets. They can be added to soup to provide flavouring or as a delicacy to prepare special traditional meals. The products are made from wet fish or shellfish by washing, optional brining in 5 per cent salt solution, and then by laying them over the traditional platform (banda) or in a kiln and smoking them. The smoking conditions, including smoke intensity and time, will depend on the size of the raw material, tradition in the area, type of equipment and the required quality of end product. Typically, products are smoked for between five and thirty hours at temperatures of 60–120°C/140–248°F.

Salted fish

Product description
This is a heavily salted product made by dry-salting (or kench-salting) fish. Variations include wet (or brine) salting and both are therefore outlined here. It is used as a source of fish in soups. It is soaked in cold water overnight or boiled for about one hour to soften the tissue and desalt it before incorporating into the soups.

Method of processing and principles of preservation
The process involves heavy salting of the fish. This removes water, and salt also has an anti-bacterial effect.

In kench-salting, salt is rubbed into the flesh and the fish is placed skin side up and not overlapping on a layer of salt in a basket. This layer is covered with salt and another layer placed on top. Gradually the basket is filled with alternate layers of fish and salt. Fish juices are released and drain away.

In brine-salting, the same procedure of filling alternate layers of fish and salt is followed (3 parts fish to 1 part salt), but this time using a bin. The fish juices are unable to drain away and the fish become submerged in concentrated brine. A lid, smaller than the bin, is weighted down with rocks to ensure that the fish is submerged at least 2–3cm below the surface, protecting it from air. Salt levels in the product may range between 12 and 20 per cent in the final product and it is stable for up

to four months under tropical conditions. After this, fat oxidation leading to rancid off-flavours is the first noticeable sign of spoilage.

The shelf-life of the product may be drastically reduced due to poor handling and contamination of the brine with dirt and other unwanted materials. The product must therefore be hygienically handled and the stored fish protected from dirt by covering the bin.

Hygiene
The hygienic requirements are:

○ Raw fish must be stored in clean containers and kept frozen or chilled if not used the same day.

○ The product must be kept covered in the plastic drums or baskets and hygienically handled to avoid contamination with dirt and other materials.

○ Process workers should be free from skin infection or stomach illness.

Raw materials
Fish must be good quality and free from disease or obvious spoilage.

Process control
Liberal amounts of salt are applied, enough to cover the fish. Between four and seven days' salting are normally allowed before selling the product. This allows for the salt to enter the fish flesh.

The dry-salted product is stored dry, whereas the wet-salted product is kept in the brine during retailing. However, small quantities are removed and displayed on open trays. At the end of the day the unsold product is placed back into the brine.

Packaging and storage
When properly handled and kept in the containers, salted fish may remain stable in storage for more than three months under normal ambient conditions, without additional packaging.

Process	Notes
Wash	Wash the raw fish in clean water.
Mix salt	Dry-salting: liberal amounts of salt (fine granules) are rubbed on the flesh and used to cover the layer of fish.
Mix salt	Wet-salting: the drums of fish are kept covered for at least seven days. During this period a strong brine forms from fish fluids and covers the fish.
Dry	Sun-dry (dry-salting only).
Store	Store in a cool, dry place, away from sunlight.

```
Equipment
No special equipment necessary
```

Product variation 'Maldive fish' from South Asia is a specially prepared, cooked, salted and dried

Meat, fish and dairy products

form of tuna fish (*Katsuwananas pelamis*). It is extremely hard with a characteristic flavour. It has a dark surface with a reddish interior and is sold in pieces (7.5–20cm in length), or sometimes as flakes, in polythene packs (50g–500g). Maldive fish is used as a flavouring in certain curries and sambals.

The tuna is gutted, washed and cleaned. Remove scales from tail to head using a scraper rather than a knife to avoid damaging the flesh. The general technique for gutting larger fish is applicable to this product: cut along gill covers on both sides, loosen and remove them. Cut along the belly from the anal end and open the fish, then remove the viscera by lifting the gills and pulling backwards. Remove blood from the spine and wash the body cavity. Remove the head and if necessary cut into fillets, cutting from head to tail keeping the knife close to the bones.

The fish is then cut into pieces of about 20–25cm in length and 10cm on the sides, in a longitudinal direction. The pieces are washed clean of blood and boiled (10–15 minutes) in a salt solution (500g salt : 4.5 litres water). The pieces are then dried for several days, during which water is periodically squeezed out by hand or with a cloth to make the product harder. Rubbing ash or spices onto the surface is optional, but may act against micro-organisms.

The production process until recently was considered to be a speciality to the Maldive Islands. The processes used in Sri Lanka are similar but not identical: some tend to miss out the cutting and instead boil the whole fish in salt water, split up into four pieces by hand, skin and then smoke for a day. The fish is then sun-dried and around the seventh or eighth day, ash is rubbed onto the surface. The result is a rather soft 'Maldive fish'.

Fried meat

Ipeere (snail snack)

Product description
This is a snack made from small, fried snails. It is in great demand and can keep for up to 12 months when dried.

Principles of preservation and processing
Preservation is by salting and drying for intermediate storage, and by frying before consumption. The process involves removing the meat from the snails, soaking in brine and sun-drying. The dried product is then deep fried. The low moisture content and the salt preserve the product.

Process	Notes
Snails ↓	Small, soft-shelled snails should be gathered.
Wash ↓	Wash in baskets in a river or clean water to remove sand.
Break ↓	Break shells manually with stones or a hammer.
Separate shell	Remove meat from shell by hand.
Mix salt	Place meat in concentrated brine (20 per cent) or in clean water with lumps of alum in it.
Wash ↓	Rinse in clean water to remove slime from the meat.
Dry ↓	Dry in the sun on drying trays, roofs etc. for 2–3 days.
Mix salt	Add a little salt to taste.
Fry in oil	Deep fry in vegetable oil, stirring regularly to prevent product becoming burned.
Drain, cool	To room temperature.
Pack	Pack in polythene bags and seal.
Store	Store in a cool place, away from sunlight.

Hygiene
It is important to keep preparation and processing areas separate to avoid cross-contamination of slimy raw material and finished product. This is a low acid food that carries the risk of food poisoning if proper hygienic procedures are not followed.

Raw material
Only live, healthy snails are used and unadulterated fresh palm oil is used for frying.

Process control
The main control points in the process are:

○ Ensure that no shell remains in the meat.

○ The snails must be thoroughly cleaned and free of slime.

○ The drying must be complete to avoid growth of bacteria or moulds during storage.

○ Frying must be thorough to completely cook the snails without burning.

Packaging and storage
The dried product can be kept in baskets without other packaging. The fried product can be drained and packed in polythene bags or kept in glass boxes and sold by the spoonful.

Equipment
Frying vessel
Glass box
Heat sealer

Meat products

Gelatin

Product description
Gelatin is a cream/brown powder which can be used as a thickener or gelling agent for table jelly and a wide range of confectionery. It is also used to clarify wines. The shelf-life is several months, depending on the packaging and storage conditions.

Principles of preservation and processing
Heat is used to destroy enzymes and contaminating micro-organisms and recontamination is prevented by drying the product to a low moisture content. The process involves a hot water extraction of gelatin after it has been dissolved out of the collagen in bones and tendons. After separation of the fat and meat, the gelatin is concentrated and dried and then ground to a fine powder.

Hygiene
Bones should be fresh and without gross contamination by soil or bacteria. The long heating period sterilizes the gelatin and normal hygienic food handling practices are sufficient to prevent re-contamination before drying.

Raw material
The yield of gelatin is determined by the amount of cartilage and the collagen in the bones. Bones that have a high collagen content (e.g. trotters, leg bones, joints) are therefore selected.

Process control

○ Cleaning bones by scraping meat from them makes separation of the gelatin solution easier. Breaking bones makes gelatin extraction more rapid and increases the yield.

○ Hot water not only extracts the gelatin but also sterilizes the product. The time and temperature of heating determines the yield of gelatin.

○ Evaporation and drying should be done quickly to prevent microbial growth on the gelatin before it is fully dried. The thickness of the gelatin layer and the drying conditions mostly determine the drying time.

○ The extent of grinding and sieving determines the fineness of the final product.

Packaging and storage
The product is hygroscopic and should be quickly packaged in moisture-proof, clean containers such as plastic bags or metal containers. It should be stored in a cool, dry place.

Process	Notes
Bones	Use fresh meat bones and tendons (e.g. legs, trotters or joints) as they contain more cartilagenous tissue.
Clean	Remove all meat from the bones by scraping. Retain cartilage tissues.
Chop	Break bones into manageable pieces using choppers.
Heat	Boil gently for 5–6 hours.
Cool	Cool to room temperature.
Separate fat	Remove floating solidified fat.
Filter solids	Decant clear liquid to separate from layer of solids at the base.
Concentrate	Gently simmer to boil off water until the liquid is thick and viscous.
Dry	Sun-dry in thin layers on metal sheets until clear and crisp.
Grind	Pound using a mortar and pestle or a manually operated mill to a fine powder (this stage is optional as the gelatin can be sold as clear flakes).
Sieve	Sieve to a fine powder using a 0.5mm sieve. This should be done quickly as the product is very hygroscopic.
Pack	Pack in sealed polythene bags.
Store	Store in a cool, dry place.

> **Equipment**
> Filter bags
> Grinding mill
> Heat sealer

Milk

Pasteurized milk

Product description

Liquid milk is always in high demand because of its nutritional value and pleasant flavour. Milk from cows has a creamy-white appearance; that from goats and other animals has a yellower colour and a higher viscosity. Milk is sold universally for domestic consumption, for use with other products (e.g. tea, porridge) and for use by other processors (e.g. to make butter, cheese and yoghurt). For small-scale processors this is a relatively difficult product to process, requiring careful control over hygiene, a relatively high capital expenditure and short distribution channels to markets as the shelf-life (at three to five days) is shorter than that of most products.

Principles of preservation and processing

The principle of preservation is the destruction of pathogenic and most spoilage bacteria and inactivation of most enzymes by heat during pasteurization at 63°C/145°F for 30 minutes. This time and temperature combination is described by regulations in some countries which should be carefully followed.

Hygiene and raw material

As milk is a low-acid food that is very susceptible to spoilage and transfer of pathogenic bacteria to consumers, the methods used to handle milk at the dairy play an important role in determining the quality of the final product.

The main hygienic requirements are:

○ Thoroughly clean and sterilize (with chlorine solution or boiling water) all equipment and utensils before and after processing. *Note* Aluminium equipment should not be cleaned with chlorine solution.

○ Strict enforcement of personal hygiene measures.

○ Filter milk after milking to remove visible dirt and any 'ropiness'—curds.

○ Cool milk immediately to control further growth of micro-organisms and enzyme activity.

Process	Notes
Filter	Filter raw milk immediately, by use of filtering pads, soon after milking.
Cool	Use surface cooler to cool the milk, to stop further multiplication of micro-organisms.
Pasteurize	Use a batch pasteurizer. Control of temperature and time is very important for correct pasteurization to give expected shelf-life. The vessel to be used should be fabricated from stainless steel or aluminium, or bought locally from hardware shops. Milk should be heated with constant stirring to prevent the product overheating or burning at the bottom.
Cool	Cool quickly to temperature below 10°C/50°F. Cooling is carried out by placing the pan containing the hot product into another vessel which contains cold water. The product is stirred continuously until the temperature drops.
Pack	Pack into sterilized bottles and seal with sterile lids, using a small filling and capping machine.
Store	Storage should be either in a cooler or in a refrigerator at below 10°C/50°F. The milk should not be exposed to sunlight as this will heat it, promote rancidity of milk fat and destroy the vitamin, riboflavin.
Transport	The transportation of milk from the storage room to the market should be in a refrigerated vehicle if the distance to be covered is long. For a short distance which takes less than an hour's drive, refrigeration is not necessary.

Process control

The main control points are the temperature and time involved in heating and cooling the milk. Overheating and slow cooling cause changes to flavour, colour and nutritional value; underheating may result in inadequate destruction of enzymes and micro-organisms leading to a reduced shelf-life and the risk of food poisoning.

Packaging and storage

During packaging the most important quality control check is to ensure that filling equipment, bottles and caps are thoroughly cleaned and sterilized to prevent recontamination of the heat-treated milk. This is especially important if the bottles are reused. Fill weights should be accurately controlled and storage temperatures should be kept below 10°C/50°F.

Equipment

Filling machine
Capping machine
Bottle sterilizing equipment
Thermometer
Filtering pads
Milk cooler
Refrigerator

Fermented milk products

Yoghurt

Product description

Set yoghurt is a smooth, firm, white gel with a characteristic acidic taste made by fermenting cow's milk. Other similar products can be made from goat's milk. It is used as an accompaniment, as a dessert or as a dressing for vegetable salads. It has a shelf-life of up to eight days, depending on the storage conditions.

Principles of preservation and processing

Preservation is due to the production of lactic acid by naturally occurring bacteria in the untreated milk. The high levels of acid inhibit the growth of spoilage bacteria and pathogens that may be present in the raw milk.

Process	Notes
Raw milk	Cow's milk.
Mix	Mix the homogenized milk and skimmed milk powder. Use cleaned, sterile milk containers which will be sold to customers.
Heat	Heat to 70°C/160°F with a holding period of 20–30 minutes.
Cool	Cool to 44–42°C/111–104°F (dip container in tub containing cold water to accelerate the cooling process).
Inoculate	Inoculate with selected strains of actively growing microbial starter cultures (*Lactobacillus, Bulgaricus* and *Streptocollus thermophilus*).
Incubate	Maintain temperature of 42–44°C/111–104°F for approximately five hours until desired degree of acidity is achieved to the correct consistency.
Cool	Cool rapidly to 8–10°C/45–50°F. Traditional cooling systems are available.
Store	Store in a cool place until next morning to check for curd formation.
Pack	Place lids on containers.
Store	Store in a cool place for up to seven days, depending on storage conditions.

Hygiene

As milk is a low acid food that is very susceptible to spoilage and transfer of pathogenic bacteria to consumers, the methods used to handle milk are important in determining the quality of the final product. The main hygienic requirements are:

○ Thoroughly clean and sterilize (with chlorine solution or boiling water) all equipment and utensils before and after processing.

○ Cool milk immediately to control further growth of micro-organisms and enzyme activity. Milk which is likely to contain antibodies should not be used as they will inhibit the action of lactic bacteria.

Raw material

Ingredients for 1kg/2.2lb of product
940g/2lb homogenized milk
60g/2oz skimmed milk powder
Starter culture

Filter milk after milking to remove visible dirt and 'ropiness'—curds.

Process control

The main control points are:

○ The temperature and time involved in heating and cooling milk. Overheating and slow cooling cause changes in flavour, colour and nutritional value; underheating may result in inadequate destruction of enzymes and micro-organisms leading to contamination.

○ Correct incubation temperature to allow rapid production of lactic acid by the inoculated bacteria. If the temperature is too high the bacteria will be destroyed; if it is too low there may not be sufficient acid production to form the yoghurt.

Product control

The main quality factors for yoghurt are the colour, taste and texture. The colour is determined mostly by the amount of heating during pasteurization. The taste and texture are both determined by the amount of lactic acid produced during the fermentation, and this in turn depends on the amount of inoculum added to the milk and the temperature and time of incubation.

Packaging and storage

The product may be sold in portions directly from the culture vessel, or alternatively the inoculated milk may be poured into pots and allowed to ferment in them. The whole pot plus the contents is then sold—with a returnable or a disposable pot. In all cases the short shelf-life of the yoghurt means that it does not require sophisticated packaging and the product only requires protection against dust and insects. Pots should be stored in a cool place away from sunlight and preferably in a refrigerator. Clay pots, gourds and wooden or ceramic bowls are all used traditionally, and are suitable provided proper hygiene is observed in their preparation and cleaning, particularly if they are to be reused. Plastic yoghurt pots are becoming increasingly available and these are more hygienic, more attractive to customers, more convenient to use and easily sealed with a foil cover.

Equipment
Cooler/refrigerator
Thermometer
Starter culture
Pot sealer (optional)

Product variation Fruit yoghurt is a semi-solid, cultured milk which has a smooth creamy texture, a sweet-sour taste and the characteristic flavour and colour of the added fruit. It has a shelf-life that is similar to traditional yoghurt (up to eight days depending on storage conditions) and is mainly used as a dessert.

Fruit pulp is prepared and mixed with yoghurt according to taste (e.g. one part fruit to three parts yoghurt). The main control points for processing the fruit base are:

○ Sorting, cleaning and peeling to remove unwanted parts of the fruit and contaminants.

○ Pulping to produce a uniform, fine pulp without large pieces that would be inadequately heated during pasteurization.

○ Adequate time and temperature of pasteurization to destroy contaminating micro-organisms (especially yeasts that are able to grow under the acidic conditions in the yoghurt).

○ Mixing of pulp and yoghurt in the correct proportions to retain a thick, creamy consistency while giving a good flavour and colour to the final product. The fruit pulp should not be too acidic or it will cause the yoghurt to separate.

Ayib (traditional cheese)

Product description

Ayib is an unfermented 'cheese' made by coagulating milk solids in buttermilk. It is used as a component of traditional dishes such as 'kitifo' and 'doro wet' (Ethiopian minced and spiced raw meat, with chicken sauce). It is white in appearance and similar to European cottage cheese, but more sour in taste and with a pronounced cheese flavour.

Principles of preservation and processing

Bacteria in the milk are destroyed by heating and recontamination is limited by the higher solids content after coagulation of milk solids. However, the product has a short shelf-life of one day unless refrigerated.

Process	Notes
Buttermilk ↓	The fermented buttermilk from which traditional butter is extracted is known as 'aryera'.
Heat ↓	Heat the aryera in a clean pot gently until complete coagulation has occurred (about 30 minutes).
Cool ↓	Allow the cheese and the whey to cool and separate.
Separate whey ↓	Collect the cheese by draining off the whey. The whey can be given to cattle. The cheese is then put on a straw or stainless steel screen to drain.
Pack	Pack in polythene bags.
Store	Put in a chill-room or refrigerator until sold.

Hygiene

The product must be handled with good, sanitary practices as even slight contamination can cause off-flavours and make it unfit for consumption. The product must be sold within 24 hours if refrigeration is not available.

The main hygienic requirements are:

○ Thoroughly clean and sterilize all equipment and utensils before and after processing.

○ Strict enforcement of personal hygiene measures.

Raw material

Aryera is a low acid product that is very susceptible to spoilage and transfer of pathogenic bacteria to consumers.

Process control

The main control points are the temperature and time involved in heating the aryera, which determine the product quality and yield: overheating results in loss of quality and off-flavours whereas underheating lowers the yield and may risk passing on food poisoning bacteria to customers.

Packaging and storage

During packaging the most important quality control check is to ensure that filling equipment and bags are not contaminated.

> **Equipment**
> No special equipment required

Milk is highly perishable and so some kind of processing is usually necessary [IT/PMM]

Ghee and butter

Ghee

Product description

Ghee is a clear, golden brown fat (below 25°C/ 77°F) or oil (above 25°C/77°F) with a characteristic flavour of milk fat. It is made from cow's or buffalo milk and is in high demand as a cooking oil for domestic use, as an ingredient for local food products and as an export commodity.

Principles of preservation and processing

The principles of preservation are to destroy enzymes and contaminating micro-organisms by heat and to remove water from the oil to prevent microbial growth during storage. Ghee has a long shelf-life due to its low moisture content. Storage over long periods requires an airtight, light-proof and moisture-proof container and a cool storage room to slow down the onset of rancidity.

Hygiene

Milk is very susceptible to spoilage and transfer of pathogenic bacteria to consumers, and hygienic methods are needed to handle milk at the dairy. The main hygienic requirements are:

○ Thoroughly clean and sterilize (with chlorine solution or boiling water) all equipment and utensils before and after processing.

○ Strict enforcement of personal hygiene measures.

○ Filter milk after milking to remove visible dirt and any 'ropiness'.

○ Cool milk immediately to control further growth of micro-organisms and enzyme activity.

The heat treatment during processing and the low water activity of the ghee reduce the risk of bacterial spoilage and food poisoning. After heating, normal hygienic food handling techniques should be used. Filter cloths should be boiled each day and thoroughly cleaned of particles to avoid contaminating the product.

Raw material

The milk used for ghee production should be fresh, good quality and free from dirt and excessive

Process	Notes
Milk	Fresh, filtered buffalo or cow's milk.
Pre-heat	Heat in an aluminium pan to 36–40°C/96–104°F to facilitate easy separation of fat.
Separate	Traditionally, milk is boiled and cooled several times and the fatty scum is skimmed off. In modern methods, pre-heated milk is separated into cream and skimmed milk using a cream separator.
Heat	The separated cream is boiled in a vessel to evaporate water. During boiling the product is stirred continuously until the milk proteins start to coagulate and the cream changes from white to golden brown. After the heating is stopped and the product is left to set, all the particles settle at the bottom of the vessel. Skill is needed to determine the end-point of boiling.
Cool	The product is left to cool so that it can be filtered easily.
Filter	The product is filtered very carefully using a cheesecloth so that it is clear without any particles.
Pack	Glass or metal containers are normally used (iron or copper pots should not be used as they incease the development of rancidity). They should be thoroughly cleaned, especially if they are reusable, and they should be made airtight. Alternative packages include ceramic pots sealed with cork or plastic stoppers.
Store	Store at room temperature, away from heat and sunlight. The shelf-life can exceed 12 months with proper packaging and storage conditions.

microbial contamination, so that it will not clot or curdle during processing. Older, spoiled milk will impart an unpleasant flavour to the final product.

Process control
The main quality control points in the process are:

○ Temperature control at 36–40°C/96–104°F during pre-heating milk before separation, to optimize the efficiency of the separator. If the milk is too hot or too cold the milk fat will be difficult to separate and the yield of product will be reduced.

○ The end point of the boiling stage is shown by the correct colour and texture of the ghee. There is no simple test for this and it is judged by experience.

○ Correct filtering is essential to produce a clear product.

Product control
The main quality factors for ghee are colour, clarity, flavour and odour. Correct colour and clarity are mainly due to proper filtering. The taste, colour and odour are determined by the time and temperature of heating. Overheating produces a burnt taste and odour and a dark colour.

Packaging and storage
Rancidity during storage is reduced by using clean, dry containers and by keeping the stored product away from light and heat. Iron and copper should not be used in any vessels, utensils or packaging as these metals promote rancidity in the product.

Equipment
Cream separator
Cheese cloth
Filler
Thermometer

Product variation In some countries the separated cream is ripened for 10–12 hours using a *Lactobacillus spp.* starter culture at 10ml per litre of cream.

Butter

Product descriptionn

Butter is a semi-solid emulsion containing approximately 80–85 per cent milk fat and 15–20 per cent water. It is white-yellow with a bland characteristic flavour and a slightly salty taste. It is a valuable product that has a high demand for domestic use and as an ingredient in other food processing (e.g. bakeries).

Principles of preservation and processing

The principles of preservation are to destroy some enzymes and contaminating micro-organisms by pasteurizing the milk and to prevent microbial growth during storage by reducing the water content, by storing the product at low temperatures and by adding a small amount of salt to the aqueous phase of the emulsion during processing.

Hygiene

Milk is a low acid food that is very susceptible to spoilage and transfer of pathogenic bacteria to consumers. The main hygienic requirements are:

○ Thoroughly clean and sterilize equipment and utensils before and after processing.

○ Strict enforcement of personal hygiene measures.

○ Filter milk after milking to remove visible dirt and any 'ropiness'.

○ Cool milk immediately to control further growth of micro-organisms and enzyme activity.

Raw material

The correct storage control of cream is necessary to prevent deterioration and the consequent formation of rancid, unpleasant flavours in the final product. The cream should be stored away from sunlight in a cool place or refrigerator. The recommended storage temperature is below 10°C/50°F. Water used for washing and salting the butter should be chlorinated or boiled to ensure that it is free from bacteria.

Process	Notes
Heat	Pasteurize raw milk at 63°C/145°F for 30 minutes to destroy most spoilage and pathogenic bacteria and some enzymes.
Cool	Cool the milk to 36–40°C/96–104°F to optimize efficiency of cream separation.
Separate	Use a cream separator.
Hold	The cream is held at 10°C/50°F for 10–12 minutes to allow crystallization of fat so that it can easily be churned into butter.
Churn	Churn in an enclosed vessel at approx. 60rpm to form butter granules. It involves the following steps: ○ Fill the churn half full, to allow movement of the product in the drum. ○ Churn for five minutes and open briefly to remove excess air. ○ Churn until fat granules are evident and then remove liquid (buttermilk) that has separated from the fat granules. ○ Wash the granules in water (very clean and sterilized if necessary). Water equivalent to the weight of buttermilk is added. ○ Churning is continued until the butter granules are properly washed. ○ 1.5–2 per cent salt is dissolved in water and the wash water is replaced by the salt water. Churning is continued for a further 5–10 minutes at 30rpm to compact the butter. ○ Remove the butter from the churn.
Form	Make the butter into blocks by tapping/pressing with butter pats.
Pack	Greaseproof paper or plastic containers can be used. Normal pack sizes are 50–250g.
Store	Store in a cool place, preferably a refrigerator, to maintain a shelf-life of several months. At room temperature it melts and gets rancid quickly, especially if exposed to sunlight.

Meat, fish and dairy products

Process control

The main quality control points in the process are:

○ Temperature control at 36–40°C/96–104°F during pre-heating milk before separation to optimize the efficiency of the separator. If the milk is too hot or too cold the milk fat will be difficult to separate and the yield of product will be reduced.

○ During churning it is important to observe the fat granulation in the cream, because over-churning will result in oily butter and under-churning will result in a reduced yield. Experience and skill are needed to determine the cut point for production of butter granules.

○ Washing and salting are needed to remove buttermilk which would accelerate bacterial growth during storage and produce off-flavours and odours and affect the colour of the product. Salt must be well-dissolved to prevent salt crystals in the product. The texture of the butter is adversely affected if it contains salt crystals or buttermilk.

Packaging and storage

Rancidity during storage is reduced by using clean, dry containers and by keeping the stored product away from light and heat in a cool place, preferably under refrigeration. Iron and copper should not be used in any vessels, utensils or packaging as these metals promote rancidity in the product.

Equipment
Butter churn
Cream separator
Butter pats
Thermometer

Milk confectionery

Channa (loose panir)

Product description

Channa is the intermediary product obtained by heat-acid coagulation of milk. The coagulum is granular, a whitish cream in colour, soft and spongy with a characteristic bland and fatty flavour. It is used in the preparation of channa-based sweets such as rasagolla, champakali, chum-chum, rasmali and so on.

Principles of preservation

The product is preserved by the heat-acid coagulation of milk to destroy micro-organisms and reduce the moisture content. Refrigeration slows bacterial growth.

Process	Notes
Raw material	Cow's milk.
Boil	Heat to boiling point and keep at that temperature for 10 minutes.
Cool	Cool to about 80°C/176°F.
Mix	Dissolve citric acid in 1 litre water, add slowly to the milk (20g per 10 litres milk), with constant and slow stirring. Continue until coagulation is complete. Maintain the temperature at 80°C/176°F.
Settle	Allow to settle for 15 minutes.
Drain	The coagulated milk is hung in a muslin cloth bag for about two hours to drain the whey. The coagulum is the finished product.
Pack	Wrap in aluminium foil.
Store	In a cool place.

Hygiene

As milk is a low-acid food that is very susceptible to spoilage and transfer of pathogenic bacteria to consumers, the methods used to handle milk at the dairy play an important role in determining the quality of the final product.

The main hygienic requirements are:

○ Thoroughly clean and sterilize (with chlorine solution or boiling water) all equipment and utensils before and after processing. *Note* Aluminium equipment should not be cleaned with chlorine solution.

○ Strict enforcement of personal hygiene measures.

Raw material

Milk should be regularly stirred during processing to avoid cream forming on the surface. Only fresh milk should be used.

Process control

The temperature of the milk is reduced to 80°C/176°F before adding the citric acid solution to achieve higher yields of channa.

Citric acid solution should be added fairly quickly to prevent the temperature falling below 80°C.

Packaging and storage

The product has a shelf-life of up to three days under refrigeration. Aluminium foil can be used for packaging.

Equipment
Steam jacketed vessel
Stainless steel vessel
Stainless steel ladle

Meat, fish and dairy products

Rasagolla

Product description

Rasagolla is a milk-based sweet made from channa (see above), flour and cardamom; round in shape, creamy white and kept suspended in sugar syrup. The product has a smooth surface, distinct spongy and springy texture and the flavour of channa. It is served as a teatime snack, and as a dessert after meals.

Principles of preservation and processing

Heat destroys contaminating micro-organisms.

Sugar syrup surrounding the product acts as a preservative for a short time, while canning is required for a longer shelf-life.

Process	Notes
Channa	Good quality fresh channa.
Mix flour	Add refined flour (20g per kilo of channa) gradually while kneading channa. Knead to smooth and pliable consistency.
Shape	Take small quantities of dough to make balls of 2cm diameter, slightly flatten by pressing with fingers, keep a cardamom seed in the centre, fold and shape into smooth balls. Keep the balls covered with a wet cloth.
Mix	Prepare sugar syrup: add about 1 litre of water to 1kg sugar.
Heat	To dissolve sugar, filter and boil.
Mix	Transfer balls to simmering sugar syrup kept ready on a low flame.
Heat	Cook the balls in syrup for about 10–15 minutes on medium flame. On cooking, the balls absorb the syrup and swell.
Cool	To room temperature.
Pack	Pack in glass jars.
Store	Store in a cool place.

Hygiene

As milk is a low-acid food that is very susceptible to spoilage and transfer of pathogenic bacteria to consumers, the methods used to handle milk at the dairy play an important role in determining the quality of the final product.

The main hygienic requirements are:

○ Thoroughly clean and sterilize (with chlorine solution or boiling water) all equipment and utensils before and after processing. *Note* Aluminium equipment should not be cleaned with chlorine solution.

○ Strict enforcement of personal hygiene measures.

Raw material

Channa should be freshly made, without any off-flavours or acidity. Channa made from cow's milk is preferred.

Cane sugar should be of good quality, without any extraneous matter, and refined wheat flour should be without any infestation, musty odour or off-flavours.

Process control

Channa balls should not have any cracks on the surface. Addition of flour while kneading channa ensures smoothness.

Throughout the cooking process the rasagollas should be immersed in sugar syrup and should have sufficient space for swelling.

Occasionally, small quantities of hot water are added to the syrup to maintain 'one-string' consistency throughout the cooking process.

Packaging and storage

Rasagolla is packed in syrup and stored in wide-mouthed stainless steel containers or glass jars. The product can be canned for long-term storage.

> **Equipment**
> Vessel of thick stainless steel
> Steam jacketed kettle (for commercial scale operation)

Khova

Product description

Khova (also called 'mawa') is a product obtained by the evaporation of milk. It is a semi-solid compact mass, creamish white in colour, granular in texture, with a milky, fatty flavour. It is used in the preparation of many sweetmeats (e.g. gulab jamun (see following), burfi, milk cake, doodh peda). It has a shelf-life of up to three days under refrigerated conditions.

Principles of preservation and processing

Heat destroys contaminating micro-organisms and the reduced moisture content helps prevent recontamination. Refrigeration slows bacterial growth.

Process	Notes
Milk ↓	Fresh buffalo milk is used, with a minimum of 5 per cent fat.
Heat (high) ↓	Boil continuously over a high heat with constant stirring. Continue boiling until the milk starts to coagulate, which is marked by an abrupt change in colour.
Heat (low) ↓	Regularly stir and scrape the milk solids from sides of the pan.
Cool ↓	The end-point of heating is marked by the solid mass leaving the sides and bottom of the pan.
Press ↓	Pat to form a compact mass.
Pack ↓	Pack in vegetable parchment paper or polythene.
Store	Store in a cool place.

Hygiene

Khova should be kept clean and cool. Operators should have no skin infections or stomach illness.

Raw material

Milk should be fresh, without any undesirable off-flavours of acid development. Buffalo milk is preferred as it yields more khova, with a better texture.

Process control

○ Continuous stirring while boiling the milk is very important to avoid cream separation.

○ Once coagulation starts the temperature should be lowered to 85–88°C/185–190°F and the process should be carefully monitored with brisk stirring and scraping.

Packaging and storage

The product can be packed in vegetable parchment paper, polythene bags or laminated pouches where these are available. It can be stored for two to three days under refrigerated conditions.

Equipment

Pans made of thick stainless steel
Stainless steel ladles
(Stainless steel steam-jacketed kettles with stirrer for commercial-scale operation)

Meat, fish and dairy products

Gulab jamun

Product description

Gulab jamun is a popular, milk-based sweet made with khova, refined flour and cane sugar. It is round or elliptical in shape with a deep brown, slightly crisp, outer surface and is dull white, soft, and porous inside. Always kept floating in sugar syrup, the product has a distinct flavour of deep-fried milk solids, sugar syrup and added flavours.

Principles of preservation and processing

Khova (see above) has increased solids and is kept under refrigeration.

Deep fat frying, crust formation on the outer surface, and suspension in sugar syrup reduce the chances of microbial spoilage.

Process	Notes
Khova ↓	Take fresh khova and break it to loosen the mass.
Mix ↓	Sieve flour and baking powder together before adding khova.
Mix ↓	Mix thoroughly to obtain a homogeneous mixture. Add a little water.
Knead ↓	Knead to smooth and soft dough. Cover the dough with a wet cloth and keep it aside.
Mix sugar ↓	Prepare sugar syrup by dissolving 3kg of sugar in an equal quantity of water and boiling it for five minutes. If desired, flavouring essence can be added.
Shape ↓	Take small quantities of dough and shape them into balls of 2cm diameter or oval forms.
Fry ↓	Heat oil in a shallow pan and fry dough balls on medium flame until they turn deep brown.
Mix syrup ↓	Remove the fried balls from oil using a perforated ladle and immediately transfer them into sugar syrup. The fried balls swell in size and become soft as they absorb the syrup.
Store	Store in glass jars.

Raw material

Ingredients
900g/2lb khova
105g/4oz refined flour
7.5g/¼oz baking powder
3kg/6.6lb cane sugar
3 litres/5⅓pt water

Khova should be freshly made and free from off-flavours. Flour should be good quality, free from musty odours and infestation and cooking oil should be fresh and not rancid.

Process control

Thorough mixing of khova and refined flour is essential to get a homogeneous product. Very little water, just enough to make a smooth mixture, is added while kneading. The balls should be smooth without any cracks on the surface.

The use of refined flour in the correct quantity is crucial for the desired texture in the finished product. Excess flour gives a leathery and soggy product while insufficient flour results in bursting and disintegration of the product during frying and syrup absorption.

Uniform frying on a medium flame is important to avoid the formation of an uncooked hard core.

Packaging and storage

Generally, gulab jamuns are stored in syrup in closed glass jars or wide and deep stainless steel containers. Sometimes they are canned for longer shelf-life and distant transportation.

Equipment
Frying pan
Perforated ladle
Deep fat fryer with temperature controller (commercial use)

---

7. HERBS, SPICES, FLAVOURINGS AND ESSENTIAL OILS

Dried herbs

General

Product description

There are very many herbs and medicinal plants which are dried and used in traditional food preparations. They include whole plants or parts of plants, such as flowers, leaves, roots, bark, seeds and parts of seeds. The general method is described below.

Principles of preservation and processing

Preservation is achieved by drying. A low moisture content prevents the growth of micro-organisms. When the product is carefully dried and packed in containers that offer protection from moisture, light, insects and rodents and stored in a cool, dry room, these products have a shelf-life of many months.

Process	Notes
Raw material	Herb/part of herb as appropriate
Clean	If roots are used, the earth has to be removed and the root cleaned before drying. All leafy materials should be washed in clean water. Seeds, stalks etc. may be cleaned by winnowing.
Dry	Place on clean mats or on concrete slabs and sun-dry for 5–10 days.
Pack	In gunny or polythene bags.
Store	In a cool, dry room.

Hygiene

The main hygienic requirements are as follows:

○ The raw material is thoroughly cleaned in clean water before drying.

○ The products are protected from dirt, dust, insects and birds during drying.

Raw material

The raw materials should be dried as soon as possible after harvest to prevent wilting and loss of flavour.

Process control

The products are dried quickly and protected from dust and dirt. Products with volatile aromas need to be dried in the shade. The products are stored in clean containers.

Packaging and storage

Herb products are usually packed for storage in gunny bags or wooden or cardboard boxes. Some plants which are woody are tied into bundles and kept in a clean store room. Seeds and leafy items are packed in polythene bags. There are also mixtures of medicinal herbs which are packaged in polythene. The products keep well if stored in a dry, cool place.

Equipment
Mats for drying
Heat sealer
Scales

Note In traditional processing the process used in drying herbs is often very basic. Not carrying out a blanching and a sulphiting step in the process makes some compounds unstable and in some cases the products are not cleaned. This permits the continued existence of microbes and other extraneous matter on the product. Each stage in the process can therefore be upgraded to improve the product quality.

For a slightly larger scale of production, tray dryers can be used which have heater/blowers attached to dry herbs faster and independent of weather conditions.

Specific examples of products made by the general process above include kowe, as follows.

Herbs, spices, flavourings and essential oils

Kowe (basil)

Product description

Kowe (*Ocimum canum* or American basil) is a strongly scented herb commonly grown in Ghana and used in many food preparations. The herb has been called 'Akoko besa', literally meaning 'All the chicken will be consumed with the herb'.

Process	Notes
Fresh leaves	Leaves may be clipped when mature, preferably after the plant has flowered. This will ensure a higher concentration of the essential oil in the leaves.
Sort	Remove any spoiled, damaged or infected leaves.
Cut	Leaves and stalks may be cut with a sharp knife into smaller pieces.
Dry	Spread to dry in the sun, occasionally mixing and turning the herbs to ensure uniform drying. The drying process may last for between three and five days to ensure a well-dried product. The fresh, leafy herb must be spread to dry in the sun as quickly as possible and soon after collection. Fresh leaves may contain about 90 per cent or more moisture and, if not quickly dried, mould infection may set in.
Pack	Pack in polythene bags and seal properly.
Store	In a dry, cool place.

Quality control

As herbs and spices are frequently used in foods that may not be fully processed to destroy micro-organisms, it is essential that hygienic practices are applied to prevent food poisoning bacteria from being transmitted to customers. This must be reflected in good manufacturing practice during raw material preparation, processing, packaging and storage. The aim is to avoid contamination of the material at each stage of the process, so as to produce a wholesome, stable product.

Raw material

The raw material should be prepared and dried as soon as possible after harvest to prevent mould growth and spoilage.

Process control

The drying process must be thorough and without delays to avoid development of moulds and growth of bacteria. The dried product should have a moisture content of not more than 10–14 per cent to ensure safety during storage, and this should be reached within five days of drying with at least six hours drying per day.

Packaging and storage

The dried product may be packed and sealed in polypropylene bags for safe storage. The leaves, seeds, etc. can be pounded using a pestle and mortar or milled to a powder before packaging. However, it should be noted that many customers prefer to buy unmilled products as they consider that the risk of adulteration is lower.

Storage must be in a cool, dry environment to ensure an adequate shelf stability. The shelf-life may be between six and twelve months under good storage conditions.

Equipment

Dryer
Heat sealer
Scales
Mill/pestle and mortar (optional)

Spices

Cloves

Product description

Cloves (or 'peple' in Ghana) are the dried flower buds of the plant *Eugenia aromatica*. They are golden brown to black in colour, about 1.7cm to 2.5cm (¾in to 1in) in length, rubbery or crisp to the bite with a strong characteristic taste on the tongue and a strong aroma. They are used as a flavouring in many traditional dishes and oil of cloves finds widespread use in the flavourings and perfumery industries.

Principles of processing and preservation

Preservation is achieved by drying to reduce the moisture content and prevent growth of micro-organisms. When the spice is packed in moisture-proof bags and protected from light, air and insects, it has a shelf-life of many months.

Process	Notes
Harvest	The flower buds are plucked when they are greenish yellow in colour. Some also fall off the inflorescence, which can be picked off the ground and cleaned.
Sort	Remove unwanted woody and leafy parts. Green, immature buds must not be collected, since they contain less essential flavour.
Dry	Place the buds on mats or woven containers in the shade for several days until a moisture content of about 12 per cent is reached. Exposure to direct sunlight can cause undesirable breakdown of flavour components.
Winnow	A traditional winnowing basket or mechanical winnower can be used to remove dirt, stones, dust and petals.
Pack	Pack in polythene sacks, plastic or metal containers.
Store	Store in a cool, dry place. If the product is mould-free and kept dry, the shelf-life can be more than one year.

Hygiene

Care and strict hygiene must be maintained during drying and storage processes. This is to protect the product from contamination with dirt, sand particles and moisture.

Raw materials

The buds should be detached from the stem by taking a cluster in one hand and pressing this cluster against the palm of the other hand and twisting. The buds will then drop off. The buds and the stems should be separated by hand and dried separately. They should be dried as soon as possible or they will start fermenting. If they do start to ferment, the final colour is pale and dull.

Process control

○ Drying is very important and must be carried out quickly and under controlled conditions to avoid mould growth and loss of flavour.

○ The final moisture content of the product is also important. Drying must continue until moisture content of the material is below 12 per cent. This may be achieved in three to five days with about eight hours sun-drying per day. If the clove is bent over a thumbnail, it should snap; if it bends, it is not dry enough. When one grasps a handful of dry cloves, it will hurt. If it does not hurt, they are not dry enough.

Packaging and storage

Product must be well packaged such as preferably in moisture-proof containers (such as polypropylene bags) and stored away from humid conditions. When well-dried and properly stored, spices may remain stable for a very long time (a year or more). However, with prolonged storage the flavour components diminish.

Equipment
Dryer
Scales

Product variations   Most spices are processed in a similar way to cloves.

Herbs, spices, flavourings and essential oils

Spices must be dried to prevent the growth of micro-organisms, and normally red-coloured chillies will turn black during storage unless they are below 10 per cent moisture content [IT/ PMM]

Chilli

Product description

This is the dried fruit of *Capsicum fruitescens*. The product is bright red in colour, flat in appearance and leathery to the touch. It has a hot flavour. It is used as a flavouring in many different cuisines. A well dried product can be kept for several months if packaged. Chilli can be marketed whole, or as a coarsely or finely ground product.

Principles of preservation and processing

Preservation is achieved by drying. Low moisture content prevents the growth of micro-organisms. When the product is carefully dried and packed in containers that offer protection from moisture, light, insects and rodents and stored in a cool, dry room, it has a shelf-life of many months.

Process	Notes
Harvest ↓	For small-scale production harvesting will be manual.
Clean ↓	The chillies should be washed in clean water quickly to remove any field dirt.
Dry ↓	The chillies need to be dried to less than 10% to prevent them turning black during storage.
	Most chillies are dried in the sun in 5–15 days. The skin of chillies can be pricked to increase drying rates.
Winnow ↓	Remove the dust and dirt accumulated during sun-drying by using sieves or winnowing baskets.
Sort ↓	Sort the dried chillies into different grades based on colour and size. Damaged fruits and extraneous materials should be removed.
Grind ↓	Care needs to be taken when grinding chilli to avoid powder coming into contact with eyes or other sensitive tissues.
Package	In polypropylene or polythene bags.
Store	Store in airtight containers in a cool room to prevent moisture uptake and volatile flavour components loss. The value of chilli is dependent on its colour and to reduce colour loss the chillies should be stored out of the sunlight.

Hygiene

The chilli fruits should be washed in clean water before processing, and it is important that the drying mats are clean and placed away from sources of excessive dirt and dust.

Raw materials

The time of harvesting depends on a variety of factors: the final use of the chilli, the time of the year and the availability of labour. A dried chilli powder needs a fully ripe, red chilli fruit. Sometimes, to produce a strong red coloured chilli powder, the fruits are not harvested until they start to wither. In India, the first chillies are picked immature to encourage further fruits to develop. After the first harvest, ripe chilli fruits are picked. In Sri Lanka and India, chillies are sometimes picked immature and allowed to mature in heaps for two to three days. The heaps are kept indoors or in the shade to avoid direct sunlight which can result in the development of white patches.

The fruit and stalk should be removed from the plant by gentle pulling. The fruit should be handled carefully to avoid bruising and cuts. Bruising shows up on the dried chilli as discoloured areas and cuts can result in the loss of seeds.

Process control

○ The most important process control is to ensure that drying is completed as quickly as possible. The final product should have a moisture content of less than 10 per cent.

○ Drying temperatures over 55°C/131°F will reduce the volatile oil content of the final product.

Packaging and storage

The chilli should be packaged in polypropylene to prevent the loss of volatile flavour components. However, polythene is often used. As with other spices the products need to be stored in the airtight containers in a cool room to prevent moisture uptake and flavour loss. If this is not possible, the chillies should be stored in a cool, dry room free from pests. The ground product will lose the volatile flavour components at a faster rate than whole products so it is often worthwhile storing the chilli in the unground form. To reduce colour loss the chillies should be stored out of the sunlight.

Herbs, spices, flavourings and essential oils

Other chilli products
Capsicum is a milder form and is usually sold in the whole, undried form.

Paprika is mild and sweet and is sold only in the ground form.

Pepper

Product description

Black pepper is the dried berry of the vine *Piper nigrum*. It accounts for a quarter in the total world trade in spices. It is black in colour and has a strong aroma and a hot taste. It is 0.25cm in diameter and has a wrinkled seed skin. The product is also sold ground.

Principles of preservation and processing

Preservation is achieved by drying. Low moisture content prevents the growth of micro-organisms. When the product is carefully dried and packed in containers that offer protection from moisture, light, insects and rodents and stored in a cool, dry room, it has a shelf-life of many months.

Process	Notes
Harvest	The pepper spikes should be cut from the vines.
Fermentation	Immediately after harvesting, the pepper spikes should be laid out in the sun to ensure that the final product has a deep black colour.
Thresh	The berries can be detached from the spikes by hand, by trampling the spikes underfoot, or beating them with sticks.
Sort	The larger pieces of the spike stem can then be picked out and smaller pieces removed using a winnowing basket. In some countries threshing does not take place until after final drying.
Wash	The berries should next be washed in clean cold water. Light berries, which are not suitable for culinary use, will float and these should be dried separately. There is a market for light berries for oil distillation.
Blanching (optional)	Blanching increases the rate of drying. Blanching can also speed up the enzymatic reaction that produces the final desired black colour.
	Blanching is carried out by immersing the berries in hot, but not boiling, water for up to 10 minutes until their colour changes to a dark green. A simple method of blanching involves placing the berries in a cloth sack attached to a stick. The sack can then be immersed and removed from the hot water with relative ease. After blanching, the raw material should be dipped immediately in cold water to prevent over-blanching or cooking. Blanching is not essential but is commonly practised in Indonesia and Sri Lanka.
Dry	The pepper should be dried to a moisture content of 12 per cent which can take up to 12 days in the sun.
Winnow	Removing dust and dirt can be carried out with winnowing baskets and sieves.
Grade	Grading by size and weight can be done using a winnowing basket.
Package	In polypropylene.
Store	In cool, dry room.

Hygiene

The pepper berries should be washed in clean water before drying, and protected from dust and dirt. The mats should be placed in the sun away from sources of excessive dust and dirt. Animals and birds should be kept away from the drying pepper as these are another source of contamination.

Raw material

Only mature pepper spikes should be harvested.

Immediately after harvesting, the pepper spikes should be laid out in the sun to ensure that the final product has a deep black colour.

Process control

○ The pepper berries should be dried as quickly as possible after harvest to prevent mould growth. Even a trace of mould can reduce the value of the pepper by half. The final product should have a moisture content of less than 12 per cent. Determining the point of adequate drying is critical. A method used in Sri Lanka to tell if it is dry enough is to put one's hand into a heap of pepper and if the pepper sticks to the hairs it is sufficiently dry. Overdrying results in the loss of flavour and, of course, weight or yield which reduces the return.

○ The drying temperature should not exceed 60°C/140°F or flavour components will be lost.

○ Secondary processing by grinding may add value to the product. However, it is fraught with difficulties. With a whole product, it is easy to assess its quality, whereas with a ground product it is difficult. Because of this, there is a consumer resistance to ground pepper which can only be overcome by consistently producing a good product and an established brand image.

○ When blanching it is important that the pepper is not left in the water for more than 10 minutes as volatile flavour components can be lost and the enzymes responsible for the colour changes may be de-activated.

Packaging and storage

Black pepper needs to be stored in airtight containers to prevent moisture uptake or flavour loss. Polythene is unsuitable as the volatile flavour components are lost, so polypropylene is required.

Equipment
Mats for drying
Packaging material
Polythene sealer
Grinder/mill
Weighing scale

Ginger

Product description

Ginger is the rhizome of *Zingiber officinale*. It is sold both fresh and in a dried, processed form. The dried pieces are an off-white colour, fibrous and crisp to the bite. Ginger has a hot flavour and pleasant aroma and is used in foods and beverages.

Principles of preservation and processing

Preservation is achieved by drying: low moisture content prevents the growth of micro-organisms.

Process	Notes
Wash	Remove sand and other extraneous materials and then wash in clean water.
↓	
Cut	Cutting large rhizomes into smaller pieces aids drying.
↓	
Dry	Sun-dry to 12 per cent moisture content.
↓	
Pack	Dried ginger is collected and packed in gunny bags. Well dried ginger can also be packed in polypropylene.
↓	
Store	In a dry, cool atmosphere.

Hygiene

Sun-drying involves the risk that the product will be contaminated by dust and dirt. The main hygiene requirements are that the drying mats are clean and kept away from areas with excessive amounts of dust and dirt (such as roads). Animals and birds must be kept away from the drying mats. The rhizomes must be washed in clean water.

Raw material

The ginger should be processed immediately after harvest.

Process control

The rhizomes must be dried to 10 per cent moisture content. An experienced processor can usually tell when the ginger is sufficiently dry.

Packaging and storage

Ginger needs to be stored in airtight containers to prevent moisture uptake or flavour loss. Polythene is unsuitable as the volatile flavour components are lost, so polypropylene is required.

Equipment
Brush for cleaning off, cleaning sand
Knife for cutting
Cutting board
Mats or woven spreads for drying
Packaging materials
Weighing scale

Herbs, spices, flavourings and essential oils

Cinnamon

Product description

The dried inner bark of *Cinnamomum zeylanicum* is known as cinnamon. It is a light brown colour with a distinctive aroma. The pieces or 'quills' range from 2.5cm to 30cm (1–12in) in length. It is used as a flavouring.

Principles of preservation and processing

Preservation is achieved by drying. Low moisture content prevents the growth of micro-organisms. When the product is carefully dried and packed in containers that offer protection from moisture, light, insects and rodents and stored in a cool, dry room, it has a shelf-life of many months.

Hygiene

The drying mats must be clean and kept away from areas with excessive amounts of dust and dirt. Animals and birds must be kept away.

Raw material

Cinnamon should be peeled on the same day as it is harvested. In India the peeled bark is left overnight before the quills are made.

Process control

○ The cinnamon must be dried to 10 per cent moisture content. An experienced processor can usually tell when the cinnamon is sufficiently dry.

○ Brass is used for cutting the cinnamon as it does not stain the product.

Packaging and storage

For retail, package in polythene or polypropylene. Cinnamon should be stored in a cool, dry place.

Equipment

Brass knives
Mats
Packaging materials
Ropes for tying bundles
Weighing scale

Process	Notes
Harvest	Cut the cinnamon branches.
Clean	Wash in clean water.
Scrape the bark	Scrape off the soft outer bark with a fine rounded rasp or a crude curved knife.
Rub the stems	Rub the stripped stems with heavy brass rods or blocks to loosen the inner bark.
Cut the stem	Cuts should be made round the stem at 30cm intervals. Two longitudinal cuts are made, one on each side of the stem. A brass knife is used, rounded with a point on one side.
Ease off inner bark	The inner bark is then eased off the hard wood using either the pointed side of the knife or a blunt knife.
Roll the bark	The pieces of peeled bark are rolled by hand one into another to form compound quills of about 1m. Use the longest quills on the outside and smallest quills and the broken pieces in the inside.
Trim	Trim the compound quills.
Dry	Dry in the shade as direct exposure to the sun can result in flavour loss and warping. The compound quills can be dried on rope strands or rush mats suspended from the roof. Hand-compress the quills daily to help acquire the tubular form.
Sort	Cinnamon quills are graded by length, colour and thickness, and bundled together after arranging into varying lengths the telescoped bark pieces (telescoped pieces in the bundles are more or less of the same size).
Bundle	Tie the quills in mats (several bundles) or place in gunny bags. The packages do not need to be airtight.
Package	For retail in polythene or polypropylene.
Storage	In a cool, dry place.

Flavourings

Daudawa (locust bean)

Product description

Daudawa (*Parkia clappertoniana*) is the West African locust bean tree which bears fruits as bunches of pods. The pods contain a yellow mealy pulp which is sweet to taste and may be prepared into a valuable drink when mixed with water, called dozim. The dehusked kernels can also be prepared into strong-smelling daudawa cakes and used as the basis for soup and as seasoning.

Principles of preservation and processing

The principle of preservation is drying to prevent the growth of micro-organisms. The yellow mealy pulp around the seed and the kernels are allowed to ferment and are then sun-dried. The resulting food may be thick, sticky, strongly or mildly smelling, dried or fermented with a moisture content of between 12 and 20 per cent. Apart from drying, the stability may also be enhanced by the acids produced during fermentation.

Process	Notes
Kernels ↓	Kernels containing seeds are collected after removal of yellow pulp by washing.
Dehusk ↓	Boil kernels until soft, then pound in a mortar and pestle to loosen husk from seeds.
Wash	Wash to remove broken testa.
Heat ↓	Boil seeds in water for about 24 hours to soften.
Ferment ↓	Load seeds into a plastic or metal container, cover and allow to ferment for two to three days.
Press ↓	Manually mould and press the fermented product into balls.
Pack	In polythene bags.
Store	In display box for sale.

Raw materials

Seeds should be mature and without mould or infection.

Process control

○ Boiling and pounding of seeds is important to help husk removal. The seeds are hard and elaborate cooking is required to soften them. The cooking process has been claimed to remove unpleasant odour from the seeds.

○ The cooking, fermenting and moulding processes must be carried out under hygienic conditions to avoid contamination of material with dirt and unwanted foreign matter. The fermentation period must not go beyond three days to avoid producing undesirable odours. Sometimes the moulded balls are given one or two days drying to further stabilize the product during storage.

Packaging and storage

The moulded daudawa balls may be kept in polythene bags and sealed. This will protect them from external contamination or moisture uptake. Since the product is fermented with a strong odour, it is difficult to know when the product has spoiled but it is claimed that the shelf-life may range between six and eight months.

> **Equipment**
> Scales
> Heat sealer

Essential oils

Citronella oil

Product description

Essential oils are the compounds that give the characteristic aroma to spices, flowers and other plants. They are present in small amounts in the plant material and, because they have a lower boiling point than water, they can be evaporated by heating the plants with steam (in a similar way to distillation of alcohol).

Citronella oil is the the essential oil extracted from the leaves of the citronella plant. It has a strong smell, slightly similar to lemon and is colourless and volatile. It is used as a flavouring and in perfumes. Essential oils are often very valuable and can form the basis for a successful small business. However, they readily spoil due to rancidity and must be properly packaged to prevent contact with light and air in particular.

Principles of preservation and processing

Harvested citronella plants are dried in the shade, collected and placed in suitably designed stills. The essential oil is steam distilled and the distillate is cooled and condensed into a collection vessel. It first appears as an emulsion, but is made to break, whereby the essential oil fraction floats on the surface. This is then collected and bottled.

Drying the plant in the shade removes some water and concentrates the oil. Drying in the shade also minimizes changes to the oil due to direct sunlight. Steam vaporizes the essential oil fraction, which has a low moisture content and is therefore preserved.

Raw material

There are few control points. The leaves should be free of mould or infection.

Process control

The temperature of distillation and the temperature of cooling water should both be monitored to ensure the optimum yield of essential oil.

Packaging and storage

Essential oil is usually packed in well-sealed bottles or in drums for transport and storage.

Process	Notes
Raw material	Citronella leaves.
Dry	In the shade.
Distil	Distil steam in specially designed distillation apparatus.
Cool	Cool the distillate using cold water on the vessel.
Collect	Collect the condensate in a receiving vessel.
Separate	Collect essential oil.
Package	In dark-coloured glass bottles or in drums.
Store	In a cool, dark place.

Coloured bottles are used to prevent loss of aroma due to rancidity caused by sunlight. The packaged product must be stored in a cool, dark place in order to prevent loss of the volatile components.

Equipment

Still for essential oil distillation
Steam generator
Storage containers
Scales

Product variation Cinnamon oil is a dark brown to black coloured oily product, with a typical smell of cinnamon. It evaporates easily and is used as an essence and also in the perfumery industry. It is also claimed to have medicinal properties.

Dry cinnamon quills are broken into smaller pieces and loaded into a steam distillation unit. Steam is generated and passed through the material to vaporize the oil. The essential oil layer separates out on cooling in the collection vessel or sometimes as a result of breaking the emulsion.

Cinnamon oil can also be distilled off dried cinnamon leaves and cinnamon root bark. However, there are compositional differences between cinnamon bark, leaf and root bark oils.

It is also possible to obtain essential oils from other spices, such as cloves, nutmeg, cardamom, using the same techniques.

Further reading

Technical advice

Appropriate Food Packaging, P. Fellows and B. Axtell, 1993, TOOL Publications, Amsterdam, The Netherlands (ISBN 90 70857 28 6)

Food Cycle Technology Source Books, series aimed at women, covering various types of food processing technology. IT Publications, London, UK

Food: The chemistry of its components, T.P. Coultate, 1984, The Royal Society of Chemistry, London, UK (ISBN 0 85186 483 X)

Food and Drink – Good Manufacturing Practice: A guide to its responsible management, IFST, London, UK (ISBN 0 905367 08 1)

Food Poisoning and Food Hygiene, B. Hobbs and D. Roberts, 1987, Edward Arnold Ltd, London, UK (ISBN 0 7131 4516 1)

Hygienic Design and Operation of Food Plant, R. Jowitt (Ed.), 1980, Ellis Horwood Ltd, Chichester, UK (ISBN 0 85312 153 2) [NB: for larger-scale food processing]

Improving Small-scale Food Industries in Developing Countries, W. Edwardson and C.W. MacCormac (Ed.), 1986, IDRC Publications, Ottawa, Canada (ISBN 0 88936 398 6)

Making Safe Food, P. Fellows and V. Hidellage, 1992, From Technical Enquiry Unit, ITDG, Myson House, Railway Terrace, Rugby, CV21 3HT, UK

Processing Tropical Crops, J.J. Asiedu, 1989, Macmillan, London, UK (ISBN 0 333 44857 X)

Small-scale Food Processing: A guide to appropriate equipment, P. Fellows and A. Hampton, 1992, IT Publications, London, UK (ISBN 1 85339 108 5)

Traditional and Non-traditional Foods, R. Ferrando, 1981, FAO Publications, Rome, Italy (ISBN 92 5 100167 7)

Business advice

Consultancy for Small Businesses: The concept, training the consultants, M. Harper, 1976, IT Publications (ISBN 0 903031 42 6)

Doing a Feasibility Study: Training activities for starting or reviewing a small business, Suzanne Kindervater (Ed.), 1987, OEF International, Washington DC, USA (ISBN 0 912917 07 5)

Entrepreneurship for the Poor, M. Harper, 1984, IT Publications, London, UK (out of print)

Marketing Strategy: Training activities for entrepreneurs, S. Kindervater and M. Range, 1986, OEF International, Washington DC, USA (ISBN 0 912917 08 3)

Monitoring and Evaluating Small Business Projects: A step by step guide for private development organizations, S. Buzzard and E. Edgcomb (Ed.), 1992, PACT, New York, USA (ISBN 0 942127 00 5)

Small Business in the Third World, M. Harper, 1984, IT Publications, London, UK (ISBN 0 471 90474 0)

Product index

legumes 39–40, 48, 80
lentils 39
lime pickle 116
lime powder 68, 70
locust bean 204
lubisi (banana beer) 113

macadamia nuts 147
maize 32, 38, 46, 50, 53, 54, 68, 70, 72
Maldive fish 174
malted grains 44
mango pickle 119
mawa 190
meat products 164, 170, 176, 177
meat tenderizer 96
metin shiro 48
milk burfi 141
milk, pasteurized 178
milk products 178–91
millet 32, 56, 86, 88
muscat 74

nacatamale 71
nectar, fruit 106
noodles 81
nuecados 78
nuts 144, 147–50, 154

ogi (fermented maize paste) 54
oils 156–9, 205
ojojo (fried yam cake) 129
orange juice 106

paddy see rice
palm sap 149
palm wine 112
palmitos (bottled palm hearts) 132
pancakes 60, 68
panela 114, 139

panir (channa) 188–9
papain 96
paprika 199
parboiled rice 36
pasteurized milk 178
peanut brittle 150
peanut butter 148
peanut oil 158
peas 39, 48
peple (cloves) 196
pepper 200
pickle 116–119, 133
pineapple peel vinegar 114
plantain 121
popcorn 72
popped sorghum 73
prawns 166
pre-packed whole grains 32

rasagolla 189
rice 34–7, 36, 44, 70, 76, 81, 86, 88
rice noodles 81
rich fruit cake 64
roasted cashew nuts 145
roasted fava beans 40
roti 60

salted fish 174
salted vegetables 126
semolina 74, 82
sesame balls 153
sesame oil 161
sesame seeds 146
shea butter 160
shellfish 166
shiro 48
shrimps 166
smoked bream 172
snackfoods 66–73, 120–21, 128–31
snail snack 176
sorghum 32, 46, 56, 73, 86, 88

soy milk 84
soy flour 48
spiced foods 47, 66, 100, 102, 116, 118, 119, 129, 133, 164, 170
spices 196–203
split cereals 38
split legumes 39
squash, fruit 107
sugar 76, 80, 114, 139–141
sugar fondant 78
sweet bread 58
syrup 108, 138

tamales, maize 70
tamarind pickle 118
tef 56
tenderizer, meat 96
thala bolo (sesame balls) 153
thala thel (sesame oil) 161
toddy, coconut 154
toffee, fruit 104
togwa 86
tomato sauce (ketchup) 100
tomato paste 102
tortilla 60, 68
tortitas 130
treacle, coconut 152
tuna 174
tuo zaafi 50

vetch 39
vinegar 114

wet 48, 56, 182
wheat 44, 56, 60, 66, 74, 78
wheat flour nuecados 78
wheat, hard 38
wheat, soft 58, 62, 78
whole grains 32
wine, palm 112

yam cake 129
yoghurt 180